BEER
&VEG

BEER &VEG

Combining great craft beer with
vegetarian and vegan food

MARK DREDGE

DOG 'n' BONE

Published in 2021 by Dog 'n' Bone Books
An imprint of Ryland Peters & Small Ltd
20–21 Jockey's Fields, London WC1R 4B
341 E 116th St, New York, NY 10029

www.rylandpeters.com

10 9 8 7 6 5 4 3 2 1

A CIP catalog record for this book is available
from the Library of Congress and the British
Library.

ISBN: 978 1 912983 40 7

Printed in China

Photographer: Stephen Conroy
Stylist: Kim Sullivan
Food stylist: Katy McClelland
Illustrators: flavor wheels on pages 11 and 24
by Andrew Henderson; other illustrations by
Nick Frith

Senior designer: Emily Breen
Art director: Sally Powell
Production manager: Gordana Simakovic
Publishing manager: Penny Craig
Publisher: Cindy Richards

CONTENTS

INTRODUCTION

Beer belongs with vegetables in a way which hasn't been properly addressed before. Beer is the ultimate plant-based drink. It's a product of the ground, the seasons, and different regions. It sprouts, grows, flowers, gets harvested, and then it begins its change into beer, helped by the hands of the brewers, and shaped by time and place. Beer is made from plants and it goes really well with plants. It's time to celebrate that.

Look around the world at the most famous dishes that go with beer and it's all meat, meat, meat: Belgian beer stews, meat and ale pies, schnitzels, knuckles, sausages, wings, fried fish, steamed mussels…. Beer food means meat. Or it meant meat, because those old, traditional dishes no longer truly reflect the modern world and the drinker who's likely to eat a broader diet, one more focused on plant-based foods.

Beer is a contextual and social drink that has brought humans together for thousands of years—in caves, by campfires, on farms, around ancient settlements, in the earliest towns, the industrializing cities, and the modern metropolis. It's a drink that's more than just hydration, more than just flavor, more than just a social enabler. It is shaped by time and place, by the past and the future; by things in the fields where the ingredients grow, and in the building in which it is made, but also far away from those places; and it's a drink influenced by culture, climate, fashion, and food.

The world of beer is always evolving and updating. It is built on a foundation of traditions but it is progressively changing with new inspirations and trends, often reflecting changes in what we eat. The traditional beer foods usually come with a classic beer style, and they are of a specific place—the British Bitter, the roast dinner, the pub; the German Lager, the plate of sausages, the beer hall—and they belong to one part of the beer industry. But beer is now way more than just its traditions and heritage, and for a lot of drinkers the idea of a Bavarian beer hall is a novelty and not a part of modern beer culture; modern beer comes in big colorful cans, or we drink it in our local brewpubs or favorite bars. And we drink styles like Hazy IPAs, sour beers brewed with tropical fruits, big strong Stouts made with peanut butter and vanilla, lagers infused with exotic spices and herbs. It's these innovations which have made beer the most exciting and varied drink in the world, and we could easily argue that the modern beer industry now commands much more attention than the traditional parts of beer culture.

Just as beer is perpetually changing and evolving, so too are the foods we eat. We know more cuisines, we're more familiar with previously exotic ingredients, we're trying new dishes, and increasingly we're eating more plants, whether we are moving fully away from animal products or just eating a more flexible diet with

less meat. And that created a gap for a book about beer which specifically looks at it in conjunction with great vegetarian and vegan food.

Having written a couple of books and countless articles about beer and food together, and having traveled the world eating and drinking, experiencing revelatory and unforgettable combinations, I felt like I had a good understanding of what things worked well together. But almost all of those experiences contained animal-based products. Almost all media about beer and food go to meat as the first-choice pairing, as if someone who likes a hearty glass of Stout could only be interested in eating a fat hunk of steak. But a lot of beer-lovers don't eat like that any more. I don't eat like that any more.

My diet is now mostly plant-based, with a bit of dairy. That might change in the future, or if I'm traveling and really want to try a local specialty (my stomach still determines most of my travel), but at home I eat a vegan diet. This change led to me eating a more varied diet, to cooking new dishes, and drinking different beers with my dinner, which gave me a new excitement about the possibilities of beer and food together. By not defaulting to animal protein, I felt like I gave myself way more options.

I also learned that I didn't need to go all the way back to the beginning of learning about beer and food. The basic ideas still apply, whether you're having turkey or tofu, and most of the time we're thinking about the sides, sauces, spices, and herbs that go with the protein, not the protein itself. What this did do was make me step away from the pairings I knew about and try new things, new cuisines, new combinations, and it's been fascinating to learn more about flavor. My realization was that "beer and veg" didn't need to be revolutionary; it just needed to work for more people with more diverse tastes to go with more diverse beers.

It was cooking with beer which excited me the most in writing this book. Without the focus being on a piece of meat, I could be more creative. I could look to the classic beer dishes and turn them vegan. I could come up with dishes that you'd never find in another book like this. And I found that beer can be an integral ingredient in vegan food in a way which is impossible if you're using animal-based foods. It made me want to "eat" more beer.

Whether you are vegan, vegetarian, or just wanting to eat less animal produce, my aim in this book is simply to bring together great beers with great food for you. To me, it's an irrelevance that there's no meat in this book because, simply, all of the dishes discussed or cooked in this book are delicious with beer. And that's what is most important.

THE HISTORY OF BEER AND FOOD

There's a common line surrounding the history of beer saying that we drank it because it was safer than water. That's absolutely true, of course, because to brew beer you boil a combination of water, grain, and hops, and boiling it kills any dangerous bacteria that might've been in the water. But if people had been aware of that, wouldn't they simply have boiled their water, rather than undertake the more complicated process of brewing beer?

There were other reasons why people drank beer, of course. First, it was nutritious and it provided vitamins, minerals, and calories (300 calories of beer was often more appealing than 300 calories of food). It had flavor, which could be sweet, tart, smoky, bitter, or herbal, and those flavors could season bland diets. If we look back just 200 years, the standard working-class diet in cities like London or Munich was bread, maybe potatoes, and some smoked fish or fatty meat. The food was dense, hard to digest, and boring; beer made it taste better. Also, turning water, grain, and hops into beer basically made water keepable, no bad thing in the days before homes had a ready supply of fresh water. Brewing was as important as smoking and salting meat and fish, pickling and fermenting vegetables, making jams, turning milk into cheese, and distilling leftover grain into whisky or gin, or potatoes into schnapps, or corn into bourbon.

Beer was a basic necessity and it was on dinner tables around the European beer-drinking nations (it took North Americans a lot longer to trade their liquor for lager). It was also on the breakfast and lunch tables, because beer was drunk steadily through the day, sipped like we might do with tea, coffee, or soft drinks. As beer was so prominent in the rural home, we can assume that it was used in a lot of different dishes too—breads, braises, stews, soups. I say assume because there's actually little written about the history of beer and food and we think that's because it was so normal to cook with beer, and to drink it all the time, that it didn't warrant writing about. Plus it was primarily a working-class drink and there's little documentation of working people's lives until into the nineteenth century, which is also when beer's role began to change.

Perhaps the most significant change in the role of beer came when cities created safe supplies of drinking water. Once the expanding populations had ready access to clean water, beer was no longer a basic necessity and could become a drink for leisure and pleasure. When that happened—coinciding with industrialization and urbanization in the beer-drinking nations—we got new beer styles and we started to value different beers, our tastes changing from hearty, sweet, and filling, to light, bitter, and refreshing.

From the late 1800s, beer was the social drink of much of the western world. By the end of the 1900s, it was the most common and most-drunk alcoholic drink everywhere in the world. Beer is the drink we're most likely to share with others, and in most cultures it's the drink we're most likely to have with food. Wine may dominate fine dining, but most of the world drinks a beer with dinner.

Beer's role on the dinner table is now a social one but it is still symbiotically linked to food. What's wonderful is how a country's common foods are so often good with beer. Stews and cheeses in Belgium with dark Monastic beer; tacos in Mexico with Dark Lagers; fried noodles in southeast Asia with cold Pale Lagers; nachos and burgers in North America with IPA. Beer has become the world's most global drink, but it's also the most local, brewed wherever you go, and with distinct local flavors and customs to go with the local dishes.

Increasingly, these local foods are being joined by dishes from all around the world, while beers have extended way beyond their old traditional regionality, meaning you could name any beer style and find it brewed anywhere in the world, and with that beer you can serve up whatever food you want. For a lot of us, that food no longer contains any animal products—or at least we're cutting down and eating a more flexible diet. It's a new shift in our ever-changing eating and drinking habits. Beer has been with humankind since we first deliberately turned grain into alcohol and drank it. Now it's something exciting and diverse that we can enjoy for entertainment, with limitless choices for bringing together beer and food, and celebrating it.

THE FLAVOR OF BEER

To understand the flavors in beer it helps to know about the ingredients that create it and the qualities and characteristics they give it. We can then can start to match those up with different foods.

GRAIN

Grains are the base of every beer. The grain will give beer its color, its sweetness, the sugars which will turn into alcohol, some mouthfeel, and flavor. Grain flavors are usually anything that you might find in a bakery: bread, toast, cookies, cake, caramel, toasted nuts, chocolate, coffee.

Barley is harvested and turned into malt, with part of that process kilning or roasting the barley kernels. Different roasting temperatures and times will create malts with different colors and flavors: think of it like bread that's toasted, as it goes from pale and bready, to toasty amber and caramelized, to bitter, dark, and burnt.

Grains contain sugars. The more grain that goes in, the more sugars are extracted, the more flavor and body we get, and the more alcohol. Different malts are combined to create the base of a beer, much like a baker would combine different flours, sugars, and ingredients to create different breads or cakes, though all beers will have a "base grain," usually pale ale or pilsner malt, which is the foundation of the recipe (like most bakes use flour).

Malted barley is not the only grain used. Wheat is common and it will give beer a richer texture, often a little (or a lot) of haze in its appearance, and a gentle, nutty flavor. Oats are another common grain. These give a fuller texture and body to a beer and might add a light, oaty flavor. Rye or spelt can be used to add a nuttier, spicier flavor to a beer, while rice and corn or maize are used to make a beer lighter and drier in body.

The brewing process begins with combining warm water with grains and letting them steep together for an hour. During this time, the sugars and other compounds in the grain are extracted into the water, leaving a sweet liquid called wort. The wort is drawn off and moved through the brewing process, while the grain is a leftover by-product and typically goes to farms as cattle fodder.

Above are some common malts and grains and the characteristics they might give to your beer.

THE FLAVORS OF GRAIN	
Pilsner malt	Bread, cookie, crackers
Pale ale malt	Toast, cereal, bread
Munich malt	Toast, toasted nuts, bread crusts
Caramalt	Toffee, sweet, toasted nuts
Crystal malt	Caramel, dried fruit, honey
Chocolate malt	Cacao, dark chocolate, coffee
Roasted barley	Dark chocolate, coffee, licorice
Wheat	Smooth, nutty, bready
Oats	Creamy, bready, oaty

HOP AROUND THE WORLD

NORTH AMERICA

Common hop varieties are: Citra, Mosaic, Simcoe, Cascade, Centennial, Chinook, Amarillo, Ekuanot, Strata, El Dorado.
North America is the largest hop growing nation in the world and the hops are mostly grown in the states of Washington, Oregon, and Idaho. The hops are generally strong in flavor and aroma and dominated by citrus (grapefruit, oranges), tropical fruits (mango, pineapple, melon), stone fruit (peach, apricot) and herbal/woody (pine, dank, allium). These hops are most often found in IPAs and hop-forward beers.

UNITED KINGDOM

Common varieties are: Goldings, Fuggles, Target, Bramling Cross, Challenger, Pilgrim, First Gold, Olicana, Endeavour, Jester.
Mostly grown in the counties of Kent, Herefordshire, and Worcestershire, British hops vary from delicate and complex through to lightly tropical, though rarely will you find the same intensity of flavor in a British hop as in an American hop. Common characteristics include citrus (orange pith, marmalade), stone fruits (apricot), berries (blackcurrant), herbal (woody, minty, tobacco, tea), floral (honeysuckle, elderflower), and modern varieties, like Jester and Olicana, give more tropical fruits (mango, passion fruit, but more subtle than American and Antipodean hops). These hops are most often found in Best Bitter, English Pale and Golden Ale, Belgian Blonde, Saison, Mild, Stout, Porter.

GERMANY AND CZECH REPUBLIC

Common German varieties are: Hersbrucker, Tettnanger, Perle, Spalt, Hüll Melon, Saphir.
Common Czech varieties are: Saaz and Kazbek.
Germany is the world's second-largest hop grower and most grow in the Hallertauer region north of Munich. In the Czech Republic they grow in the west, around the town of Žatec. Hops also grow in surrounding countries including Poland and Slovenia. Most of these hops have an elegant, subtle character, though they can be expressive and enticing, and are prized for how they give a firm, clean bitterness. They will be citrusy (lemon, pithy, zesty, mandarin), tropical (melon), herbal (grassy, juniper), floral (elderflower, jasmine, pepper). They are most often used in Lagers, Wheat Beers, and Belgian Ales.

AUSTRALIA AND NEW ZEALAND

Common Australian varieties are: Galaxy, Ella, Vic Secret, Topaz and Enigma.
Common New Zealand varieties are: Nelson Sauvin, Motueka, Riwaka, Rakau.
The main growing regions are in South Australia and Tasmania, and the Nelson region of New Zealand. The hops are known for being abundantly fruity and tropical, with citrus (grapefruit, tangerine, lime, pomelo), tropical (passion fruit, mango, pineapple), stone fruit and berries (gooseberry, grapes), floral (elderflower). These hops are most often used in Pale Ales, IPAs, Pacific IPAs, and Hoppy Lagers.

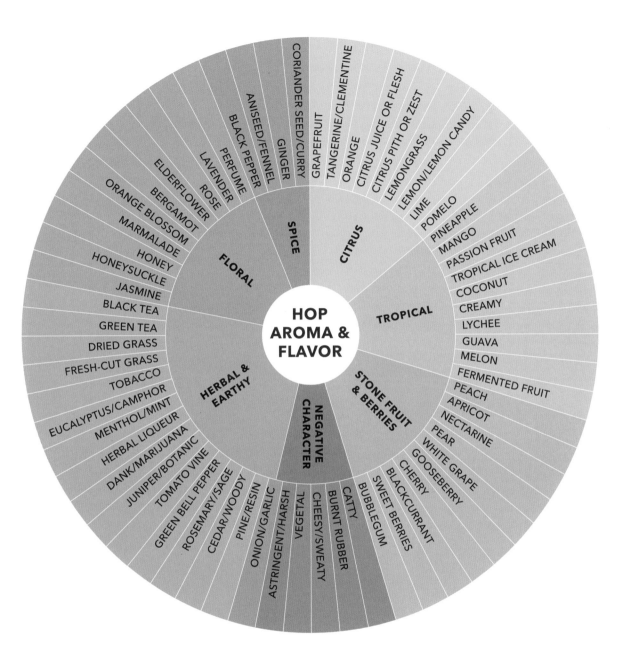

HOP AROMA & FLAVOR

- SPICE: CORIANDER SEED/CURRY, GINGER, BLACK PEPPER, ANISEED/FENNEL, PERFUME, LAVENDER, ROSE
- CITRUS: GRAPEFRUIT, TANGERINE/CLEMENTINE, ORANGE, CITRUS JUICE OR FLESH, CITRUS PITH OR ZEST, LEMONGRASS, LEMON/LEMON CANDY, LIME
- FLORAL: ELDERFLOWER, BERGAMOT, ORANGE BLOSSOM, MARMALADE, HONEY, HONEYSUCKLE, JASMINE
- TROPICAL: POMELO, PINEAPPLE, MANGO, PASSION FRUIT, TROPICAL ICE CREAM, COCONUT, CREAMY, LYCHEE, GUAVA, MELON, FERMENTED FRUIT
- HERBAL & EARTHY: BLACK TEA, GREEN TEA, DRIED GRASS, FRESH-CUT GRASS, TOBACCO, EUCALYPTUS/CAMPHOR, MENTHOL/MINT, HERBAL LIQUEUR, DANK/MARIJUANA, JUNIPER/BOTANIC, TOMATO VINE, GREEN BELL PEPPER, ROSEMARY/SAGE, CEDAR/WOODY, PINE/RESIN, ONION/GARLIC
- STONE FRUIT & BERRIES: PEACH, APRICOT, NECTARINE, PEAR, WHITE GRAPE, GOOSEBERRY, CHERRY, BLACKCURRANT, SWEET BERRIES, BUBBLEGUM
- NEGATIVE CHARACTER: ASTRINGENT/HARSH, VEGETAL, CHEESY/SWEATY, BURNT RUBBER, CATTY

HOPS

Hops are the seasoning and spice of a beer, and they can vary from delicate to intense. Hops give beer its bitterness and much of its flavor and aroma. The flavors we expect from hops are similar to anything that we might find in the fruit and vegetable aisle: orange, grapefruit, lemon, lime, tropical fruits like mango and pineapple, stone fruits like peach and apricot, berries, fresh herbs, mint,

pepper, plus more earthy flavors like grass or a woody quality.

It's the flower of the hop plant which is used and hops are varietal, with each different variety having different characteristics and strengths. Where the hop grows also affects its flavors—just as the same grape variety grown in California and southeast England will have different qualities. Hops contain acids, which give them bitterness, and they contain aromatic oils, many of which are also found in different fruits and spices. The most prevalent hop oil is myrcene, which is also found in mango, lemongrass, bay, and pine (and marijuana). Citra hops are especially high in myrcene. Humulene is another important hop oil—it's more herbal and resinous, and is also found in sage, ginger, pine, and orange.

Brewers add different hops for different characteristics; some are primarily used for bitterness, while others are reserved to add aroma and flavor. In the brewing process, the sweet wort is brought to a boil and then the hops are added. The boil usually lasts 60 minutes and hops can be added throughout that time, with any hops going in at the beginning of the boil giving the beer its bitterness, and the hops going in later giving it aroma and flavor. Once the beer has fermented, which takes three to nine days, it's left to mature. More hops can still be added during maturation. This is called dry-hopping and it's done to give even more aroma and flavor to a beer—it's the equivalent of putting fresh herbs on your food before serving it.

The main characteristics we get from hops can be seen in the hop wheel on page 11.

YEAST

Yeast is the magical microorganism which makes the alcohol and bubbles in beer. All yeasts produce some aroma compounds (typically fruity), and while most are neutral, some are prominent.

Fermentation is the process where yeast consumes the grain sugars and converts them into alcohol and carbon dioxide, while also producing some aromatic compounds called esters and phenols, which we smell and taste as being fruity or spicy. The fruitiness is often banana, pear, stone fruit, vanilla, or bubblegum, while the spiciness is pepper or clove. Belgian beers and Wheat beers often have a strong ester aroma profile.

Sour beers are made acidic by yeast and/or bacteria (the good kind of bacteria, like in yogurt). These beers are brewed with different strains of yeast which work with bacteria to produce a tartness or sourness, plus a range of aromas which could be fruity, spicy, or more rural and funky. This acidity in beer can be thirst-quenching and refreshing, but can also be more intense and challenging. Some beers, like Belgian Reds

and Browns have an acetic flavor, which is like balsamic vinegar compared to the lemony acidity of most sours.

Not all aromas or flavors from the yeast are positive. If we have a Pale Lager that smells of banana and clove then it's unintentional and a sign of a bad fermentation. Likewise, there are numerous off-flavors which are produced by the yeast during fermentation, like diacetyl (butter, popcorn), acetaldehyde (apples) and sulphur (eggs, struck match). While the yeast produces those compounds, it will also remove them if given enough time to do so.

WATER

Beer is a liquid and water is really important to each beer, but as a drinker considering what beer to have with dinner, we don't really need to know anything about water. Even the most hardcore beer nerds will very infrequently comment on the water profile in a beer, though if you're interested, a softer water profile (meaning fewer minerals in it) will give a beer with a softer, rounder mouthful (as in a classic Pale Lager), while a harder water profile will lead to a drier, leaner body (as in a British Bitter or Stout).

OTHER INGREDIENTS AND PROCESSES

SUGARS

Grain provides beer with most of the fermentable sugars which become alcohol, but brewers can also add other sugar sources. A contemporary trend is for lactose to be used in several different styles. Lactose is milk sugar, so vegans should be aware of that, and it's used to give a creamy depth, texture, and sweetness to beer. It used to be found only in Milk Stouts but it's now in some Hazy IPAs, some Fruit Sours, and some strong Stouts. In Belgium, you'll find lots of beers brewed using regular sugar—pale or dark—and this adds a lot of fermentable sugars without adding body to a beer, so they can produce strong beers with a lean, light body. Maple syrup and honey (another thing to watch out for if you are vegan) are also used in some beers—maple syrup would most commonly be found in strong Stouts as an additional flavoring.

FRUITS

Brewers can add any fruit you can think of to their beers. The fruits could be fresh, frozen, purée, pulp, peel, or syrup, depending on what flavors the brewers are trying to achieve. Some fruit beers will be subtle, others will be like juice. Berries (cherries and raspberries) are the most common fruit in Slow Sour beers. Tropical fruits (mango and passion fruit) are used in heavily fruited Fast Sours. You'll regularly see citrus fruits used in IPAs. Belgian Witbiers traditionally contain dried orange peel. Pumpkin beers are a seasonal special for many North American breweries, often also including spices.

CHOCOLATE, COFFEE, NUTS, AND VANILLA

Chocolate, cacao, and/or coffee will add extra richness, more roasted flavors, and perhaps some sweetness, and are most often found in strong Stouts and Porters. Nuts will also most commonly be found in Stouts, usually strong ones, but sometimes in regular-strength beers (like Peanut Butter Porters). Coconut is used in a wide range of styles, from light sours, to IPAs, to Imperial Stouts, and gives a tropical creaminess. Vanilla is another common flavoring, again most often (but not exclusively) found in dark strong beers. A trend for "pastry" or "culinary" beers has seen even sweeter ingredients being used.

SPICES AND HERBS

Like chefs, brewers can take whatever they want from the spice rack. The most common spice in traditional brewing is coriander seed, which is used in traditional Gose, wheat beers, and some other Belgian styles, and gives an orangey-floral fragrance and flavor. Any other spices and herbs can be used as a seasoning in beer: pepper, grains of paradise, cardamom, cinnamon, lemongrass, ginger. Tea or floral ingredients like elderflower, jasmine, hibiscus, and juniper are brewed into styles ranging from Saisons and Sours to IPAs. Gose will be brewed using salt to give it a richer flavor. And chili is regularly used in beers.

BARREL-AGED BEER

Beers can be matured in wooden barrels to develop new flavor profiles. There are two main types: sour and not-sour. The sour beers often go into old wine barrels and they are encouraged to acidify, turning tart and vinous; sometimes fruits are also added. The non-soured beers are most often Imperial Stouts or other strong ales, and these go into barrels which previously held bourbon, another spirit, or sometimes wine. The previous liquid, plus the wood itself, will impart characteristics to barrel-aged beers, where common flavors are vanilla, oak, woody spice, and coconut.

HOW TO TASTE BEER

There are no right or wrong ways to taste beer
(unless you spit it out—that's wrong) and it's a
uniquely individual experience, which only comes
from actual experience of doing it. The best advice
I can give to be a better and more confident taster
is simply: drink more, drink more broadly, eat more
broadly so you know more flavors, and really try to
think about what you're drinking. Like learning a
language or playing a sport, we can practice and
improve at tasting beer if we focus a little.

The hardest part of tasting beer is usually
connecting your flavor experience with the right
words in your brain (you smell something fruity, but
what exactly is that fruit?) Finding the words to
describe beer is difficult. I tend to focus more on the
balance of the beer: how do the malts and the hops
interact, what's the body of the beer like, what's the
first impression and the last, and most importantly:
is it delicious and does it make me happy?

Flavor is the combination of smell and taste.
Without a sense of smell, we can only get a limited
appreciation of what we're eating and drinking,

though we should still be able to pick out the tastes
(sweet, bitter, sour, salty, or umami). Memory,
emotion, and experience are closely linked to
flavor, and certain smells and tastes elicit different
emotional responses such as nostalgia and
happiness. The neuro-wirings of smell and taste
are connected to the nervous system, which is why
some smells can make us thirsty or hungry (fresh
coffee brewing, the smell of bread baking) while
others can make us feel disgust (rotting vegetables,
sour milk). Personal experience is also key: if two
people drink the same beer and one tastes papaya,
pomelo, and grains of paradise, but the other
person has never eaten those ingredients before,
then they might taste melon, grapefruit, orange, and
pepper. Neither drinker is wrong, because of the
individual nature of taste and flavor.

Scientifically, there are some useful things to
know about taste. The tongue is a sensitive
muscular organ that we can train, but it also has
important innate functions. For example, we have
the five tastes of sweet, sour, salty, umami, and
bitter, but our tongue doesn't treat them equally:
there are significantly more taste receptors for
bitterness than sweetness. When we eat something
sweet, it's almost always good and our brain doesn't
need to worry about it. But something bitter could
potentially be a toxin, so our brains need more time
and information to decide whether it's safe to
swallow or not. A lot of people don't like IPA or
black coffee for this reason, but the tongue is
adaptive and we can grow to like them.

Beyond smell and taste, the sensation of touch
is important to our enjoyment of food and drink.
Trigeminal sensations will pick up on the beer's
carbonation (flat or fizzy); its temperature (ice cold,
too warm); its texture (thin and dry like soda water,
thick and smooth like milk); they'll sense spice and
heat; they can pick up on cooling sensations like
mint and cucumber; they'll feel tannins, which are
dry (think about unripe bananas or a woody dryness
in some wines).

Want to be a better beer taster? Just drink
more beer.

THE IMPORTANT CHARACTERISTICS OF BEER

While thinking about the flavors of beer we also need to consider other qualities, including its strength, its intensity, and its mouthfeel. All of these will contribute to the overall appreciation of the beer and then how it might work with food. Here are some common words used to describe a beer, and what they really mean.

Mouthfeel: The body or texture of the beer. This could range from light (think soda water) to heavy (think syrup); light beers are often refreshing, whereas heavy beers are more filling. "Smooth" is a word used often and it's an indicator of a beer that has a low carbonation and low-to-moderate hop bitterness, while "creamy" will usually be used when describing a sweeter, richer beer.

Finish: The flavor or character at the end of the beer. It'll normally be on a scale from dry and bitter to sweet, and from short to long. Most mainstream lagers have a short, dry finish, whereas a quality Pilsner will have a long, dry, and bitter finish. An Imperial Stout will probably have a long sweet finish.

Carbonation: How fizzy the beer is. Some beer, like classic British cask ales, will naturally have a low carbonation (but they shouldn't ever be flat like water), while other beers, like Belgian ales and Slow Sours, will have a brisk, lively fizz to them. The carbonation can have an uplifting impact with food, being refreshing against stronger flavors and high fat content.

Clean: For me, a "clean" beer is one that's free from negative characteristics and also has a flavor profile that's really defined. Imagine a really good photo—a perfectly in-focus image is like a really clean beer, whereas a shot that's a little (or a lot) out of focus, isn't clean. In my experience, all the best beers have a "clean" taste and flavor balance.

Balanced: A beer which has a balance of flavors between the sweetness, bitterness (or acidity), and alcohol. This doesn't mean it's low in flavor and boring, and even the strongest Stouts should still have a balance to them, while a very bitter Double IPA can still be balanced if it has an appropriate malt profile and the bitterness isn't overwhelming. The best beers in the world all share a great balance, which leads to you wanting to drink more of them.

Dry: Champagne is a dry drink, while Irish cream liquor is the opposite—it's sweet. Dry describes the finish of the beer, which will be crisp, refreshing, and not sweet. Most good lagers (and most cheap ones, actually) are dry. Crisp is another word often used in place of dry. It's a beer with a snappy, clean, refreshing finish.

Juicy: A word most often used to describe very hoppy and hazy beers which have a juicy quality. The juiciness could be the appearance (orange and opaque), the aroma (lots of juicy fruits), or the flavor (a tangy citrus quality).

Spicy: Spice is usually a combination of peppery yeast, perhaps some cloves, ground spices like coriander, and also a dryness to the beer which enhances the spiciness. It's most commonly tasted in Belgian ales and wheat beers.

COMPLEMENTARY FLAVORS IN BEER AND FOOD

When we are bringing together beer and food, we are usually most interested in the sauces, side dishes, or seasonings, rather than a protein element. Think about Thai fried noodles: it doesn't matter if it's chicken, prawn, or tofu because the soy sauce, garlic, fresh herbs, chili, and lime have way more impact. Here are some common ingredients, with beer styles which might naturally work well with them. Below and over the page is a group of primary beer flavors and the foods which might complement them.

FOOD FLAVORS	BEERS
Butter	Pale Lager, Pilsner, Dark Lager, Kölsch
Black pepper	Belgian Blonde, Saison, Tripel, Dubbel, Pale Ale
Lemon	Pilsner, Pale Lager, Smoked Beer, Slow Sours, Tripel, American IPA, Hazy IPA
Soy sauce	Stout, Porter, Dark Lager, Black IPA, Dubbel, Dunkelweizen
Lime, Thai basil, cilantro (fresh coriander)	Pacific Pale, Hoppy Lager, Belgian Blonde, Fast Sours
Dill, basil, fennel	Saison, Belgian Blonde, Tripel, Slow Sours, Hoppy Lager, Pacific Pale
Rosemary, thyme, sage	Saison, Tripel, Pale Ale, IPA, Double IPA, Hazy DIPA
Roast garlic, sweet onions	Pale Ale, IPA, Double IPA, Porter
Salsa/hot sauce	American Pale Ale, Dark Lager, Amber Lager, Porter
Tomato ketchup	Pale Ale, IPA, Black IPA, Dark Lager, Porter
Mustard	Hefeweizen, Saison, Dark Lager, American Pale Ale, Pilsner
Yogurt	Wheat Ale, Hefeweizen, Fast Sours
Smoke	Porter, Smoked Beer, Pale Ale, Dunkelweizen, Dubbel
Cinnamon, nutmeg, clove	Dubbel, Quadrupel, Dunkelweizen
Caramel	Imperial Stout, Red IPA, Weizenbock

BEER AND FOOD: SOME GREAT FLAVOR COMBINATIONS

Beer Flavor	Found In	Complementary Foods
Bready/toasty	Pale Lager, Kölsch, Pale Ale, British Pale Ale, Golden Ale, Amber Lager, Dark Lager, Strong Lager	Bread, hot dog/burger buns, pizza, pasta, fried batter, mild cheese, white beans, potatoes, savory pastry, rice
Caramel/toffee	Pale Ale, IPA, Red IPA, British Bitter and Mild, Porter, Imperial Stout	Roasted vegetables, roast onion and garlic, fried foods, toasted nuts, aged cheeses, miso, dried fruit, sweet potato/squash, maple syrup, ketchup
Nutty	Amber Lager, Dark Lager, Amber Ale, Red Ale, Brown Ale	Aged cheese, toasted nuts, roasted vegetables, whole grains, beans, sesame/tahini, wild rice, wholegrain pasta, nutritional yeast, white miso, coconut, corn, corn tacos, cauliflower, lentils
Roasted	Stout, Porter, Dark Lager, Black IPA, Brown Ale	Roasted and barbecue vegetables, root vegetables, roasted nuts, smoked tofu, mushrooms, black beans, soy sauce, miso, dried fruits, chocolate
Dried fruit	British Bitter, Dubbel, Quadrupel, aged beers, Red IPA	Dried fruit, balsamic vinegar, miso, caramelized onions, cooked orchard fruit, tamarind, chutney, tagine
Smoky (wood and spice)	Smoked beer, some Porters and Stouts, Hefeweizen, Saison	Smoked tofu, barbeque sauce, paprika, all spice, cloves, chipotle chili, roasted nuts
Sweet	Imperial Stout, Sweet Stout, Strong Lager, Hazy DIPA	Sweet potato/squash, gochujang, hoisin, bread, cakes, pastries, chocolate, vanilla cream, pancakes, sweet onions, root vegetables, cooked stone/orchard fruit, vanilla, honey, maple syrup
Creamy	Sweet Stouts, Weissbier, Hazy DIPA	Cream cheese, cheese sauces, avocado, egg yolks, eggplant (aubergine), cashew nuts, risotto, beans, mayonnaise, yogurt, coconut and coconut cream, chocolate
Oak/barrel-Aged	Barrel-aged beer	Vanilla, coconut, woody spices, toffee, chocolate
Spicy (from yeast)	Witbier, Weissbier, Saison, Belgian Blonde, Dubbel, Tripel, Quadrupel	Cloves, ginger, ground spices, fennel, chili, miso, Thai basil, basil, aniseed, black pepper, arugula (rocket), celeriac, carrot
Fruity (from yeast)	Pale Ale, British Ale, Hazy IPA	Chutney, olive oil, dried fruit, stone fruit, mature cheeses, ginger
Acetic	Slow Sours	Balsamic vinegar, tomatoes, marinara sauce, ketchup, tamarind, pickles, chutney, mustard
Acidic	Slow Sours, Fast Sours	Fermented foods (sourdough, yogurt, kimchi), citrus fruit, wine or cider vinegar, fresh cheeses, goat cheese, tomatoes
Fermented	Most beers	Miso, aged cheese, sauerkraut, kimchi, sourdough, Sriracha, dark chocolate, coffee
Earthy	Slow Sours, Saison, English IPA	Farmhouse and blue cheeses, goat cheese, potatoes, root vegetables, olive oil, berries, cauliflower, beetroot, turmeric, cumin
Citrus hops	Pale Ale, all IPA and DIPA, Red IPA, Hoppy Lager	Citrus fruit, ginger, onion, chive, mint, cilantro (fresh coriander), ground coriander, tropical fruits, Cheddar cheese, roasted onion and garlic, avocado, lime, Szechuan pepper, lemongrass
Tropical hops	Pale Ale, all IPA and DIPA, Pacific Pale, Hoppy Lager	Mango, passion fruit, pineapple, roasted garlic, ginger, sweet potato, aged cheeses, mint, Thai basil, lime, mirin
Stone fruit hops	Pale Ale, all IPA and DIPA, Pacific Ale, English Pale Ale	Ginger, dried apricots, avocado, toasted nuts, honey, ground cilantro (coriander), nutty cheeses
Herbal hops	Saison, Tripel, Pilsner, British Ale, Red IPA, American IPA	Basil, thyme, garlic, pepper, cinnamon, mustard, ground coriander, oregano, sage, rosemary, citrus peel, arugula (rocket), Brussels sprouts
Floral hops	Saison, Pilsner, British Ale, Golden Ale	Aged cheeses, mushrooms, truffles, cumin, potato, eggplant (aubergine), cilantro (fresh coriander), dill, rosemary, lemongrass, avocado, bell peppers

HOW TO PAIR BEER WITH VEGETARIAN AND VEGAN FOOD

So how do you pair vegetarian and vegan food with beer? The good news is that the existing approaches to beer and food pairing are still totally relevant. Here I'll give a few tips and some considerations and then we'll jump into specific ways to focus on veggie and vegan food with beer, using the Three Bs of beer and food pairing: **Bridge**, **Balance**, and **Boost**.

Before even thinking about the Three Bs, the most important consideration in any beer and food pairing is the **intensity**. A Dark Lager and an Imperial Stout have shared flavors of dark malts, toasted nuts, and chocolate, but they are completely different strengths. If you have a bowl of mushroom fried rice followed by a chocolate brownie, then the Dark Lager will match the rice and the Imperial Stout will match the brownie, but swap them around and something is overpowered. We always want to make sure that we find a balance of intensities.

Another consideration is the **mouthfeel** and **texture** of a beer. This can range from light to thick; it could be low in carbonation or really fizzy; it could be creamy and sweet, or dry and refreshing.

GOOD EXAMPLES OF BALANCING INTENSITIES

Pale Lager	Tomato and mozzarella salad
Golden Ale	Green vegetable risotto
Pale Ale	Grilled vegetable pizza
IPA	Roasted vegetable lasagna
Double IPA	Smoked tofu and BBQ veg sandwich

A Pilsner is going to be dry, well-carbonated and light in body; a Belgian Golden Ale will be similar but with more structure and body behind it; a Double IPA will be rich, rounded in the body, and lower in carbonation, with a prominent bitterness.

Mouthfeel works differently with different foods. If you've got something with a high fat content, like a creamy curry or farmhouse cheeses, then you often want carbonation to lift and cut it so you'd have a Pilsner with the curry and a Belgian Gueuze with the cheese. Sweeter foods often want a richer, more luxurious mouthfeel, like having a Hazy DIPA with roasted peaches. Chili heat can be softened with a smooth, creamy, sweeter beer.

The **alcohol content** will affect the intensity and the mouthfeel of a beer, while the alcohol itself can also be a strong flavor with food. Typically, the stronger the beer, the stronger the dish you want with it. You'll also find that very strong beers are best balanced by fat (cheese), salt (fries), or sweetness (cake).

Red Tomato Tart with Oven-Dried Beer Tomatoes, page 138.

Beer Chick'n Tenders, page 132.

Watch out for **chili heat**. It's the capsaicin in a chili that makes it feel like we're being burnt and it's a temporary irritation that might last a few seconds or a few minutes. You want to find a beer which can soothe that irritation, not make it worse. Typically, a very hoppy beer will ignite the fire of hot chili, and a highly carbonated beer can feel like it's poking the burn, whereas a sweeter beer with a full body, like a Hefeweizen or Sweet Stout, can wrap around the heat and cool it down.

And think **local** when pairing beer and food. Look around the world and you'll find local dishes served with local beers or beer styles. Many of these come from the traditional beer-drinking nations and one challenge we have matching beer and veg is that most of those classic dishes are animal-based (stews, sausages, and so on), but we can find many more examples that are vegetarian (usually with cheese) or which can become vegan, while we can also look at seasonal dishes. Local beers have a way of reflecting local cuisines, cultures, and climates.

Some great local pairings include:
- American Pale Ale with bean and avocado tacos
- American IPA with mac 'n' cheese
- Munich Helles with pretzels
- Amber Lager with *Käsespätzle* (German mac 'n' cheese)
- Italian Pilsner with pizza
- Trappist ales paired with the monastery's cheeses
- Pacific Pale Ale with a superfood salad bowl
- Witbier with fries and mayo
- English Golden Ale with asparagus risotto
- British Bitter with a nut roast

THE THREE Bs OF BEER AND FOOD

1: BRIDGE

A zesty Witbier with a Thai coconut curry. A caramelized Red Ale with roasted root vegetables. A coffee-infused Stout with a chocolate chip muffin.

By finding shared flavors in the food and the beer we can build a bridge between them. Sometimes you'll focus on the main flavor, like trying to match a cherry beer with a cherry cake, while other times you'll want to look at the additional ingredients or what's served with it, like having a tropical Pacific Pale Ale with a herby, citrusy Thai salad. There might also be additional ingredients in the beer which can help the bridge, like a Witbier, brewed with orange peel and coriander seed, paired with a tagine or falafel. By pulling together similar flavors, we're drawing the food and beer closer to one another.

Some flavor bridges:
- American IPA with rosemary, thyme, citrus, caramelized onion
- Pacific Pale Ale with fresh cilantro (coriander), lime, lemongrass
- Pilsner with fresh herbs, lemon, pepper, fresh bread
- Amber Lager with toasted bread, pizza dough, nutty cheese
- Witbier with lemon, earthy spices, peppery herbs
- Fast Sours with citrus, yogurt, fresh cheese
- Hefeweizen with coconut, toasted bread, creaminess
- Saison with pepper, fresh green herbs, lemon
- Dubbel with miso, aniseed, dried fruit
- Stout and Porter with roasted foods, soy sauce, chocolate

Take the bridge between beer and veg:
- Pacific Ale with summer rolls and sweet chili
- Belgian Dubbel with lentil bolognese
- Porter with roasted eggplant (aubergine)
- Witbier with lemongrass and chili tofu
- American IPA with garlic and herb focaccia
- Dunkelweizen with vegetable and bean tagine
- Pale Ale with caramelized onion tart
- Raspberry sour beer with lemon cake
- Quadrupel with baked apple
- Slow Sours with goat cheese

Stout Shakshuka, page 116.

2: BALANCE

Oatmeal stout with bean chili. Hefeweizen with spicy fried rice. Hazy DIPA with mushroom risotto.

It's good to aim to harmonize and create balance with beer and food, and there are several ways to do this. One is to think about spiciness and trying to cool it down, like having a malty Dark Lager with bean tacos and hot sauce. Another is to create balance between intense flavors, for example a bowl of salty garlic fries will be well matched by a really bitter IPA. While we can also use beer to create a balanced eating experience and to leave us feeling refreshed, like having a Pilsner with deep-fried foods.

What balances what?
- Bitterness balances salt: Pilsner and pretzel; Session IPA and loaded nachos
- Sweetness balances spice: Hefeweizen and Thai red curry; Dubbel with bean tagine
- Sweetness balances umami: Porter with miso eggplant (aubergine); Bock with veggie lasagna
- Roast balances acidity: Stout and huevos rancheros; barbecued mushrooms with Gose
- Bitterness balances fat: Pale Ale and guacamole; Coffee Stout with chocolate cake
- Carbonation balances fat: Pilsner and arancini; Saison with fried tofu
- Alcohol balances fat: Tripel with farmhouse cheese; Doppelbock with apple strudel
- Sweetness balances sweetness: Hazy DIPA with sweet potato fries; Quadrupel with cherry pie

Some brilliant balance pairings include:
- Amber Ale with a quesadilla
- Pale Lager with salt and pepper tofu
- Dark Lager with spicy bean tacos
- Pale Ale with mac 'n' cheese
- Hazy IPA with avocado on toast
- English Pale Ale with cauliflower cheese
- Tripel with fennel risotto
- Brown Ale with massaman curry
- Weizenbock with a crème brûlée
- Imperial Stout with a blueberry muffin

Cherry Beer Pancakes, page 119.

3: BOOST

American IPA with grilled cheese. Belgian Blonde with vegetable and bean tagine. Double IPA and carrot cake.

A Boost pairing comes when the beer and the food can enhance each other and boost the experience. It's usually a powerful combination of flavors, and sometimes an unusual and unexpected one, but the results are always great. There are no simple rules to finding a match like this, but when you get it just right, you'll have something extra delicious in front of you.

Boost your beer and veg experience:
- Hazy Pale Ale with lemongrass and chili tofu
- Hazy DIPA with peach cobbler
- Pilsner with pan con tomate (or just pizza)
- Amber Lager with vegan mac 'n' cheese
- Dark Lager with mushroom fried rice
- Dunkelweizen with roasted cauliflower
- Dubbel with pasta and marinara sauce
- Tripel with apricot and pistachio cake
- Barrel-aged Imperial Stout with toasted PBJ
- Imperial Stout and coconut cheesecake

COOKING VEGETARIAN AND VEGAN FOOD WITH BEER

Cooking veggie and vegan food with beer is way more fun than using meat, and the best thing about it is how beer can become a more integral ingredient in many of the dishes. For example, my vegan cheeses are made with beer in them; you can't make a block of cheddar with beer in it. Likewise, beer sausages can contain a significant amount of beer in the actual mixture. Want to avoid baking with eggs? Mix up some ground flax seeds with beer and you have an alternative (it doesn't taste like egg, obviously, but it binds like one). I love that it's possible to integrate beer into vegan dishes way more prominently than with non-veggie dishes.

There are some common ingredients used in many recipes as flavor boosters. Most of the time they are umami-enhancers, capable of adding more depth and deliciousness to what you're cooking. There are also a lot of fermented foods, as they naturally work with the flavors of beer. Here are a few of the most important ingredients to have in your cupboard.

Vital wheat gluten is what you'll want to buy if you're trying to make the meatiest meat-free food. It's made from wheat which has had its starches and gluten separated. You use it like a flour, but when mixed with other ingredients, it becomes amazingly meat-like with a dense texture and a nice chewiness. You have to get the cooking right or it can be oddly spongy. The key is to knead it for a really long time.

Nutritional yeast (made from a strain of *Saccharomyces cerevisiae*, which is the same family of yeast which makes beer) adds a cheesy, nutty flavor and can be used in place of Parmesan or just as a general all-purpose seasoning for a savory flavor.

Miso is a brilliant ingredient and I use it in a lot of recipes. It's fermented soy beans and might also contain rice or barley. The fermented flavor enhances the beer qualities and adds a richness and depth, with the white miso adding a sweet flavor and the brown ones giving more oomph and richness. Soy sauce and tamari are similar and also give a savory flavor, plus they work well with a lot of different beers.

Sweetness is often used to balance some of the bitterness and enhance other flavors. Malt extract is a good ingredient and mirrors some beer flavors, but sugars, honey and agave are all good to have. You'll see a lot of cashew nuts used to give a creamy texture to foods. And if you avoid dairy then you'll want to find great alternatives to milk, butter, and yogurt. I use Vegan Block for cooking with butter, or Flora if I'm baking; I like Oatly Whole Milk and unsweetened almond milk; Oatly's cream is also really good for desserts; soy yogurt tastes pretty gross but it's fine to cook with. For nearly all the recipes which use milk or butter, you can use dairy or a vegan alternative (I always use the vegan alternatives as it's my personal preference, even if the rest of the dish contains cheese or eggs).

THE BEST BEERS TO USE

There are a few styles of beer which are particularly good for cooking with: most lagers (but not really bitter or aromatic ones), most Wheat beers, Belgian Blondes, Brunes, Dubbels and Quadrupels, Stout and Porter, Sour beers. Hoppy beers are rarely worth cooking with because they will likely add too much bitterness and the thing which is so good about those beers—the hoppy aroma and flavor—is volatile, so will disappear when cooked.

The important consideration for any cooking with beer is hop bitterness—and you want to avoid it. It's only in a few dishes that this can be good to cook with. Generally, the sweeter the beer, the better it'll work and the more flavor it'll impart. One more thing: I will sometimes save beer in the bottom of the can or bottle and cover the top in plastic wrap

Imperial Jackfruit Dirty Fries, page 187.

(clingfilm) to be able to use it a day or two later. That's fine for beer you are going to cook with.

Just because we're cooking with beer, it doesn't mean that every recipe should taste strongly of beer. Some recipes will have a dominant beer flavor, while sometimes it'll be subtle and beer will be just one of a number of different seasonings and ingredients used. Some recipes use specific styles, while others are great with just a cheap can of mainstream lager. And while some recipes might take a couple of hours to make, others take minutes and allow you to drink while cooking—I don't know about you, but I love to open a beer while I'm in the kitchen.

Finally, a really good high-speed blender is a useful piece of kitchen equipment for a lot of these recipes.

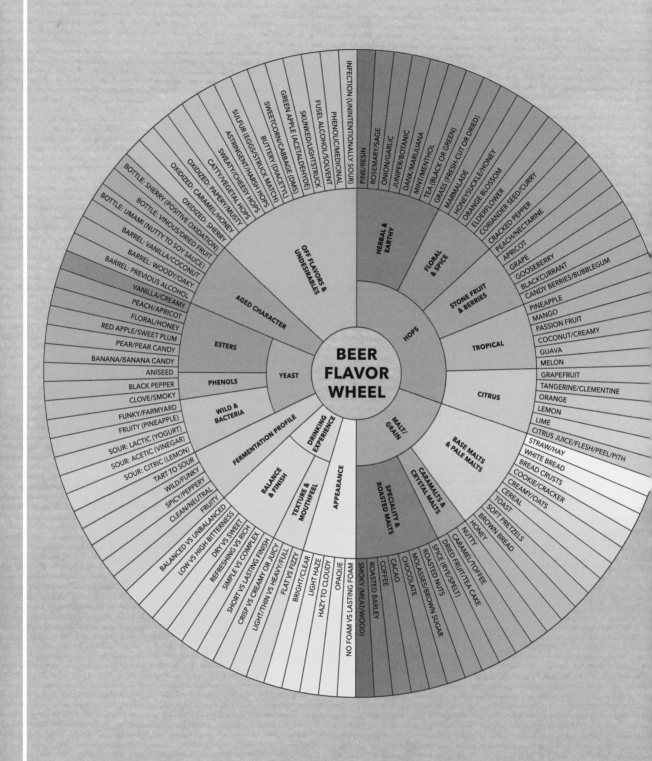

BEER STYLES

In this section there are over 200 suggestions for different beer and food combinations. I've tried to select beers which are considered classics of their type, or which are readily available in different countries. Some of the combinations will be very specific to each other, but most of the time they are suggestive rather than instructive and the aim is that you can use any similar beers with the dishes mentioned.
The most important consideration is that taste is individual: we all like different things in different combinations, so use these ideas as a guide to suit your own preferences in bringing together beer and veg.

HOPS

PALE ALE

American-style Pale Ale is notable for its hop content, being aromatic and bitter with American and modern hops, giving lots of citrus with some support from tropical and resinous aromas, plus a strong bitterness. Beneath all the hops is often a robust base of malt, which won't be sweet but could have some toasty and toffee-like flavors to hold all the hops in place. Complementary ingredients include bread, roasted vegetables, hard herbs, cooked alliums like onion and garlic, citrus, semi-hard cheese.

BRIDGE: Sweet-citrus dressings, bitter vegetables, caramelized onion

BALANCE: Fried foods, pizza, salty snacks

BOOST: Roasted vegetables, mac 'n' cheese, avocado

AVOID: Desserts, gravy dishes, too much chili

FIVE POINTS PALE

TRY WITH: **VEGGIE PIZZA**
BREWED IN: **LONDON, ENGLAND**
ABV: **4.4%**

The Pembury Tavern, in Hackney, London, is one of my favorite pubs and it's run by Five Points Brewing Co., who are based just over the road. I usually start with a pint of Five Points Best on cask and drink it quickly enough that I have time to order a pint of Pale before my pizza arrives (because I always order a pizza when I'm there). The beer will be on cask and keg and I like both equally, though in the Pembury I'll have the cask. It has the toasty body you'd expect in a Pale Ale and it's hopped with Amarillo and Citra, giving it orange and grapefruity aromas, and a firm bitterness. The pub has one of the best selections of veggie and vegan pizzas, including one with zucchini (courgette), cavolo nero, pesto, lemon oil, and chili, and all those flavors love the hops in the Pale.

HALF ACRE DAISY CUTTER

TRY WITH: **BEAN AND GUACAMOLE BURRITO**
BREWED IN: **CHICAGO, ILLINOIS, USA**
ABV: **5.2%**

Daisy Cutter is a brilliant example of a Pale Ale that's supremely balanced, with enough malt to give it structure but not sweetness, then American hops giving it mandarin, pithy citrus, and some pine, before it cuts right through to a bitter finish. The brewery serves up Mexican food in its taprooms and that's the direction to go. A bean burrito with guacamole is a great choice, with the avocado able to be the balancing ingredient between hops and hot sauce. Add some cheese and roasted mushrooms into the burrito and it'll be even better, as they'll emphasize some of the malt sweetness.

TOPPLING GOLIATH PSEUDO SUE

TRY WITH: **NAM JIN EGGPLANT (AUBERGINE)**
BREWED IN: **DECORAH, IOWA, USA**
ABV: **5.8%**

Pseudo Sue is in the modern style of American Pale Ales, one which begins to cross over to the hazy-juicy brews, but it strikes a balance between all the hop flavor and aroma and a tighter, cleaner, drier-bodied beer, one that's more elegant than exuberant, poised perfectly on the point of exciting and everyday. It's solely Citra-hopped and from that you get plenty of mango, some citrus juice and zest, some woody pine, and a herbal depth. Not many strongly hopped beers go with a salad, but they can be great with roasted eggplants (aubergines) covered in nam jin, a Thai dressing made with soy sauce, sugar, garlic, chili, lime juice, and orange juice. The recipe I like serves it on wild rice and I add roasted smoked tofu (Citra hops love smoke) and lots of cilantro (fresh coriander), mint, and Thai basil.

FERAL BREWING HOP HOG

TRY WITH: **MUSHROOM AND AIOLI BURGER**
BREWED IN: **BASKERVILLE, AUSTRALIA**
ABV: **5.8%**

They used to call Hop Hog an IPA but the palate shift of drinkers has tucked it a little closer into the expectations of a Pale Ale. It's a wonderfully balanced beer with sweetness, bitterness, and lot of pomelo, mandarin, pine, pulp, and pith, and it's all ripened by a juicy kind of malt character that plumps up the fruitiness. If you're in Western Australia, try out Feral Brewing's brilliant brewpub with its big backyard. They have a mushroom, cheese, and bell (sweet) pepper burger with aioli, which is a great match—the hops love the garlicky aioli and the bitterness (which shares some flavors with bell pepper) gives you the balance. Plus it comes with a load of proper pub-style chips and every beer is good with chips (they are definitely British-style chips, by the way, not fries).

BOULEVARD BREWING PALE ALE

TRY WITH: **VEGAN RIBS**
BREWED IN: **KANSAS CITY, MISSOURI, USA**
ABV: **5.4%**

Brewed since 1989, this is a classic-tasting American Pale Ale that has a prominent malt middle to it, with caramel malts giving the beer a chewy, toasty sweetness to go alongside the grapefruity, peppery, zesty Cascade hops. Kansas City is well known for its barbecue, and we're going to go for the vegan version with seitan ribs in a thick, smoky, tomato-based sauce. The malt in the beer works really well the sauce, while the hops and the spices complement each other then enhance the smokiness around the seitan. Add some crunchy coleslaw on the side and it's even better— and if you want to make something similar for yourself, check out the recipe on page 155.

SESSION IPA

Session IPAs are lower-alcohol IPAs, usually 4–5% ABV. The difference between a Pale Ale and Session IPA usually comes down to the malt, with a Session IPA often less sweet and toasty, which allows the hops to present more aroma and bitterness. The best Session IPAs have the right balance between hop flavor, malt structure, and moderate alcohol, and most are brewed using modern hops. Ingredients like avocado, beans, cheese, lime, and fragrant herbs can all taste good with this style, while salty or fatty dishes will provide balance from the bitterness.

BRIDGE: Vietnamese dishes, pesto and herb sauces, sweet-citrus dressings

BALANCE: Fried cauliflower wings, fresh cheeses, spiced tomato sauces

BOOST: Grilled vegetables, bar snacks, roasted garlic

AVOID: Chocolate, gravy-based dishes

THE KERNEL TABLE BEER

TRY WITH: **VIETNAMESE NOODLE SALAD (BUN CHAY)**
BREWED IN: **LONDON, ENGLAND**
ABV: **3.0%**

"Table" has become a synonym for lower alcohol beer in a similar way to the prefix of "Session." Table comes from the old tradition of having a low-strength beer which people drank through the day, including with their meals. The Kernel's Table Beer is like a mini Pale Ale, one that's light yet smooth in body and blooming with aromatic hops—they use a rotating range of hops which are always brightly aromatic and leave a lasting bitterness. My favorite of their beers always contain Mosaic hops, which I often think smell like fermented tropical fruits, the kind of fermenting fruity aroma that's evocative to me of Hanoi; perhaps because of that I find Mosaic-hopped beers often go well with the flavors of Vietnamese noodle salads with their sweet-savory dressing and lots of fresh herbs and lime.

BALTER BREWING XPA

TRY WITH: **ROAST VEG, MOZZARELLA, AND PESTO SANDWICH**
BREWED IN: **CURRUMBIN, AUSTRALIA**
ABV: **5.0%**

The XPA has become a contemporary Aussie style, standing for Extra Pale Ale, with most having lots of aromatic hops, a light malt body, and a refreshing bitter to suit the local climate and thirst. Balter's XPA is one of the best. It's super-fruity with lots of tropical hops, some mandarin, lemon, and pineapple, plus something more floral like elderflower. Its crisp bitterness makes it the sort of beer you open, drink, then quickly find yourself reaching for another. Roast up some veg—bell (sweet) peppers and zucchini (courgettes), perhaps—and serve in a sandwich with mozzarella and pesto. The hops in this are really good with the oil and herb in the pesto, while the cheese sweetens everything up.

CRAK BREWERY MUNDAKA

TRY WITH: **BURRATA, PEACH, OLIVE, AND LEMON**
BREWED: **CAMPODARSEGO, ITALY**
ABV: **4.6%**

Crak's Mundaka uses modern European hops, which bring elegant mandarin, lemon, and blossom, and powerful American hops, which give grapefruit, pineapple, and pine, and they combine into a summery sort of Session IPA, one for beaches and beer gardens. They have a garden in the brewery taproom (unfortunately no beach though), and they serve up briciola, which are large slabs of bread somewhere between Roman pizza and focaccia topped with different local ingredients, like cheeses, hams, and vegetables. It's the sort of beer food that's simple but always good, and you can choose different toppings based on what you're drinking. My dream bread topping for Mundaka would be burrata, rosemary-grilled peaches, olives, and some grated lemon peel, and the bread would be fresh focaccia. A sensationally good combination of flavors for a Session IPA.

Korean Cauliflower Bites, page 188.

BEAVERTOWN NECK OIL

TRY WITH: **HALLOUMI FRIES**
BREWED IN: **LONDON, ENGLAND**
ABV: **4.3%**

Neck Oil deserves to be seen as a defining example of what a true British Session IPA is: very light, crisply refreshing, the sort of bitterness which gets your attention but doesn't need to yell at you, and it's really aromatic with zesty tropical and citrus fruits, but not so hoppy that it gets perfumey and overwhelming, meaning it's actually properly sessionable. It's a beer for the pub and for bar snacks, like mozzarella sticks or halloumi fries. Add some sweet chili or spicy ketchup to dip and it's even better, elevating the beer's fruitiness while letting the bitterness keep it balanced.

BREWDOG DEAD PONY CLUB

TRY WITH: **CAULIFLOWER WINGS**
BREWED IN: **ELLON, SCOTLAND**
ABV: **3.8%**

BrewDog are a hero of beer and vegan food. Their bars have some of the best vegan dishes you'll find, and they've really focused on making them excellent. I like their burgers a lot and my particular favorite thing to eat are their cauliflower wings—they are incredible. They're beer-battered, crispy and yet still soft, and smothered in buffalo sauce. Their Lost Lager works really well with them, as does Punk IPA, but Dead Pony is the best choice. It's a Session Pale, so lower in alcohol and with a bit more malt sweetness than a Session IPA, and that sweetness balances out the intense flavor in the sauce. Any veggie and vegan beer lovers will be very happy in a BrewDog bar.

AMERICAN IPA

American IPAs, or what are becoming defined as West Coast IPAs, are beers with a strong aroma of citrus and resinous hops, and a lasting, powerful bitterness. They have more malt, more bitterness, and more pithy hops than the tropical, smooth, low-bitter Hazy IPAs. American IPAs are usually 6-7% ABV, so have some strength behind them, meaning they need some stronger dishes to go with them. High fat and high salt—like in typical bar foods—are going to work well to balance the hop bitterness and accentuate the hop flavor. Cooked onion and garlic, roasted vegetables, strong cheeses, and toasted breads are good go-to ingredients.

BRIDGE: Sandwiches, veggie burgers, garlic and herb sauces

BALANCE: Fried potatoes, blue cheese, avocado

BOOST: Quesadillas, mature Cheddar, salt, and garlic

AVOID: Light salads, heavy desserts, too much chili

FAT HEAD'S HEAD HUNTER

TRY WITH: **LOADED FRIES**
BREWED IN: **MIDDLEBURG HEIGHTS, OHIO, USA**
ABV: **7.5%**

This is a classic West Coast-style IPA. It's one of those beers which every beer lover should try to see just how punchy and yet balanced the best IPAs can be. You get a beer that has a little sweetness in the body, though that comes across more as a full texture for the hops, which jump out as orange, grapefruit, pineapple, and pine. The bitterness is big and long, which is why you want something savory and salty. Loaded fries are a dream bar snack with IPAs. Salted fried potatoes, onion, chili, cheese— all these things love the flavor of hops.

DIEU DU CIEL! MORALITÉ IPA

TRY WITH: **BAGEL, CREAM CHEESE, AVOCADO**
BREWED IN: **MONTREAL, CANADA**
ABV: **6.9%**

Dieu du Ciel! is a must-visit brewpub in Montreal, and when you're there have a Moralité IPA. It's a hazy-looking IPA, but it's not full New England. The hops are tropical and bright, with lots of fresh pineapple and mango, with grapefruit and tangerine backing them up and leading to a persistent, pithy bitterness. The local match would be a Montreal bagel. You could go simple with just some cream cheese, and that's good, but add some avocado and a sweeter chili sauce and it's even better—the hops love the creaminess of cheese and avocado, which are able to enhance the hop flavor. Replace the chili sauce with some blue cheese and it's also great. Grab a few extra bagels, as once you leave Dieu du Ciel! you'll probably need an extra snack after all the beer.

BREAKSIDE WANDERLUST IPA

TRY WITH: **BURGER & FRIES**
BREWED IN: **PORTLAND, OREGON, USA**
ABV: **6.2%**

Breakside are one of those breweries who excel at everything they brew, whether it's the cleanest lager, the hoppiest IPA, or the most complex Sours. I love their IPAs. Wanderlust is what they call a Golden IPA and it's hopped with Amarillo, Cascade, Mosaic, Simcoe, and Summit, which combine into pineapple, orange, papaya, and some verdant pine and resinous hard herbs. I think it's always good to see what food a brewpub serves, as surely they're choosing the dishes that taste best with their beers. Breakside serve up the classics and it's hard to find a better, more natural match than burger and fries. Beyond Meat-style patty and all the toppings, like ketchup, mustard, and pickles, really resonates with fruity hops, plus the danker, resinous notes in Wanderlust pick out some of the herbal seasoning before the bitterness refreshes it. A beer and burger—an American IPA and a burger—is simple but it's always a good match.

BENTSPOKE BREWING CO. SPROCKET

TRY WITH: **CHEDDAR CHEESE**
BREWED IN: **CANBERRA, AUSTRALIA**
ABV: **7.0%**

Sprocket pours a pale gold and it's full-on-fruity right away, with mango, tangerine, and really ripe stone fruits from the Mosaic and Amarillo hops. That fresh aroma stays alongside a tight body of malts which don't give any sweetness before a long, gripping kind of bitterness, the sort of bitterness that's disappeared from a lot of beers nowadays. That bitterness wants some fat content and the combination of American IPA and Cheddar is one that's hard to beat. Get a tangy mature Cheddar and an IPA will bring out a sweet fruitiness in the cheese that's reminiscent of tangy pineapple, while the beer's bitterness will be softened and balanced. Put the cheese in a sandwich, grill it, make a quesadilla, mac 'n' cheese, or just eat a wedge of cheese on its own.

HAMMER WAVE RUNNER

TRY WITH: **ARANCINI**
BREWED IN: **VILLA D'ADDA, ITALY**
ABV: **6.5%**

The thing I love most about Wave Runner is the tight balance that it achieves; it's one of those rare IPAs that's supremely light yet still intensely packed with hop flavors. The hops are all citrusy and tropical, with some lemon, orange, peach, and pine, plus a pithy Campari-like bitterness which ends really dry. You need some fat to cut through those hops and I think arancini are ideal. Fried balls of risotto, often stuffed with cheese or marinara sauce, they soak up the booze and soften the bitterness, while giving a savory depth and creamy texture which really hoppy beers love. Another choice would be the Italian-American dish of pasta alfredo, especially if you use fresh herbs like basil and sage and plenty of Parmesan or Grana Padano.

AMERICAN DOUBLE IPA

Strong, bitter, and very aromatic, American Double IPAs are impactful beers. They are beers which demand some attention, which have a thrilling, powerful depth, charged with alcohol strength, and impressing with the intense hop flavors. American Double IPAs differ from Hazy DIPAs (I'm going with Double IPA vs DIPA to try and differentiate the two) by being more bitter, having a tauter malt depth though sometimes going into a caramel-like sweetness, and by being more orange and resinous than melons and juice. With food, you need big flavors, salt, and fat to stand up to them. Smoked food can sweeten the bitterness. Strong cheese can be brilliant. Bread helps soak up bitterness. Citrus desserts can work well.

BRIDGE: Roasted vegetables, citrus, toasted bread

BALANCE: Barbecue, avocado, strong cheese

BOOST: Smoked foods, blue cheese, carrot cake

AVOID: Light salads, gravy dishes, too much chili

WARPIGS BIG DRUNK BABY

TRY WITH: **BARBECUE SMOKED TOFU SANDWICH**
BREWED IN: **COPENHAGEN, DENMARK**
ABV: **9.0%**

Warpigs is a brewpub specializing in Texas-style barbecue, which means huge hunks of smoking meat. It's a great place, but it's not the best place to eat for vegetarians (vegans probably shouldn't even bother trying to eat). Thankfully the beer is worth going for, and Big Drunk Baby is their American Double IPA. It's unfiltered and cloudy, it's resinous, intensely hoppy, oily with orange, marmalade, caramelized tropical fruit, and big bitterness. Smoke is a good flavor with Double IPAs as it works well with citrus, so get some smoked tofu, cover it in as much smoky barbecue sauce as you like, pile on some slaw (you'll want that to cut the bitterness and smother the sweetness), and a little hot sauce, and squash between sliced white bread.

DOGMA CERVEJARIA HOP LOVER

TRY WITH: **VEG FEIJOADA**
BREWED IN: **SAO PAULO, BRAZIL**
ABV: **8.5%**

Dogma are a top Brazilian craft brewery, known for their expansive use of hops. Their Hop Lover is an amber-colored Imperial IPA. It's a big beer, one with a lot of malt sweetness but the kind of sweetness which amplifies the hop fruitiness. There's mandarin, peach, lemon, some bitter honey, and a general hop intensity which swirls out of the glass. Feijoada is the famous Brazilian dish of stewed black beans, usually cooked with different cuts of meat. Make it with roasted veg and smoked tofu instead and it's a hearty, comforting, and deeply savory hug of a stew. An Imperial IPA is going to be a powerful pairing, one that needs the richness of the beans to soften the hops, but those hops in turn add a citrusy freshness to the stew.

Black beans and deep-fried avocado from the Four-Beer Taco Feast, page 140.

BURNT MILL GREAT BITTER LAKE

TRY WITH: **CHEDDAR, EGG, PICKLED CHILI**
BREWED IN: **BADLEY, ENGLAND**
ABV: **8.0%**

Great Bitter Lake is one of the best British Double IPAs that I've ever had. As I'm writing this, I don't even know if Burnt Mill will brew it again, but I'm putting it in here as it's a textbook example of a West Coast Double IPA: orange oil, grapefruit, pithy and zesty, some orange candy, mandarin, and a mineral-clean, punchy bitterness. There's a bakery near me that makes my favorite sandwich: it's Cheddar, scallions (spring onions), cilantro (fresh coriander), chili, and a fried egg in spongy focaccia. I replicate it at home and add in pickled chilis (try the recipe on page 156). Cheddar makes the hops in a Double IPA naturally taste fruitier while also easing up the bitterness, then the pickled chili comes in and adds an extra fruity-sweet spike of flavor. You can do the same combo of ingredients on toast, in a taco, as a grilled cheese sandwich, or an omelet.

TO ØL DANGEROUSLY CLOSE TO STUPID

TRY WITH: **BLUE CHEESE RISOTTO**
BREWED IN: **COPENHAGEN, DENMARK**
ABV: **9.3%**

There's a crossover zone between Double IPAs and American Barley Wines. It happens only in the strongest Double IPAs, and often when they're a little bit old and the intensely pithy and bitter citrus fruits have turned toward sticky marmalade. While we want to drink most Double IPAs fresh for their maximum aromatic intensity, some—like Dangerously Close to Stupid—can taste good a little old. That flavor is like a bitter-sweet chutney and it's brilliant with a wedge of strong blue cheese. Even better, mix that cheese into a risotto with leeks, onion, thyme, and garlic, and you get something that's powerful, creamy, and pungent, and which tastes great with the sweet beer and its bitter orange hops.

BELL'S HOPSLAM ALE

TRY WITH: **CARROT CAKE**
BREWED IN: **COMSTOCK, MICHIGAN, USA**
ABV: **10.0%**

Hopslam is appropriately named for being a massive wallop of sticky, resinous, piney, pithy, orangey hops, and it's an intense beer which saturates the senses with sweetness and bitterness. It's brewed with honey, which gives it a full body with some caramel flavors, and softens the huge bitterness. Carrot cake is one of the best matches for a Double IPA. Citrus bridges the beer and cake, the sweetness in both match up, the cream cheese frosting eases the bitterness (but not too much, as you still want some), and the hops and the spices share similar flavors. Other citrus or fruit cakes can also work with Double IPA, and there's a recipe for Carrot and Pineapple Upside Down IPA Cake on page 221.

HAZY PALE

Hazy hoppy beers are now found in bars, pubs, and taprooms all around the world, and they have become a new defining flavor for craft beer. That's a good thing for thinking about food to go with beer, as they are surprisingly versatile and interesting beers to match to, with low bitterness, a smooth texture, and a lush fruitiness with a citrus quality, which is able to highlight or boost many different flavors, almost like adding a squeeze of lemon or a handful of herbs to a dish. Good ingredients with Hazy Pales include citrus, fresh herbs, feta or creamy cheese, avocado or guacamole, grilled vegetables, and fermented foods.

BRIDGE: Thai and Vietnamese dishes, citrusy sauces

BALANCE: Avocado on toast, Middle Eastern spices, smoked foods

BOOST: Coconut curries, soy-based sauces, most tacos

AVOID: Sweet desserts, gravy dishes

BELLWOOD'S BREWERY JUTSU

TRY WITH: **SMOKY REFRIED BEAN AND VEG TACOS**
BREWED IN: **TORONTO, CANADA**
ABV: **5.6%**

Hazy Pale Ales seems to be almost universally good with tacos. I think it's the classic toppings which makes it work, as flavors like lime, white onion, cilantro (fresh coriander), avocado, mild cheese, and salsa have an amplifying effect on the hops, while the smooth texture of the beer and the moderate bitterness creates a balance. Smoked paprika-infused refried beans with all the toppings is a great choice with the lime, melon, pomelo, and stone fruitiness in Jutsu really enhancing the flavor of smokiness, then jumping around with the fresh ingredients. I also think that there's an underlying grassiness in the hops, which picks out some of the green flavors in the herbs and avocado.

HILL FARMSTEAD EDWARD

TRY WITH: **MIDDLE EASTERN MEZZE**
BREWED IN: **GREENSBORO, VERMONT, USA**
ABV: **5.2%**

Edward is a beer which straddles the classic flavors of an American Pale Ale with the modern hazy style, and Hill Farmstead are one of the breweries touted as being responsible for the popularity of what's become known as the New England IPA. I don't think it's necessarily fair to compare this one to the fully juicy brews, and while it's hazy, it's still light for the style and has a subtle elegance. Edward uses Centennial, Chinook, Columbus, and Simcoe to give classic (old-school, even) tangerine, lemon, grapefruit, and pine American hop aromas. The varied flavors of a Middle Eastern mezze are ideal for Edward. Whipped feta brings some acidity; smoky baba ganoush with flatbreads; cooling tzatziki; grilled veggie pide; big fresh salad bowls with roasted vegetables, tahini, lemon, and pomegranate. A light Hazy Pale Ale can sit in between these flavors and work with them all, enhancing the citrus present in most of the dishes.

BEHEMOTH BRAIN SMILES

TRY WITH: **FRIED CHICK'N BURGER**
BREWED IN: **AUCKLAND, NEW ZEALAND**
ABV: **5.4%**

Brain Smiles is a Citra- and Mosaic-hopped Hazy Pale Ale that looks like a glass of mango juice. It's sweetly juicy and tropical with papaya and tangerine, and a clean, refreshing finish which keeps it light for the style. Fried chicken is one of the foods I most miss now I don't eat meat, but there are some brilliant meatless alternatives. With a spicy-crumbed piece of fried chick'n, a smoky mayo or hot sauce, some fresh salad, and a soft brioche-style bun, a Hazy Pale Ale is going to add lots of fruitiness and will bring the refreshment you want. Vegan tenders, nuggets, and wings are also all good here, and it's the little bit of beer sweetness which helps it—most of the time we eat these foods with a sweet or fruity sauce anyway.

TRILLIUM BREWING COMPANY FORT POINT

TRY WITH: **THAI BARBECUE**
BREWED IN: **CANTON, MASSACHUSETTS, USA**
ABV: **6.6%**

Trillium have become one of the best-known brewers of this modern kind of American beer, and Fort Point is their go-to Pale Ale. It's brewed with Citra as the primary aroma hop and it's a silky-bodied brew, a little like orange juice without the sweetness or tang. There's no discernible grain taste, it's just hops hops hops—oranges, melon, pulpy mango—then a balanced, dry finish. That juicy perception wants some big flavors, like citrus, salt and smoke, and Thai barbecue, cooked over coals, is an amazing match. Eggplant (aubergine) with chili, garlic, and lime. A creamy-spicy Southern-style curry with veg and Thai basil. Greens sautéed in soy sauce and garlic. Papaya salad and some sticky rice to bring it all together. It's a match of citrus intensity and power for a full-flavored feast.

DEYA STEADY ROLLING MAN

TRY WITH: **KIMCHI FRIED RICE**
BREWED IN: **CHELTENHAM, ENGLAND**
ABV: **5.2%**

Steady Rolling Man has become the hazy hoppy beer that's most likely to be in my fridge. It's consistently excellent, vibrant with pineapple and mango and a little melon, it's crushable, pleasing, balanced, dry, and bitter, totally nailing the balance between lots of fruitiness and a crisp refreshment. Kimchi fried rice (I make my own kimchi or buy a fishless one) is a dish I eat ofte,n and Hazy Pale Ale is a really good match for it. It's able to mellow the pungent ingredients and heat, plus the shared fruity-fermented flavors between the cabbage and beer really work well. A fried egg or gochujang-fried tofu on top is a good addition.

HAZY IPA

Hazy IPA, also known as New England IPA, has become the new star of the craft beer world. It's the beer everyone is brewing now, and a lot of people are drinking it as their standard everyday beer. These beers are hazy to cloudy yellow-orange in appearance, and very aromatic with modern hops giving lots of tropical fruits, melon, and sweet citrus, with a smooth, full texture and a finish which, in the best, intersects alcohol, dryness, carbonation, and bitterness (and in the worst is sweet like juice). They are versatile food beers capable of working broadly with a lot of flavors: they like a little acidity, whether a tangy cheese or citrus; sweetness and spice are nice; creamy foods like coconut and avocado are good. I think it's the low bitterness and the fuller textures which make these Hazy IPAs surprisingly versatile food beers.

BRIDGE: Sweet-and-sour dressings, citrusy herbs, fermented foods

BALANCE: Avocado, mild cheese, creamy coconut

BOOST: Vietnamese and Thai food, veggie barbecue, lentil dal (or dhal, daal)

AVOID: Heavy desserts, gravy-based dishes

SIERRA NEVADA HAZY LITTLE THING

TRY WITH: **HALLOUMI AND SWEET CHILI BURGERS**
BREWED IN: **CHICO, CALIFORNIA, USA**
ABV: **6.7%**

Hazy Little Thing quickly became one of Sierra Nevada's top-selling beers when it was released in early 2018, and it's easy to see why: it jumped into the trend of hazy hoppy beers but it did it the Sierra Nevada way, meaning it was a supremely well-done crowd-pleaser of a beer, brightly fruity with mandarin, pineapple, and mango, with a dry, refreshing finish for a relatively strong beer. The texture really likes mild cheeses, and grilled halloumi in a burger with some sweet chili and perhaps some bitter leaves like arugula (rocket) is a great match, which highlights the fruity hoppiness but doesn't overpower the mild cheese.

MUMFORD BREWING LA LIKE...

TRY WITH: **KOREAN TOFU TACOS**
BREWED IN: **LOS ANGELES, CALIFORNIA, USA**
ABV: **6.8%**

The culinary coming together of Korean barbecue and Cal-Mex is a triumph of diverse cultures and flavors. Tofu covered in a sweet and spicy Korean sauce, sticky with gochujang, then cut through with kimchi and some slices of cucumber, all on top of corn tacos is a lot of flavor to put a beer with, but a Hazy IPA can handle it, and given how this style of taco was made famous in LA, it's fitting to pick LA Like… by Mumford Brewery. The beer's juicy malt and juicier hops bridge over to the kimchi, while there's a fresh juice fruitiness in the beer which works with the barbecue sauce. It's a mix-up of big flavors which come together brilliantly.

STRANGE BREW JASMINE IPA

TRY WITH: GRILLED VEG SOUVLAKI
BREWED IN: ATHENS/CHIOS, GREECE
ABV: 6.2%

I ran the Athens Marathon at the end of 2019, and within a few hours of finishing I was in the Strange Brew taproom drinking a Jasmine IPA. It's on the light side of the juicy style. It's zingy and tropical, there's some melon and fleshy fruits, some mandarin, and a crisp bitterness. I took some bottles with me and, suddenly hit by a huge post-run hunger, I found a souvlaki place near my apartment and ordered flame-grilled veg in a chewy pitta along with some raw onion, tomato, tzatziki, and some fries (in the pitta, as all the best souvlaki are). The beer really worked well, and I think it was made great by the tzatziki, with the cucumber, mint, and garlic enhancing the hop fruitiness while also softening the bitterness.

CLOUDWATER IPA

TRY WITH: COCONUT DAL
BREWED IN: MANCHESTER, ENGLAND
ABV: 6%

Cloudwater have an ever-changing range of Hazy IPAs, often highlighting a specific hop variety or combination of hops. While they might vary in content, the quality is always very high and the beers have the characteristic soft and smooth texture of the style; they always achieve that crossover balance of bitterness, dryness, and alcohol, and they always impress aromatically. Hazy IPA is a nice contrast to the earthy spiciness of a dal cooked with coconut milk. The beer's freshness lifts up the lentils (add a squeeze of lemon to the dish as that helps, too), while the coconut cools it all down and enjoys the fruitiness. I think it's improved if you add some grilled paneer or roasted red bell (sweet) pepper, and a garlic naan bread is always welcome on the side.

BEARDED IRIS HOMESTYLE

TRY WITH: LEMONGRASS CHILI TOFU
BREWED IN: NASHVILLE, TENNESSEE, USA
ABV: 6.0%

This is one of my favorite IPAs and I wish I could drink it more often. It's a singular showcase of Mosaic hops and it's judiciously juicy, not over-done, not over-saturated, just the right amount of the hop to let the flavors of fermenting tropical fruit, light citrus, lime, lemongrass, mandarin, and herby pine come through, before the dry and very clean finish. Those hop flavors are really good with lemongrass chili tofu, served on rice or noodles with fresh herbs like holy basil, cilantro (fresh coriander), and perilla, and a dressing of soy, sugar, garlic, chili, and lime. The dish and the hops amplify each other's aromatics.

HAZY DOUBLE IPA

These are some of the most flavor-intense beers you can buy. They are strong in alcohol, usually in the 8–9% ABV range (though Triple IPAs can pass 10% ABV)- and are usually double dry-hopped to get as much hop aroma and flavor through the beers as possible. They are typically thick with tropical fruit, citrus, lots of juice and zest, a ripe fruitiness that it's hard to believe comes from a hop flower, sometimes a savory depth (think onion or hard herbs), and, like the best Hazy IPAs, they end with alcohol, dryness, carbonation, and bitterness intersecting to create its own kind of amplified balance. With all that flavor, we need big dishes. We can bring out desserts here, often with citrus, tropical fruits, coconut or ginger, or we need some oily, salty foods.

BRIDGE: Pineapple and other tropical fruit, fermented vegetables, fragrant herbs

BALANCE: Guacamole, white bread or rice, high-fat dishes

BOOST: Ginger cake, Bolognese, creamy coconut

AVOID: Light salads, gravy dishes

GAMMA BREWING BIG DOINK

TRY WITH: **KIMCHI GRILLED CHEESE**
BREWED IN: **GØRLØSE, DENMARK**
ABV: **8.0%**

If you've never had kimchi and strong Cheddar together then you've been missing out on a huge umami-bomb of flavor. Grill it between slices of some good bread and it gets even better. It's a strong flavor combo which wants something equally powerful to go with it, like the DIPAs brewed by Gamma, which add plenty of alcohol to go with the tangy fermented cabbage flavors. Big Doink uses hops which give a mix of pungent tropical fruit and some more resinous, funky depth, plus the beer has a rich texture and a snappy, tangy finish (a tang that bridges the cabbage and cheese), which together help to make this an impressive pairing. Just one thing: kimchi is usually made with fermented fish, so make your own or get a vegan version.

OTHER HALF ALL GREEN EVERYTHING

TRY WITH: **BLOOD ORANGE CAKE**
BREWED IN: **BROOKLYN, NEW YORK, USA**
ABV: **10.5%**

All Green Everything is a Triple IPA, meaning it's everything you expect in a regular IPA, tripled. It's 10.5% ABV, so it's very strong, though the brewers at Other Half can magically hide the strength in their beers (until you've had half of it, when you'll already be half drunk). It's as dramatically hoppy as you'd imagine, blasting overripe tropical fruit, pithy citrus, orange juice, pineapple, pine, floral honey, and sweet papaya into your face. You want something with a similar sweetness and bitterness to the beer, and a blood orange cake with candied orange on top works to soften the booze like a literal sponge (cake), adding back some strong citrus flavors into the beer.

VERDANT BREWING ALLEN

TRY WITH: **JERK TEMPEH AND PINEAPPLE SALSA**
BREWED IN: **FALMOUTH, ENGLAND**
ABV: **8.0%**

Verdant are one of the best hazy hoppy brewers in Britain and they were one of the first to properly focus on perfecting this modern type of beer. They make a lot of exceptional Hazy Pales, IPAs, and DIPAs, each with a full-on fruitiness, a ton of tropical juice, and the all-important balanced finish at the end. Allen is hopped with some of the juiciest hops, like Citra, Mosaic, and Nelson Sauvin, and it's a bright, soft, smooth, tropical, and melony DIPA. Cover some tempeh or tofu (smoked tofu is good) in jerk spices (garlic, ginger, thyme, allspice, cinnamon, red pepper flakes, black pepper, Scotch bonnet chili), grill it, and serve with a pineapple, chili, and lime salsa and some coconut rice. There are a lot of overlapping flavors, including the fruitiness of the Scotch bonnet (just watch out for the heat), with the rice helping to cool everything down.

THE ALCHEMIST HEADY TOPPER

TRY WITH: **SPAGHETTI BOLOGNESE**
BREWED IN: **STOWE, VERMONT, USA**
ABV: **8.0%**

Heady Topper is held up as one of the originators of the Hazy DIPA style, though for me this beer is not like most of the others. Heady is not heavy or slick, it's not creamy, it's not juicy, instead it's dry and well bittered, lean, aromatic, and herbal, dank and resinous alongside some of the stone fruit and citrus you expect from a heavily hopped beer like this. It's a surprisingly good match for a veggie Bolognese, especially one with plenty of pepper, basil, garlic, and umami-flavor boosters like yeast extract and soy sauce, and not too tomatoey. It's brought together with the crossover of herbal flavors, with the umami-rich sauce softening some of the booze. Sweeter juicier DIPAs don't work here; you need them to be on the savory side.

TREE HOUSE KING JULIUS

TRY WITH: **MANGO STICKY RICE**
BREWED IN: **CHARLTON, MASSACHUSETTS, USA**
ABV: **8.2%**

King Julius is one of America's best-known and most sought-after DIPAs. The beer is sticky with tropical fruits—mango, pineapple—and sweet orange. The Tree House texture is something the brewery are known for; it's slick and thick, literally juice-like, and it holds onto all the hop oils. I like the combination of Hazy DIPAs with mango sticky rice—the rice is cooked in coconut milk, though it's not sweet and has a slight saltiness, then ripe mango (ideally alphonso mangoes—they are the best) is placed on top. The coconut adds a good creaminess, while the beer's juiciness and the sweet mango pull together. If you want a savory dish, cook a mild vegetable and coconut curry and have some mango chutney on the side.

ENGLISH PALE ALE AND IPA

The combination of toasty British malts and tangy, floral, lightly orangey English hops creates a flavor profile distinctly different from American Pale Ales and IPAs. The best English-style brews have a rich but not sweet malt character, they are dry and bitter, and have a mellow and inviting hop aroma. As the beers get stronger, so the hops turn from floral to herbal, and from orange pith to marmalade, and the malt goes from toast to toffee. Good flavor matches include cruciferous vegetables, earthy flavors like whole grains, beetroot, mushrooms, asparagus, potatoes, turmeric, ground coriander, ginger (so mild curries can be good), and strong cheese.

BRIDGE: Root vegetables, Indian spices, whole grains

BALANCE: Sharp salad dressings, salty pub snacks, creamy curries

BOOST: Cauliflower cheese, mature Cheddar, ginger cake

AVOID: Chocolate desserts

MEANTIME LONDON IPA

TRY WITH: **VEGGIE SCOTCH EGG**
BREWED IN: **LONDON, ENGLAND**
ABV: **7.4%**

Meantime's London IPA is hopped with Fuggles and Golding, the old stalwarts of British hops, and they give some bitter honey and marmalade and the kind of floral aroma you smell in British woodlands. The malt gives the beer an amber color and a toasted depth, without much sweetness as it leads to a strong bitterness. Try it with a veggie scotch egg with English mustard or some piccalilli (curry-spiced pickled veg) on the side. It's a classic bar snack and the veg version is usually made with lentils, giving a nutty flavor which is good with the malt.

IPA Bhaji Bakes and Mango IPA Chutney, page 195.

FIRESTONE WALKER DBA

TRY WITH: **TANDOORI CAULIFLOWER**
BREWED IN: **PASO ROBLES, CALIFORNIA, USA**
ABV: **5%**

DBA is brewed using a version of the Burton Union System, an old technique used to collect yeast while the beer ferments. The Firestone version updates it for flavor, letting the beer spend some time in wood, picking up an underlying complexity which comes through with the peachy, peppery hops and alongside some bready, creamy malts. Try with Tandoori cauliflower, which is roasted in a curry-spiced yogurt sauce and it's soft, earthy and fragrant. The malts in the beer add some sweetness and balance out an underlying earthiness in both beer and food. British-style ales like this are typically good with cauliflower dishes and you could serve with a veg biryani or in a naan bread wrap.

CHESHIRE BREWHOUSE GOVINDA

TRY WITH: **GINGER CAKE**
BREWED IN: **CONGLETON, ENGLAND**
ABV: **6.8%**

Govinda is a heritage IPA based on a recipe from 1843. It uses Chevallier, a heritage malt, and a lot of East Kent Golding hops. The recipe involves a three-hour mash and then it's boiled with the hops for three hours, which is at least double the time a regular beer would get, and the beer pours a dark amber thanks to all the time in the brewhouse. The malts are rich, toasty, caramelized; it's a little sweet to begin before all the hops comes through, powerfully bitter, with tangy marmalade, roasted stone fruits, and pears, peppery and complex. It's an extraordinary beer. It's really good with tomato-based curries or dals (or dhals, daals), and also with cauliflower cheese, while a slice of ginger cake is also good with this one as the earthy spice really likes the flavors of the malt and the spicy, orangey hops.

ST AUSTELL TRIBUTE

TRY WITH: **CHEESE SANDWICH (OR SUPERFOOD SALAD)**
BREWED IN: **ST AUSTELL, ENGLAND**
ABV:**4.2%**

Tribute is a wonderful beer that's supremely balanced between lush Maris Otter malt, fresh citrusy hop aromas, and a clean bitterness. It's a beer that reminds me of drinking pints outside in the Cornish sunshine, but it's equally great from the bottle or can (by the way, the cask version of this beer uses isinglass, which is derived from fish). A simple West Country Cheddar and pickle sandwich would be ideal with Tribute, as would a summery superfood salad with roasted sweet potato, quinoa, avocado, feta, and a lemon, honey, and chili dressing. It's a versatile food beer.

COOPERS SPARKLING ALE

TRY WITH: **EGGPLANT (AUBERGINE) PARMA AND CHIPS**
BREWED IN: **ADELAIDE, AUSTRALIA**
ABV: **5.8%**

An Aussie classic, Coopers Sparkling Ale is English-styled with the addition of Pride of Ringwood hops from Australia. It's a lightly hazy deep golden beer. The hops give a little orange and floral honey but it's not a hop-forward brew. It's got a good body of toasty malts but remains clean and dry through to a crisp finish which, when served cold, is really refreshing—it's reminiscent of a classic British Ale, only served sparkling. The Aussie pub is much like the British pub, and foods cross over, too: pies, sandwiches, burgers, fish and chips, a roast lunch on a Sunday. But then there's the uniquely Aussie parm, typically a breaded chicken breast topped with ham, marinara sauce and cheese, served with chips and salad. The veggie version loses the ham and uses fried eggplant (aubergine), and a Sparkling Ale has the malt, the bitterness, and the fizz you need to balance it nicely.

PACIFIC PALE ALE AND IPA

These beers all have in common the use of hops from Australia and New Zealand. Those hops have abundant tropical qualities, giving a varied fruit bowl of mango, pineapple, grapes, gooseberries, berries, lemon, and lime. The underlying beers are often similar to the American-hopped equivalents, ranging from dry to malty, and from sessionable to strong, though one important category of Australian beer, called Summer Ale, is light in body and with a general sunny disposition. When it comes to food, the lighter beers are great with salads, sandwiches, fresh herbs, and citrus, while stronger versions match up nicely to Southeast Asian flavors.

BRIDGE: Fresh salads, Vietnamese and Thai, jackfruit

BALANCE: Fried noodles, creamy cheeses, coconut curries

BOOST: Savory brunch dishes, avocados, citrus salads

AVOID: Most desserts, gravy-based dishes

STONE & WOOD PACIFIC ALE

TRY WITH: **SUPERFOOD SALAD**
BREWED IN: **BYRON BAY, AUSTRALIA**
ABV: **4.4%**

Pacific Ale is the originator of the Aussie Summer Ale style. It's made with all-Aussie ingredients, it's soft-textured, super-refreshing, and tropical with Galaxy hops. This is the sort of beer that goes with those beautifully composed brunch dishes on lifestyle Instagram accounts and in travel magazines. You know the kind with perfectly ripe avocado, some scattered grains and seeds, micro herbs, smoothies and flat whites on the side. That's not to be dismissive of this kind of brunch, because those dishes are fresh, wholesome and delicious, and the vibrant yet gentle fruitiness in a Pacific Ale is perfect, especially if you've spent some of your morning on the beach. Go for the superfood salad, or a brunch bowl, and you'll be happy.

GARAGE PROJECT HĀPI DAZE

TRY WITH: **SALT & PEPPER TOFU**
BREWED IN: **WELLINGTON, NEW ZEALAND**
ABV: **4.6%**

Brewed with Southern Cross, Motueka, Wai-iti, Riwaka, and Nelson Sauvin, this is an all-star Kiwi-hopped Pale Ale, named after the Maori word for hop: hāpi. It's a golden-colored beer with some juicy malts, the jammy kind that plump up the hop fruitiness and give the beer some weight. The hops come out with lots of lime, grapefruit, gooseberries, a bit of Riesling wine, and some stone fruits, and it ends dry and refreshing. Fish and chips would be a go-to pairing for a Pacific Pale in a local pub, and a good vegan alternative would be salt and pepper tofu, seasoned with zingy Szechuan pepper, fresh chili, and a squeeze of lime. The hops add a really nice fruitiness to the tofu and pop with the Szechuan pepper.

ALPINE BEER COMPANY NELSON

TRY WITH: **JACKFRUIT TINGA TACOS**
BREWED IN: **ALPINE, CALIFORNIA, USA**
ABV: **7.0%**

Tinga is typically cooked with shredded chicken in a tomato and chipotle sauce that's sweet, spiced, and smoky. Jackfruit is an ideal veggie replacement to suck up all that tasty sauce, and you can put the tinga in tacos or burritos, on tostadas or salad bowls, and it's best topped street-style with diced onion, cilantro (fresh coriander), lime, and avocado. Given the light tropical flavor of jackfruit, plus the zesty toppings, a New Zealand-hopped IPA is a great choice, and Alpine's Nelson is all Nelson-hopped, giving lime, mango, and papaya, plus some sweeter malts accented with sweet, spicy rye, an addition which marries well to the smoky chipotle in the recipe.

GAGE ROADS SINGLE FIN

TRY WITH: **AVOCADO ON TOAST**
BREWED IN: **PALMYRA, AUSTRALIA**
ABV: **4.5%**

Single Fin is the sort of beer that's very much of its place: a beer for the sunshine and for chilling out by the sea. With this Summer Ale brewed with Galaxy

and Enigma and left unfiltered, you get a glass of tropical-scented, easy-going, super-refreshing beer. It's good for lunch and dinner, but also breakfast and brunch, being a simple quencher of a beer. Have it with the Aussie brunch staple of avocado on toast. Add some fresh chili, squeeze over some lime, perhaps crumble on some tangy cheese and toasted seeds, and the beer adds some of its own citrusy flavors, with the unfiltered body adding a soft texture alongside the avocado, and the gentle bitterness lifting it at the end.

YOUR MATES LARRY

TRY WITH: **LAKSA**
BREWED IN: **WARANA, AUSTRALIA**
ABV: **4.5%**

Brewed by Your Mates on the Sunshine Coast, Larry is a glass of tropical Aussie ale, lush with pineapple, passion fruit, lemon, and lime, and it's one of those easy-drinking, light-bodied, crisp, dry, subtle beers, which is elegantly balanced but still bursting with hops. Those flavors are really nice with coconut and the aromatics of a curry like a laksa, made with lemongrass, lime, ground coriander, cilantro (fresh coriander), ginger, and chili. Larry brings an extra zing of hops to those ingredients, while the coconut brings its creaminess and some balance. Other Malaysian recipes are also good here, like nasi goreng and satay.

AMBER, RED, AND RED IPA

The Amber and Red part of these beers comes from the malts, which bring a mix of toast, toffee, caramel, roasted nuts, dried fruits, and perhaps some more heavily roasted flavors. That extra depth and sweetness often come with more body, meaning these beers can handle richer flavors, especially ones where the Maillard reaction has impacted cooking flavor (toast instead of bread, fried food instead of boiled), and here we're looking for more roasted, toasted, and barbecued food, for sweeter and richer sauces, aged cheeses, meaty mushrooms. I've grouped together a wide range of beers, from lighter Ambers to Imperial Reds, so consider the flavor intensity when pairing to these styles.

BRIDGE: Roasted root veg, caramelized food, sandwiches

BALANCE: Barbecue, fried food, tomato-based sauces

BOOST: Sausages, roasted mushrooms, mature cheese

AVOID: Light desserts, citrusy dressings

NEW BELGIUM FAT TIRE

TRY WITH: **VEGAN MAC 'N' CHEESE**
BREWED IN: **FORT COLLINS, COLORADO, USA**
ABV: **5.2%**

Fat Tire is a classic American Amber Ale, and it's been one of the most important American craft beers since long before IPAs became the most-drunk kind of beer (Ambers were initially the most popular craft beer style, before the hops took over). It has subtle malt, with toast and a nuttiness, then the hop bitterness is gently balanced, fresh, and refreshing— it's a beer that was perfected long ago, and remains subtly brilliant rather than in-your-face. The malt character is ideal with a vegan mac 'n' cheese (see my recipe on page 129), matching the nuttiness in the sauce, adding some of its own sweetness, then able to balance it at the end with its peppery and light citrus-pith bitterness and crisp carbonation. New Belgium's Abbey Dubbel would also be a great match for vegan mac 'n' cheese.

GALWAY BAY BREWERY BAY ALE

TRY WITH: **SAUSAGES AND HERB-ROAST POTATOES**
BREWED IN: **GALWAY BAY, REPUBLIC OF IRELAND**
ABV: **4.4%**

Galway Bay's Bay Ale is a modern example of an Irish Red Ale, a style which has a lot of toasty, caramely, lightly roasted malts, though restrained and refined into a light-tasting beer, and it's balanced by a crisp, spicy, peppery hop character but not a huge amount of hop aroma. To go with it, grill some veg sausages and roast some potatoes with garlic, thyme, and rosemary; the herbs match up with the hops, and the potatoes balance the malt. Roasted carrots and an onion gravy would also be good on the side.

BATH ALES GEM

TRY WITH: **CAULIFLOWER CHEESE**
BREWED IN: **BATH, ENGLAND**
ABV: **4.8%**

Bath Gem is a British Amber Ale, brewed with Maris Otter malts and Golding hops. It's more on the malty side than hoppy, showcasing the marvelous Maris Otter and its deeply toasted, almost chewy, character which together with additional grains gives a base beer that's slightly caramelized and lovely and smooth. The hops add a peppery, ground coriander-like finish. The malt in this is excellent with cauliflower cheese—regular or vegan—and adds a little sweetness to the dish while also being able to cut through the richness. Cauliflower typically works well with Amber Ales, as do nutty and mature cheeses like Cheddar, gouda, and Comté.

TRÖEGS BREWERY NUGGET NECTAR

TRY WITH: **MUSHROOM GOUDA POLENTA OR GRILLED CHEESE**
BREWED IN: **HERSHEY, PENNSYLVANIA, USA**
ABV: **7.5%**

Nugget Nectar is an Imperial Amber Ale, one with an abundance of malt giving us some sweeter caramel flavors and a stickiness on the lips. It's also very hoppy, being verdant with pine, grapefruit pith, roasted citrus, honey, and woody herbs, and they give a powerful, lasting bitterness. Those malt and hop flavors are really pleasing with the meaty flavor of roasted mushrooms with thyme and garlic, and nutty aged Gouda. Have them in a grilled cheese sandwich or on cheesy polenta. The sweeter malts want some umami, which comes from the mushroom and cheese, and the hops like the onions, thyme, and garlic.

MODUS OPERANDI FORMER TENANT

TRY WITH: **TOMATO AND HERB FOCACCIA**
BREWED IN: **MONA VALE, AUSTRALIA**
ABV: **7.8%**

Red IPAs bring a lot of malt flavor to the dinner table, being caramelized, a little sweet, and edging into a roasted quality. Those malts will also change the way the hops taste, and in Former Tenant, which uses a lot of Mosaic and Galaxy hops, the malt makes those usually juicy-fruity hops more like roasted tropical fruit, with some hard herbs and resinous flavors. It's strong, yet nothing overpowers, though it needs a flavorsome dish with it and ingredients like extra-virgin olive oil, rosemary, basil, garlic, tomato, and salt all work well, so make a focaccia, flatbread, or pizza topped with all those and you'll match up hops and herbs, while the bread will bridge across to the malt.

BLONDE AND GOLDEN ALE

Gentle and refreshing yet still well hopped, Blonde and Golden Ales sit somewhere between Pale Ales and Pale Lagers. They usually have bready and toasty malt flavor, a small amount of alcohol—often in the 4% ABV range—a gentle to medium hoppiness, and a balanced, refreshing bitterness. Their easy-going nature wants similar simple foods which also have similar qualities to the golden malts used—sandwiches, tarts, salads, mild cheeses, potatoes, whole grains. Dishes with a small amount of acidity—lemon, vinegar, mustard—will help to highlight the hop flavors.

BRIDGE: Sandwiches, potato salad, lemon-dressed salad

BALANCE: Creamy risotto, quiche, curry spices

BOOST: Grilled halloumi, veggie burgers, veggie sausages

AVOID: Sweet and heavy desserts

BOXCAR GOLDEN ALE

TRY WITH: **ENGLISH ASPARAGUS RISOTTO**
BREWED IN: **LONDON, ENGLAND**
ABV: **4.2%**

Brewed using English Golden Promise malts and Golding and Pilgrim hops, Boxcar's Golden Ale is based on traditions but presents them to a modern drinker. It's entirely and elegantly English, so the malt is gently toasty and perfectly balances the hops, which give stone fruit, apples and pears and something lightly floral. Serve it with English asparagus risotto: the beer's light fruitiness is a nice match for the green flavors in the asparagus, while the beer's lasting bitterness refreshes the creaminess in the rice. If you add cheese, go for a Cheshire cheese, Cornish yarg, or something a little tart. It's a wonderful seasonal pairing.

FYNE ALES JARL

TRY WITH: **JACKFRUIT BURGER**
BREWED IN: **CAIRNDOW, SCOTLAND**
ABV: **3.8%**

Jarl is a much-loved British beer that's able to get the beer geeks excited whenever they see it on tap. This Citra-hopped Session Blonde is pale gold in color and ripe with all the good stuff you expect from Citra, only made a bit more subtle: lemon, orange peel, grapefruit pith, some distant tropical fruits. It's the fruitiness in the beer which makes this work with jackfruit, which has its own tropical, tangy flavor. You can pull jackfruit apart like pulled pork, and it soaks up sauces really well, so cook it like the Imperial Jackfruit Dirty Fries recipe on page 187 and serve it in a bun. The spiced-sweet-savory sauce is boosted by the Citra fruitiness and the beer's bitterness keeps it balanced.

UINTA BREWING GOLDEN ALE

TRY WITH: **ROAST VEG AND HUMMUS TORTILLAS**
BREWED IN: **SALT LAKE CITY, UTAH, USA**
ABV: **5.0%**

Some beer and food pairings work in specific places and moments, and this is one of them. Uinta's Golden Ale was brewed and packaged to celebrate America's national parks, and it's the sort of beer you'd happily pack on a hike. It's pale gold, the malt is bready and a little honeyed, the hops are delicate with some light, refreshing citrus. Also pack a tortilla stuffed with hummus, roasted bell (sweet) peppers, and zucchini (courgettes), and you've got a snack to fill you up and to go with the beer. The lemony hop flavor is really nice with the hummus, and it's a quenching and satisfying combo that's also good eaten on the sofa or in the back yard, for the less adventurous.

ALASKAN BREWING CO. KÖLSCH

TRY WITH: **PANEER KEBABS**
BREWED IN: **JUNEAU, ALASKA, USA**
ABV: **5.3%**

This is called a Kölsch but it isn't much like the golden beers of Cologne, and instead I think it deserves its own designation of an Alaskan-style golden ale. It's soft-bodied and has an intangible lightness, which in my mind comes from the glacier-fed water. The malt is honeyed, nutty, and gives some chewy crackers, while the hops, which are from both Europe and the Pacific Northwest, bring subtle citrus and some light, peppery herbs. It's refreshing yet satisfies in a really simple, pleasing way. It's great with paneer kebabs. Grill them with curry spices, mushrooms, and red bell (sweet) peppers, and serve in a warm naan bread with a little raita and chili.

GAFFEL KÖLSCH

TRY WITH: **GOUDA TART AND POTATO SALAD**
BREWED IN: **COLOGNE, GERMANY**
ABV: **4.8%**

Kölsch is the beer specialty of Cologne, and it's a bright, golden, dry, bitter lager-like ale. It's served in small 7 US fl oz (200ml) glasses, and it's the kind of beer that you can drink all day, enjoying its perfected balance of malt-hop-alcohol. Being Germany, the food offer is typically pork heavy, but at Gaffel am Dom, a large restaurant next to Cologne's incredible cathedral, they cater well for veggies. There's vegetable *Flammkuchen* (a kind of pizza), fried potato cakes, a veggie burger, and the local beer snack specialty of Gouda cheese and rye bread. All are good choices with the beer. At home, I think a Gouda tart served with potato salad is a great choice, as the beer's crisp bitterness will cut nicely through the cheese in the tart, while the malt sweetness matches the creamy potato.

LAGERS

PILSNER

Pilsners are pale, crisp, and well-hopped lagers. Czech-style Pilsner tends to be more malty, caramelized, and bitter-sweet, while German-style Pilsner is drier, leaner, and often tastes more bitter, with a floral, spicy bitterness. Generally lighter foods work well—breads, pasta, rice, potatoes, pastry—but the high hop content also allows for rich, fatty, or creamy dishes to work. Ingredients like basil, thyme, parsley, avocados, fresh lemon, black pepper, garlic, olive oil, tomato, and fresh cheeses are complementary flavors.

BRIDGE: Bread, fresh herbs and lemon, lighter salads

BALANCE: Potato dishes, creamy pasta sauces, chips and salsa

BOOST: Fresh tomatoes, basil, aromatic spices

AVOID: Most desserts

TRUMER PILS

TRY WITH: **ONION TART (OR LEEK RISOTTO)**
BREWED IN: **SALZBURG, AUSTRIA**
ABV: **4.9%**

Trumer Pils is a classic German-style Pilsner brewed in Salzburg, and also in Berkeley, California. It's bright gold, has some toasted malts in the middle, then an assertive, fragrant, floral, herbal hop bitterness, and a very dry finish. Onion tart is a popular dish in Bavaria and into Austria (often cooked with bacon, though, so watch out) and the pastry and sweetly earthy onions are really good with the hops. You can make your own as it's easy: buy puff pastry, slow-cook onions in garlic, thyme and black pepper for as long as possible, then bake. Alternatively, make a risotto using the same flavors as the pie and add a leek, then grate in some Parmesan at the end – that's a great flavor combo for a Pilsner.

NOTCH BREWING CO. THE STANDARD

TRY WITH: **POTATOES**
BREWED IN: **SALEM, MASSACHUSETTS, USA**
ABV: **4.5%**

The Standard is a properly authentic Czech-style Pilsner. It has the smooth, caramelized malt character, which is a little chewy and bready. The body has some sweetness, giving a fuller body than most low-ABV lagers, then there's a long, defined, lasting bitterness, giving the kind of balance that means you want to drink beer after beer. "Try with: Potatoes" might be a little broad, but this is a beer which wants to be with potatoes: fried potato hash (with a couple of eggs on top); a tortilla (Spanish omelet); bramboracky (Czech fried potato cakes); gnocchi in a creamy sauce; potato salad; potato chips (crisps); fries. The sweeter malts in a Czech-style Pilsner just work perfectly with a well seasoned potato. The best potato for Pilsner? Try potatoes roasted with garlic, thyme, and rosemary, with lots of salt and pepper.

LOST & GROUNDED KELLER PILS

TRY WITH: **PERSIAN JEWELED RICE**
BREWED IN: **BRISTOL, ENGLAND**
ABV: **4.8%**

I love how the German hops blast out your glass when you get a fresh Keller Pils, coming forward as herbal and floral with citrus pith and pepper. The hops—Magnum, Perle, Hallertauer Mittelfrüh—make you work a little, make you think, make you engage with the beer more (rather than the in-your-face orangey obviousness of Citra and Mosaic), and you're rewarded with all their snappy, spicy, almost-savory bitterness. Lost & Grounded's Keller Pils has become the go-to lager for a lot of British beer geeks thanks to that elevated hop character and thanks to it being really bloody good. It's a beer which can nicely complement aromatic spices: Persian jeweled rice is beautifully spiced and fragrant with ingredients like saffron, cinnamon, cardamom, allspice, orange, carrots, dried fruits, and pistachios. It's a perfumed dish and Keller Pils brings its own floral freshness, highlighting the saffron and the citrus in the dish. Grill some vegetable and halloumi kebabs to go on the side.

ROTHAUS PILS

TRY WITH: **MUSHROOMS IN HERB CREAM SAUCE**
BREWED IN: **GRAFENHAUSEN, GERMANY**
ABV: **5.1%**

Rothaus Pils, sometimes also called Tannenzäpfle (it's the same beer but the brewery has different names for the different bottles), is a cult-favorite German-style Pilsner. It's brilliant gold with bright white foam. The hops are prominent but not overpowering, and they are floral, herbal, piney (perhaps suggestively so as Tannenzäpfle means pine cones), while the malt gives a little sweetness to  balance the high bitterness. Brewed in the Black Forest, this is not a beer for gateaux, but it does suit something foraged; the brewery restaurant's menu features pasta with chanterelle mushrooms in a herby cream cheese sauce, and that's perfect: the herbal hops and the herbs in the sauce match up well, while the bitterness lifts the richness in the sauce. Lots of black pepper and some lemon zest are the key to getting the match just right.

SUAREZ FAMILY BREWERY QUALIFY PILS

TRY WITH: **FRESH BREAD, TOMATO, BURRATA, BASIL**
BREWED IN: **HUDSON, NEW YORK, USA**
ABV: **5.0%**

Suarez Family Brewery make some of the best lagers I've drunk, and their brilliance comes from their understanding of the classics, and of how complex it is to make something so seemingly simple. Qualify Pils is a dry, lively, lovely, nuanced Pilsner. It has a cracker-like malt character, loads of tiny refreshing bubbles pop and carry with them herbal, lemon pith, floral, and peppery hops, and it has an elegant, dry finish. It's a beer that deserves a considered and balanced simplicity on the side. Get some fresh burrata, sun-dried tomatoes, fresh bread, extra-virgin olive oil, and lots of fresh basil, and the beer's hop depth and its ethereal dryness pull everything together magically. The lazy version of this match would be chips and salsa, which is less refined but just as tasty.

PALE LAGER

Similar to Pilsners in that they are clean, refreshing, and light beers, these Pale Lagers differ by having more malt and less hop. They are bready and toasty, the hops are clean and not overly strong or impactful (but certainly there to give their bitter balance), and they are epitomized by the kind of classic German Helles lagers you drink by the liter mug. They are drinking beers, best found in the pub, beer garden, or just your back yard, and they seek easy-going foods. They can handle pungent flavors like mustard and pickles, they are usually fine with spice, and they love bread and cheese.

BRIDGE: Breads (pretzels), semi-soft cheese, buttered vegetables

BALANCE: Indian curries, Vietnamese salads, hot dogs

BOOST: Mild cheese, pizza, potato dishes

AVOID: Most desserts

AUGUSTINER HELLES

TRY WITH: **OBATZDA**
BREWED IN: **MUNICH, GERMANY**
ABV: **5.2%**

Augustiner Helles is a favorite lager of many drinkers. It's a beautiful bright golden color. The yeast offers a little fruitiness, a little hint of freshly baked bread, then the malt body is toasty, lightly caramelized, roundly satisfying but not at all sweet, with a lip-smacking finish. It's universally good with German beer hall food, which doesn't help us because that's universally porky. The few meatless meals will be cheese-based (sorry vegans), and obatzda is a classic Bavarian snack which is a dip made from cream cheese, Camembert, butter and onion, served with bread, and it's delicious with lager (there's a recipe on page 183, including a really good vegan version). Order a pretzel, too. And maybe some potato salad; you'll need it to soak up the next beer (because there's always a next beer with Augustiner).

BUDWEISER BUDVAR ORIGINAL

TRY WITH: **FRIED CHEESE (OR VIETNAMESE SALAD)**
BREWED IN: **ČESKÉ BUDĚJOVICE, CZECH REPUBLIC**
ABV: **5.0%**

This could sit in the Pilsner section but I'm putting it here as it has a toasty body of malt but it's not as caramely or rich as other Czech-style lagers, instead leading to a dry, crisp finish. It's the Saaz hop aroma which I like the most—a little floral, a little lemony, apples—and it's backed up by some fresh toasty malt. The Czech Republic is a place where vegetarian choices are limited, and vegans should take their own snacks. One beer food on most menus will be "*smažený sýr*," which is breaded and fried mild cheese, usually served with fries. You really need a beer with it, and the light toastiness of malt and the refreshingly dry bitterness in a Budvar is ideal to lift the richness. Fancy something lighter? There's a

Obatzda (page 183)

BIERSTADT LAGERHAUS HELLES

TRY WITH: **MASALA DOSA**
BREWED IN: **DENVER, COLORADO, USA**
ABV: **5.0%**

This Helles is reverentially Bavarian and it nails the essential malt-hop balance of the style. It's a brilliant golden color, the body has some bread crusts and a moreish maltiness, while it eases its way to the cleanest and most refreshing finish. Helles is a naturally hearty kind of beer, so it can handle some big dishes. Fragrant spices and chili heat are often good with a Helles, thanks to the little bit of malt sweetness which can wrap itself around the spice. Try masala dosa, which are chickpea flour pancakes with a spiced potato mix inside (there's a recipe on page 152). The beer is great with potatoes, it cools down the spice without dulling it, and lends some sweetness to any chutneys you add. Most chickpea, potato, or lentil-based Indian dishes will work well with Helles.

21ST AMENDMENT EL SULLY

TRY WITH: **GRILLED VEG TORTA**
BREWED IN: **SAN FRANCISCO, CALIFORNIA, USA**
ABV: **4.8%**

Mexican-style lager has grown in popularity and it's typically a Pale Lager brewed with maize which fully ferments to give a lighter, drier, and more refreshing beer. The idea is to make the kind of crisp, simple, easy-going lagers that so many people love, only to give it just a little bit more flavor. El Sully is a great example of that. It's light, there's some delicate citrus, a bright carbonation, and a quenching finish which makes you drink another gulp. Most Mexican dishes will work, but I think a grilled vegetable torta is ideal. Mushrooms, bell (sweet) peppers, eggplant (aubergine), beans, avocado, some hot sauce between the toasted bread, and El Sully comes in and fully refreshes you between each bite.

large Vietnamese population in the Czech Republic and a bun chay and banh mi chay (tofu noodle salad or tofu banh mi) would both be good alternatives.

STIEGL-GOLDBRÄU

TRY WITH: **VEGAN SCHNITZEL & POTATO SALAD**
BREWED IN: **SALZBURG, AUSTRIA**
ABV: **5.0%**

There can only be a few beer halls in Bavaria and Austria that don't sell schnitzel, and rightly so, as it's one of the best beer foods going: fatty, salty, crisp, delicious. I like them so much that I worked on a couple of vegan options (see page 144) to keep me happy while I chug through bottles of Helles at home. Stiegl's Goldbräu is the Austrian equivalent of a Munich Helles. It's gold and has that essential toasted malt and herbal bitter hop balance. The malt matches the fried schnitzel, the hops and the carbonation balance the fat, and the floral-herbal hop works with the pungent ingredients in the potato salad, like onion and mustard.

AMBER LAGER

By using malts which have been kilned a little longer, you get lagers with a richer color and body of malt. Usually they give bread crusts and toast, and in classic German-brewed or inspired versions they'll have a little chewy caramel flavor from the decoction brewing process, which separates part of the mash and boils it before returning it to the overall wort, which gives caramelized flavors. The best Amber Lagers balance the malt flavor with bitterness, which will usually be herbal and peppery, and not many are hop aromatic, so these are beers to pair to grilled, roasted, and toasted flavors. They like semi-hard cheese, bread, marinara sauce, and hearty flavors like mushrooms and potatoes, and they can work well with Mexican spices. In the Amber Lager category you might find Vienna Lagers and Märzen.

BRIDGE: Veggie sausages, cooked onions, pizza and bread

BALANCE: Creamy pasta, most tacos, potato dishes

BOOST: Wild mushrooms, roast cauliflower, cheese pasta dishes

AVOID: Citrus desserts, dark chocolate

MAHRS BRÄU AU

TRY WITH: **KÄSESPÄTZLE**
BREWED IN: **BAMBERG, GERMANY**
ABV: **5.2%**

Mahrs Bräu's brewery tavern is one of my favorite places to drink—in fact, I've probably drunk there more often than any brewery outside of London. Their aU is always the first beer I order. The U stands for Ungespundet, which means unbunged, and it's an old German brewing term relating to the barrels in the cellar which aren't "bunged" and so have a softer carbonation. The beer is traditional of the region, being amber in color, with a chewy, toasty malt depth, some light caramelization, and a crisp bitterness. On the menu, they'll have Käsespätzle, a kind of Bavarian mac 'n' cheese made with small egg noodles, a cheese sauce and grilled onion on top. It's belly-filling food, and the Amber

Lager gives some nutty sweetness to match the cheese while the hops cut through the richness to keep it refreshing. It's one of the world's top beer pairings.

DOVETAIL BREWERY VIENNA LAGER

TRY WITH: **DEEP DISH PIZZA**
BREWED IN: **CHICAGO, ILLINOIS, USA**
ABV: **5.1%**

Dovetail's Vienna Lager is one of those moreishly malty beers that has a bread crust, toast, cracker and caramel-like body to it without ever being sweet. It's the sort of soothingly satisfying lager that keeps its balance thanks to the dry bitterness at the end, showing how the match-up of bitterness and sweetness is so crucial in all the best lagers. I suggest picking up some cans to go and ordering a deep dish pizza (or any kind of pizza you like, actually). Thick dough, loads and loads of mozzarella, tomato on top, some garlic and herbs all through it, and you need a beer that's going to be able to stand up to the flavor, cut through it, but not overwhelm it with hops. The Vienna's malt structure is definitely up to the job with any kind of pizza you prefer.

GREAT LAKES BREWING ELIOT NESS

TRY WITH: MUSHROOM FETTUCCINE
BREWED IN: CLEVELAND, OHIO, USA
ABV: 6.1%

Eliot Ness is a superb example of an American update on the Vienna Lager style. In a way, Vienna Lagers persist because of American craft brewing: it was a beer that originated in Vienna in the 1840s but was largely replaced by other styles by the end of the 19th century. As craft brewing was emerging, this was one of the original styles to be brewed, and Great Lakes's version is a modern classic. Amber-colored, nutty, and lightly caramelized, a little sweet, plenty of tasty toasty malts, a very smooth and almost creamy texture before the dry finish. The combination of pasta, mushrooms, a garlicky-buttery sauce and plenty of Parmesan allows the sweeter malts to balance the richness, while seasoning with plenty of black pepper matches the hop presence in the beer.

BRAYBROOKE KELLER LAGER

TRY WITH: CAULIFLOWER CHEESE PASTA
BREWED IN: MARKET HARBOROUGH, ENGLAND
ABV: 4.8%

Initially guided by Stephan Michel of Mahrs Bräu in Bamberg, Braybrooke's Keller Lager is a beautiful British rendition of the type of beer you'd drink all around Franconia. It uses just Pilsner and Munich malt and it's decocted so you get a moreish malty and toasty flavor from the grain before it dries down to a snappy bitterness. It's a really good food beer, especially with pizza and pasta, while I've really enjoyed it with a cauliflower cheese. Combine that and make a cauliflower cheese pasta bake or lasagne (I personally think a vegan version tastes better than dairy with this beer, see the recipe on

page 130). The toasty, nutty malt flavor loves the cauliflower, balances the cheeses, then the hops balance the richness at the end.

NASHVILLE BREWING CO. AMBER LAGER

TRY WITH: HOME FRIES, BISCUITS, WHISKEY AND COUNTRY MUSIC
BREWED IN: NASHVILLE, TENNESSEE, USA
ABV: 5.2%

Nashville Brewing Company began brewing "Lager Beer" in 1859. By the end of the 1890s it was known as the William Gerst Brewing Company, which brewed until the 1950s. In 2017, Scott Mertie resurrected the historic old brand and brought lager brewing back to Nashville. This Amber Lager is a pre-prohibition style of beer. It's a gleaming amber color, it's very clean with an underlying toastiness of malt, and a dry bitterness in perfect balance. It's one of those versatile beers which work with lots of foods and in lots of situations. Find vegan Nashville hot chicken, have some biscuits (the American kind) with home fries and eggs, get pizza, nachos, onion rings, or just have a bottle on its own with a glass of Tennessee whiskey on the side while listening to live country music.

DARK LAGER

Dark Lagers are some of the best beers for pairing with food. The use of more caramelized and roasted malts bring subtle background flavors like toast, caramel, roasted nuts, cocoa, coffee, and an umami-like savoriness. There's often a delicate balance between the hop bitterness, the dry finish, and the moderate alcohol content. Dark Lagers are a broad range of beers, from Munich-style Dunkel, which is toasty and only ever-so-slightly roasted, through to Schwarzbier or Black Lager, which tends to have a more pronounced coffee-like flavor, with Czech-style Dark Lager, (Černý Ležák or Tmavý Ležák, brown or black lager respectively) being more caramelized and full-bodied. They are best with darker flavors: roasted foods, barbecue, toasted bread, whole grains, earthy mushrooms, nut oils, squash and pumpkin, tomato-based sauces, and they are usually good with spice.

BRIDGE: Barbecued vegetables, toasted breads, fried rice

BALANCE: Fresh cheeses, creamy sauces, chili heat

BOOST: Mushroom tacos, tomato-based sauces, soy sauce

AVOID: Heavy desserts

HOFBRÄU DUNKEL

TRY WITH: **STIR-FRIED NOODLES**
BREWED IN: **MUNICH, GERMANY**
ABV: **5.5%**

Made by Munich's Hofbräuhaus, the brewery founded by the Bavarian royal family and now state-owned, this is a perfect example of a Dunkel, or Dark Bavarian Lager. If you drink this in the Hofbräuhaus then it'll come in a 1 liter mug and it's everything you expect of this great style: toasted malts, some chewy caramelization from the brewing process, some roasted nuts and just a hint of savory cacao, and a refreshing finish, almost like a Helles with a suntan. The food in the Hofbräuhaus is unapologetically meaty, so perhaps order one of the huge pretzels as it's ideal with the beer thanks to being golden-brown and well-toasted. If you drink Dunkel at home have it with something very un-Bavarian: stir-fried noodles with sesame oil, soy

sauce, peanut butter, tahini, chili, garlic, Chinese vinegar, and some green veg. The additional nuttiness is ideal with the beer, which in turn will add some toasty sweetness to the dish.

BERNARD ČERNÝ LEŽÁK

TRY WITH: **WILD MUSHROOMS ON TOAST**
BREWED IN: **HUMPOLEC, CZECH REPUBLIC**
ABV: **5.0%**

Černý Ležák is the traditional Czech-style of dark lager. It's somewhere between a caramely, medium-bodied Czech-style Pilsner and a German Schwarzbier, meaning you get a lager with a rich body of malts, a full and round texture which is pleasing to drink, some caramel and cacao, then a lasting hop bitterness. Mushroom hunting is a popular seasonal pastime for a lot of Czechs and Dark Lager is the beer that I think works best with the fungi: it'd taste great with wild mushrooms and garlic on toast, with creamy mushroom sauces, a mushroom goulash, mushroom risotto, basically anything with mushrooms. Add on some Jihočeská Niva, which is like a Czech Roquefort, and it's even better.

MOONLIGHT BREWING DEATH & TAXES

TRY WITH: **MISSION-STYLE BURRITO**
BREWED IN: **SANTA ROSA, CALIFORNIA, USA**
ABV: **5.0%**

Moonlight call this one a San Francisco-style Black Lager as it's not quite a Schwarzbier and leans towards the West Coast with an enhanced hoppiness. It's a lighter-tasting Black Lager, one that looks black but tastes a lot lighter, with a crisp, clean body, some distant cacao, salted licorice, and a dry and bitter finish where the dark malt and some herbal hops come together. It's refreshing, it's a little savory, it's certainly well hopped, and if it's an SF-style Black Lager then let's have this one with a Mission-style burrito. The tortilla is densely packed with rice, beans, sautéed veg, cheese, sour cream, avocado, salsa, and the beer is going to add its own roasted flavor like an additional seasoning, then give some bitterness to try refresh the hefty burrito.

VON TRAPP BREWING DUNKEL

TRY WITH: **WILD MUSHROOM STROGANOFF**
BREWED IN: **STOWE, VERMONT, USA**
ABV: **5.7%**

The Von Trapp Brewery—yes, the same Von Trapps as in *The Sound of Music*—is one of those destination breweries that anyone traveling for beer in New England should visit. It's a beautiful lodge of a beer hall, surrounded by blue sky and green rolling hills, all with some impeccable European-style lagers made on site. Their Dunkel deserves a lot of praise. It's got some bread crust malts,

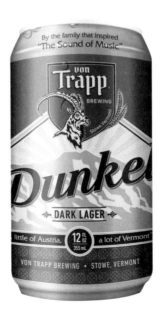

some fresh toast, a little malt sweetness, cocoa, and then the savory depth that comes from using darker malts. I had a great wild mushroom stroganoff when I was there and the combination of meaty mushrooms, sour cream, herbs, and pasta was a revelation—the flavor of the malt and the mushrooms harmonized together.

SCHLENKERLA RAUCHBIER MÄRZEN

TRY WITH: **BARBECUED CAULIFLOWER**
BREWED IN: **BAMBERG, GERMANY**
ABV: **5.1%**

Rauchbier is a smoked lager and the smokiness gets into the beer because the malts are kilned over beechwood fires, where the kernels of grain soak up the smoke. Schlenkerla's Rauchbier Märzen is the most famous example of this type of beer, and it's an evocative and unusual beer which tastes like smoked sausages, but can be especially good with food thanks to the flavor-enhancing abilities of smoke. Roast or barbeque a whole cauliflower, so that it picks up char, smoke, and sweetness, as that's a great match for Rauchbier. I love it with a tahini and lemon sauce as both of those ingredients are delicious with the veg and with smoke. If you're in Bamberg and at the brewery then veggie food options will be limited to cheese (while everyone around you eats knuckles of pork), though it's still a must-visit beer destination.

STRONG LAGER

There are several styles which fit under the Strong Lager umbrella. There's Festbier, which are inspired by the lagers of Oktoberfest and are typically like Munich-style Helles only stronger at about 6% ABV, though some will be amber in color (and sometimes called Märzen). There's Pale Bock, Maibock, or Helles Bock, usually 6–7% ABV, pale in color, malty and toasty but still balanced and dry. Regular Bocks are often amber-brown in color and more caramelized, while Doppelbocks are stronger versions of Bocks, often brown in color, upward of 7.0% ABV and with a strong malt flavor. Good ingredients include breads, grains, pasta, and potatoes to help with the higher alcohol content.

BRIDGE: Pizza, roasted vegetables, lentil stews

BALANCE: Whole grains, tomato-based sauces, chocolate cake

BOOST: Strong cheeses, mushrooms, apple and stone fruit desserts

AVOID: Light salads, citrus desserts

SCHELL'S BOCK

TRY WITH: **DETROIT-STYLE PIZZA**
BREWED IN: **NEW ULM, MINNESOTA, USA**
ABV: **6.5%**

Schell's have been brewing since 1860 and they make a range of lager styles. Their Bock is a seasonal and it's the ideal mix of sweet toasty malts and fresh-baked treats, with a spicy hop depth beneath. Put it with a Detroit-style pizza, which has all the elements of a normal pizza only more of all of it. It's cooked into a deep pan and loaded with brick cheese and tomato sauce. You need a lager with all the classic character, only more of it, and a Bock is ideal. The malt sweetness matches the pizza's dough, the dark malt is great with tomato, and the hops can handle the cheese and herbs. Like regular lager and pizza, only more of it.

PAULANER SALVATOR

TRY WITH: **KAISERSCHMARRN**
BREWED IN: **MUNICH, GERMANY**
ABV: **7.9%**

Salvator is considered the classic German Doppelbock and it was a special beer brewed annually by the Paulaner monks for the feast day of Saint Paola. The common story about this beer is that it was drunk by monks in place of food during the Lenten fast, but that's probably not entirely true. Regardless, we can take that idea and combine it with the British Shrove Tuesday tradition of making pancakes. *Kaiserschmarrn*, which translates as something like "emperor's scramble" and is named after Franz Josef I, is an Austrian and Bavarian dish of shredded pancakes (there's a recipe on page 210). Imagine fluffier American pancakes which have been pulled apart into bite-sized pieces, dusted in powdered sugar, and served with a fruit compote usually made from plums or apples. It's light but comforting, and sweet but not too sweet, and Salvator's caramel, dried fruit, toasted nuts, and roasted apple depth is a great match.

TRÖEGS BOURBON BARREL TRÖEGENATOR

TRY WITH: **BLACK FOREST GATEAU**
BREWED IN: **HERSHEY, PENNSYLVANIA, USA**
ABV: **9.8%**

Tröegenator is an American Doppelbock, one with loads of malt flavor, chocolate, dried fruit bread, and a roasted nuttiness to it. Put that in a bourbon barrel—put any Doppelbock in a bourbon barrel, in fact—and it comes out way richer, more chocolatey, luxurious, smooth, and slick with vanilla cream, coconut, and fruit cake. It's a dessert beer and one which wants chocolate. Black forest gateau is ideal: chocolate sponge, but not too sweet, then cherries and whipped cream and some extra booze from cherry liqueur; the beer has the ability to make the dessert taste more chocolatey (and more boozy), but it also refreshes it as it's not too sweet.

BIRRIFICIO ITALIANO BIBOCK

TRY WITH: **APRICOT AND RICOTTA FRIED PIZZA**
BREWED IN: **LURAGO MARINONE, ITALY**
ABV: **6.2%**

My trips away usually focus on food and drink. One year the focus was pizza. We started in Rome and then went down to Naples before spending a night in a tiny little village called Caiazzo to eat at a restaurant called Pepe in Grani, which is regarded as one of the best pizza restaurants in the world. We sat on their terrace with spectacular views over the countryside, eating pizza after pizza, and it was perfection. They served beers from Birrificio Italiano and I was drinking Bibock, a nutty, caramelized, lightly herbal, and lemony Bock, when a

dessert pizza arrived: a fried slice of dough topped with apricot jam, ricotta, lemon zest, and toasted hazelnuts. It was an incredible combination Next time you make pizza, save a bit of dough for dessert.

EPPIG BREWING FESTBIER

TRY WITH: **EGGPLANT (AUBERGINE), CHICKPEAS, HARISSA, FETA**
BREWED IN: **SAN DIEGO, CALIFORNIA, USA**
ABV: **6.0%**

Festbier has become a common style of Pale Lager and Eppig's is a great example. What makes this type of beer so appealing to me is that it has the qualities of a regular Helles-style lager, only there's more malt, a little more alcohol and richness, and usually a more noticeable bitterness which exaggerates all the other qualities. They are often a late-summer seasonal, overlapping with Oktoberfest, but some are brewed year-round. I think you can pair them with a substantial Middle Eastern salad. Grill some eggplant (aubergine), cook some fresh tomatoes and garlic in olive oil, add a can of cooked chickpeas, some harissa, then mix in the eggplant, crumble plenty of feta on top, and serve with warm flatbreads. Festbier likes the nutty chickpeas and the alcohol is good with the acidity and spice in the dish.

HOPPY LAGER

Here the combination of classic lager brewing meets the modern taste for hops, and there are several defined styles: Italian Pilsner is like a German-style Pilsner with a large dry-hop of German varieties to give more herbal and citrus-pith aromas; New Zealand Pilsner usually has a toastier body of malt, like a light Golden Ale, and is then aromatic with tropical New Zealand hops; and the IPL, or India Pale Lager, has emerged as a clean, dry, and lagered version of an IPA, which can range from session strength to imperially strong. The fresh hop aromas and flavors like fresh herbs, woody herbs, chili, lemongrass, ginger, fried foods, light citrus, bread, and salty bar foods.

BRIDGE: Hard herbs, Thai salads, Italian dishes

BALANCE: Light dairy, fresh chili, avocado/tacos

BOOST: Vietnamese flavors, pizzas and sandwiches, fried/salty foods

AVOID: Chocolate desserts, gravy-based dishes

BRLO HAPPY PILS

TRY WITH: **VEGAN CURRYWURST**
BREWED IN: **BERLIN, GERMANY**
ABV: **4.9%**

Brlo's Happy Pils is a lightly hazy gold, the hops—Citra and Huell Melon—give it lemon, stone fruit, and a little melon, and it's got a deep, lasting, dry bitterness, and those qualities are really good with vegan currywurst. There are increasing vegan options for currywurst in Germany, which is good news as it's a great beer snack. It's a fat sausage with an important "snap" to its skin, mild in taste, covered in a curry-flavored ketchup and served with fries. I think it's best eaten standing up at a street-food kiosk, with a bottle of bitter Pilsner, but add some modern hops to that Pilsner and it's even better, because the fruity beer and the fruity-spiced ketchup share some similar flavors, while the hop bitterness can balance the high sweetness of the sauce.

Vegan Beer Sausages, page 161.

BIRRIFICIO ITALIANO TIPOPILS

TRY WITH: **NEAPOLITAN PIZZA**
BREWED IN: **LURAGO MARINONE, ITALY**
ABV: **5.2%**

Tipopils is the defining and original example of an Italian Pilsner. It's a "kind of Pilsner" inspired by herbal, bitter German Pils, then dry-hopped with German hops. Tipopils has floral, pepper, stone fruit, lemon peel, and verdant green aromas, and the body is both very lean and dry yet also teasingly toasty. It's a beer that's superb with pizza (most beers are, actually). Go with a proper Napoli-style pizza. I'm a marinara man, loving how the German hops work with the garlic, oregano, and peppery extra-virgin olive oil. The beer is also great with olives and capers, with the brininess working with the hops, or add some fried eggplant (aubergine) as the hops are also really good with that. The creaminess of good mozzarella provides some extra fat to balance the hops.

JACK'S ABBY HOPONIUS UNION

TRY WITH: **EGGPLANT (AUBERGINE) PARM SANDWICH**
BREWED IN: **FRAMINGHAM, MASSACHUSETTS, USA**
ABV: **6.5%**

IPL has become a beer style brewed all around the world, and it combines the crisp, dry refreshment of a lager with the strength and the bold aromatic hops of an IPA. If any single brewery can be cited as the pre-eminent IPL brewers, it's Jack's Abby, who've been specializing in making them since 2011. Hoponius Union is also one of the world's best IPLs. It's super-clean, bright, gloriously aromatic with oily citrus, resinous herbs, and some stone fruit, with a lasting citrus bitterness. Try this one with an eggplant (aubergine) parm sandwich. Fried eggplant, Parmesan, mozzarella, marinara sauce with garlic and basil—all things which are tasty with American hops. I ate something similar in the brewery when I visited and it's a really good combination, with the oiliness cut by the beer's pithy bitterness.

SIREN CRAFT BREW SANTO

TRY WITH: **TOFU COM TAM**
BREWED IN: **WOKINGHAM, ENGLAND**
ABV: **5.0%**

Santo is a very pale hazy yellow lager that's heavily dry-hopped with American varieties like Mosaic, Citra, and Simcoe. The beer is bursting with peaches, pineapple, grapefruit, orange sherbet, with a light, crisp texture and a lively, refreshing finish. There's a great Vietnamese dish called com tam, which means broken rice. It's a grilled pork chop on broken rice with some salad and nuoc cham dipping sauce. To make it veggie, marinade some tofu or tempeh in soy sauce, brown sugar (or honey), garlic, chili, and lemongrass, and grill it until it's crispy, then just remove the fish sauce from the nuoc cham dressing. Put some pickled carrots on the side, plus an optional fried egg, and regular rice. The beer's hops love lemongrass, chili, and the salty-sweet dressing, with the acidity in the carrots able to perk up the hop fruitiness.

EMERSON'S NZ PILSNER

TRY WITH: **PAD KRAPOW**
BREWED IN: **DUNEDIN, NEW ZEALAND**
ABV: **4.9%**

This is the original example of the New Zealand Pilsner. It has a golden body of malts with some toastiness and structure which gives a little malt sweetness to accentuate the aromatic hop varieties, including Riwaka, Motueka, and Nelson Sauvin. Those hops give lots of stone fruit, gooseberries, passion fruit, and tangerine to the beer, and it's both fresh and a little jammy and sweet, which is great. It's a good beer for spicy Thai food as the malt can cool down the chili and the hops can add their own citrus. Pad krapow, cooked with tofu or another veggie protein, is bright with Thai basil's aniseed flavor, hot with chili, pungent with garlic and rich with soy. The beer helps to pick out the sweetness in the Thai basil, which is the key ingredient in the dish.

WHEAT ALE

In the world of Wheat Beer, there are three main kinds: Belgian, German, and what's come to be called American or just Wheat Ale. Wheat Ales use a significant amount of wheat in the brew, usually 30–60%; they typically have a neutral yeast, though sometimes it'll be a spicy or fruity yeast; and hops could be anything from light to IPA-like. It's a broad category but what brings them all together is the smooth and almost creamy wheat base, and usually a balanced hop character which is refreshing, so lighter dishes, light spices, fresh herbs, and citrus are all good ingredients alongside a Wheat Ale.

BRIDGE: Vietnamese dishes, salads, rice and white bread

BALANCE: Egg dishes, avocado, olive oil

BOOST: Middle Eastern spices, coconut curries,

AVOID: Rich desserts

BOULEVARD BREWING UNFILTERED WHEAT

TRY WITH: EGG BANH MI (OR EGG AND AVOCADO MUFFIN)
BREWED IN: KANSAS CITY, MISSOUR, USAI
ABV: 4.4%

This is the best-selling craft beer in the Midwest. Its popularity is thanks to its reliable easy-drinking simplicity. It's a hazy sunshine yellow, light-bodied yet with a satisfying texture and a little bit of grainy sweetness, with a gentle lemony fruitiness and a peppery finish. It's a good all-rounder for food: veggie sushi, brunch dishes, light salads but also hefty barbecue or burgers. Try it with an egg banh mi, with cilantro (fresh coriander), pickled carrot, and sriracha, as the lemony note in the beer will work with the cilantro, and wheat and eggs have an affinity, especially when in a sandwich. A breakfast egg and avocado muffin would be a good alternative.

SUAREZ FAMILY BREWING CRISPY LITTLE

TRY WITH: **AGLIO E OLIO**
BREWED IN: **HUDSON, NEW YORK, USA**
ABV: **4.7%**

Crispy Little is a beer which is ethereally light with lively Champagne-like bubbles, and those bubbles carry some fruitiness, like elderflower, lemon, fresh grass, and floral herbs. It's crisp and subtle and yet it's phenomenally interesting, and it deserves a dish which is greater than its seeming simplicity. *Aglio e olio* suits that. Olive oil, garlic, red pepper flakes, parsley, lemon, and linguine combine to become a super-satisfying dish, which wants a light, effervescent, gently lemony beer like Crispy Little to balance the olive oil's natural peppery fruitiness. And if you don't know this dish, then watch the movie *Chef*.

THREE FLOYDS GUMBALLHEAD

TRY WITH: **GUACAMOLE AND NACHOS**
BREWED IN: **MUNSTER, INDIANA, USA**
ABV: **5.6%**

Gumballhead is the leading example of a hoppy Wheat Ale, one which sits between a Pale Ale and a Wheat beer, and is aromatically hopped to give it a lemon, stone fruit, orange and grapefruit aroma. The base brew is a little sweet to begin and very bitter at the end. We can pair this one as we would a Pale Ale, which means we can pair it with bar food, so get yourself some guacamole and nachos. The creaminess in the avocado cuts the bitterness, while the chili, lime, and salt enhance the hop fruitiness. Avocado tostadas or tacos would also be

great. Or go fully loaded nachos with salsa, cheese, and sour cream. Gumballhead can handle it. It can also handle tacos, wings, loaded fries, hot dogs…. Like I said, it's a beer for bar food.

BRASSERIE EFFET PAPILLON WHEAT ALE

TRY WITH: **RAS-EL-HANOUT ROASTED ROOTS AND TAHINI SALAD**
BREWED IN: **MÉRIGNAC, FRANCE**
ABV: **5.1%**

Effet Papillon's Wheat Ale is a beguiling brew, one that's a mix of tropical hops with a peppery and clove-like yeast, with hints of dried orange peel, black pepper, and fermenting stone fruits, and it all combines to be spicy, zesty, and lively. It's a beer that works with earthy, sweet, and spicy flavors. Ras el hanout is a spice mix including cumin, cinnamon, clove, allspice, ground coriander, ginger, and black pepper, so put that on some carrots and beets (beetroot) and roast them, adding some honey five minutes from the end. Serve on quinoa with a tahini and yogurt dressing, plus feta and fresh mint. The peppery, clove-like spice in the beer intensifies the flavors in the ras el hanout, and the dairy works with the wheat in the beer to keep everything cool and balanced.

CIVIL SOCIETY BREWING PULP

TRY WITH: **JERK SWEET POTATO AND BLACK BEANS**
BREWED IN: **JUPITER, FLORIDA, USA**
ABV: **6.3%**

This American Wheat Ale is at the hoppy extreme of the style, somewhere near a Hazy IPA. It's hazy orange with a thick white foam, there's a lot of pulpy orange and grapefruit, then some tropical vibes, stone fruits, and a dank, savory depth, all from Mosaic hops. The texture is really good, and that's where the wheat is helping out, giving us something creamy-smooth before a high bitterness cuts it at the end. It's a beer which can handle some spice and some herbs, so cook sweet potatoes, bell (sweet) peppers, and black beans in Caribbean jerk spices and serve with coconut rice and fresh lime—the rice is the bitterness buffer while the hops are going to jump around with the jerk seasoning, especially if there's some fruity Scotch bonnet in there.

WEISSBIER

German-style Wheat Beers—Weissbiers, Weizen, or Hefeweizen; different names for the same kind of beer—are some of the most food-friendly beers, both to pair to food and to cook with food. The wheat in them gives them a full yet light texture, the bitterness is low, and the refreshing carbonation is high, plus they present a range of fruity and spicy aromas from the distinctive yeast, often banana, vanilla, bubblegum, pepper, and clove. There's regular Weissbier, which is pale, and there's Dunkelweizen, which is dark and might be even better than the light one to go with food. A less-common style is Weizenbock, a stronger version of the style. Weissbiers are generally good with chili heat, they work well with a range of different spices, they can handle strong flavors, and they are uniquely refreshing while being satiatingly smooth and full.

BRIDGE: Clove-like spice, creamy sauces, apple desserts

BALANCE: Chili spice, Indian food, tagines

BOOST: Roasted roots and cauliflower, Thai food, creamy curries

AVOID: Gravy-based dishes

WEIHENSTEPHAN HEFE WEISSBIER

TRY WITH: **THAI FOOD**
BREWED IN: **FREISING, GERMANY**
ABV: **5.4%**

This is the classic Hefeweizen and a beer which I find so satisfying and pleasing to drink. It's wonderfully smooth, yet also lively with carbonation. It has a banana cream depth, but it's not sweet, and there's some playful peppery spiciness which perks it up. In Germany you'll most often see this beer in summer or on the breakfast table, where it's served with *Weisswurst*, or white sausages. We're going to the other side of the world, though, as Weissbier is really good with most Thai food: red curry, massaman curry, pad Thai, fried rice, drunken noodles. Flavors like soy sauce, chili, coconut, and Thai basil really suit the creamy, spicy qualities of Weissbier.

BRAUEREI GUTMANN DUNKLES HEFEWEIZEN

TRY WITH: **ROAST CAULIFLOWER AND TAHINI**
BREWED IN: **TITTING, GERMANY**
ABV: **5.2%**

Brauerei Gutmann specialize in Weissbiers. Their classic Hefeweizen is wonderfully refreshing. It's creamy-smooth, fruity with banana and a little citrus depth. Their Dunkles Hefeweizen, or dark wheat beer, is a deep amber-brown color and has a similar creaminess, plus cacao and toasted nut flavors, with a more noticeable peppery spice at the end. I've become a little obsessed with roasted cauliflower and tahini, and no beer is better with that combo than Dunkelweizen. The darker malts sweeten the veg, while the nutty tahini is amazing with the yeast in the beer. Roast the cauliflower florets in a little ground cumin, ground coriander, salt, and black pepper, then when cooked pour over a dressing of tahini (dark tahini is even better with the dark beer) with a little lemon juice, natural yogurt (soy or dairy), and olive oil. Serve it in a wholemeal wrap or on a wholegrain salad, or just treat the cauliflower like wings as a beer snack to dip in the sauce.

URBAN CHESTNUT SCHNICKELFRITZ

TRY WITH: DAL, ROAST CELERY ROOT (CELERIAC), AND FRIED EGGS
BREWED IN: ST LOUIS, MISSOURI, USA
ABV: 5.1%

The pretzels at Urban Chestnut's Bierhall in St Louis are some of the best I've ever eaten, so that's a good starting point for their Weissbier, or any of their great lagers. I'd then take cans or bottles home and serve the beer with a dal. Cook the lentils in curry spices, including aromatics like clove, cinnamon, cardamom, and lots of black pepper, and use coconut milk. Serve it with some curry-roasted celery root (celeriac) and a couple of fried eggs or grilled tofu. Schnickelfritz is a lighter Weissbier, it's crisply refreshing but still has some creaminess in the body, there's the expected banana, some vanilla, plus a clove spiciness all through it, then it's really dry at the end. The smooth brew lightens the hearty lentils, while the spice in the beer and in the dal boost each other. The celery root's aniseed flavor also loves those spices, while the egg is there because dal and eggs are really good together and Weissbier loves eggs, too.

HAKONE ASHIGARA WEIZEN

TRY WITH: TOFU KATSU CURRY
BREWED IN: ODAWARA, JAPAN
ABV: 4.5%

Hakone's Weizen is a multiple award-winning brew that's very pale yellow, fruity, and spicy, with some foam banana candy aroma. It's nicely sweet and refreshingly light. Try it with katsu curry. You can katsu—breadcrumb and fry—anything you like, so use tofu, eggplant (aubergine), or cauliflower. The curry sauce is spiced, savory, and sweet, a thick mix of curry powder, broth, garlic, and ginger. Weissbier works well with this dish because you need some sweetness and texture in the beer, plus the natural spiciness from the yeast creates a more complex

Weissbier Dosa with Spiced Potatoes, page 152.

flavor out of the sauce. This beer would also be good with tempura vegetables or soba noodles with a dashi-based dipping sauce.

SCHNEIDER WEISSE AVENTINUS WEIZEN DOPPELBOCK

TRY WITH: BANANA BREAD
BREWED IN: KELHEIM, GERMANY
ABV: 8.2%

Schneider Weisse's regular wheat beer is usually talked about alongside Weihenstephaner's as a classic example, though it's quite different: an amber color, ripe banana, a bit more sweetness and richness. Imagine those flavors intensified into a version at 8.2% ABV and that's what Aventinus is like. It's a glowing amber color. There's a huge aroma of roasted bananas, spiced pears, caramel, dried fruit, and festive spices, and it's an impactful, impressive beer. Have a slice of banana bread and you've got a great match. The beer's sweetness intensifies the banana flavor in the beer, then lifts that with its cardamom and nutmeg-like spiciness. This beer is also good with a hearty tagine or a kebab of grilled veg and halloumi.

WITBIER

Where German-style Weissbier gives a banana-like aroma and a soft, smooth, rich texture, Belgian-style Witbier, or white beer, gives citrus and spice; they are zesty, refreshing, and dry beers. They are classically brewed with orange peel and coriander seed which emphasize the fruity-spice flavors from the Witbier yeast, though some beers feature other additional ingredients. Witbier is another style that's really good with food thanks to its combination of low bitterness, smooth texture, and yeast-derived fruitiness and spice. Certain flavors are especially good: ginger, lime, lemon, lemongrass, cilantro (fresh coriander), mint, ground coriander, aniseedy veg, coconut, and mild and tangy cheeses.

BRIDGE: Ground coriander, Vietnamese herbs, lemon and citrus

BALANCE: Creamy sauces, tangy cheeses, Indian curries

BOOST: Middle Eastern dishes, coconut curries, fries and mayo

AVOID: Chocolate desserts, gravy-based dishes, rich tomato sauces

ST BERNARDUS WIT

TRY WITH: **FRITES AND MAYO**
BREWED IN: **WATOU, BELGIUM**
ABV: **5.5%**

St Bernardus is brewed with the usual additions of coriander seed and dried orange peel, plus it has an expressive yeast which adds some clove, vanilla, and lemon. Together the yeast and spices are able to amplify each other, giving a depth of lemon, orange, the fruity-earthy-orangey coriander, some light pepper, and a lot of refreshing bubbles to uplift the cracker-like malt base. This could go with a lot of typical Belgian beer snacks—a cheese sandwich, an omelet or tart, a vegetable quiche—but you can't beat a Witbier with a cone of fresh fries, or frites, and a fat dollop of mayo.

UNIBROUE BLANCHE DE CHAMBLY

TRY WITH: **ASPARAGUS AND GOAT CHEESE TART**
BREWED IN: **CHAMBLY, CANADA**
ABV: **5.0%**

Blanche de Chambly pours a pale yellow and gives an inviting aroma of stone fruit, fresh bread, and floral honey. The body is creamy, honeyed, dry, and a touch tart and zesty, making it wonderfully complex, with spices giving hints of pepper, cardamom and coriander. Fresh asparagus is a great flavor for Witbier, especially if you add some dairy, like goat cheese or hollandaise, or make an omelet. The sweetness in the beer brings it all together, with the spiciness adding its own seasoning to the combo. Spanakopita, the Greek spinach and feta pastry, would also work really well with this beer.

ALLAGASH WHITE

TRY WITH: **FALAFEL AND HUMMUS SANDWICH**
BREWED IN: **PORTLAND, MAINE, USA**
ABV: **5.2%**

Allagash is the classic American-brewed Witbier. It's been brewed since 1995, totally inspired by the traditional brews and made with coriander seed and Curaçao orange peel.
The coriander is immediately evident in the aroma, giving its floral, orangey, savory quality. The body is soft, clean, and creamy yet it's light and ends dry and infinitely refreshing. Flavors of sweet orange, lemon pith, coriander, nutmeg, pepper, and anise weave through it, and those flavors bridge perfectly to a falafel and hummus sandwich. The beer's spices complement the food and can also enhance the seasoning in the falafel and the hummus, adding some extra lemon freshness.

WESTBROOK BREWING WHITE THAI

TRY WITH: **THAI YELLOW CURRY**
BREWED IN: **MT PLEASANT, SOUTH CAROLINA, USA**
ABV: **5.0%**

Thai yellow curry, made yellow from turmeric, is ideally matched with Witbier. The recipe uses many herbs and spices which all love the beer: ginger, lime, kaffir lime leaves, lemongrass, ground coriander, cilantro (fresh coriander), chili, plus creamy coconut. The beer adds some of its own spice, while its citrus depth and a bright carbonation lift up all the flavors in a brilliant way. That's made even better if the beer itself uses more crossover ingredients, which is why White Thai is such a good choice: it's brewed with lemongrass, ginger, and some hops which give a lemon and coconut aroma. The beer has a more prominent bitterness than other Witbiers, but it's all well balanced and fragrantly tasty with a Thai curry.

EINSTÖK ICELANDIC WHITE ALE

TRY WITH: **CARROT AND FENNEL SALAD**
BREWED IN: **AKUREYRI, ICELAND**
ABV: **5.2%**

I've always been impressed with the clarity of flavor in this beer and I associate that with the glacial water used to brew it; there's a purity to it, a lightness, despite it having a decent body of malt bulked out and made extra-smooth with oats and wheat. It's brewed with coriander and orange peel, and it's a particularly orangey Witbier, leaving a little dry, peppery spiciness. Witbier works well with a lot of salads, and you just need to bring a few ingredients together for the best matches. Roast some carrots and fennel with ground coriander and black pepper, squeeze over some lemon and honey at the end, scatter on plenty of dill, and serve with tabbouleh and whole grains, perhaps with some feta crumbled on top.
The orange and coriander in the beer work like an additional dressing with the food.

BELGIAN PALE, BLONDE, AND AMBER

Belgian beer styles give us some of the best for food matching. With the Pales, Blondes, and Ambers we usually get beers with a noticeable malt character, whether it's bready Pales or more toasted Ambers, and then we'll either get beers with a pronounced herbal, crisp bitterness, or beers with a fragrant, spicy yeast character. They almost always have a high carbonation, too, and altogether these qualities make them naturally food-friendly: fizz to lift flavors, malt to add sweetness, and hops or spice to bridge to different flavors. Ingredients like pepper, hard herbs, lemon, earthy spices, ginger, potatoes, plus fried or grilled foods, naturally work well.

BRIDGE: Black pepper, root vegetables, dried apricot

BALANCE: Soy- or miso-roasted veg, creamy sauces, Moroccan spices

BOOST: Indian curries, mac 'n' cheese, fried potatoes

AVOID: Chocolate desserts

LA TRAPPE BLOND

TRY WITH: **VEGETABLE TAGINE**
BREWED IN: **BERKEL-ENSCHOT, NETHERLANDS**
ABV: **6.5%**

A Dutch Trappist Blond, this beer is immediately fruity with yeast—banana, stone fruit, vanilla, almond, and pear, with a little hint of spiciness. The body is on the sweeter side to begin, a little honeyed and toasty, then it has a peppery, lemon zest and lightly bitter finish. Blonds are really good with a vegetable tagine or Moroccan-style stew where aniseedy root veg (like carrot or parsnip), eggplant (aubergine), zucchini (courgette), olive oil, garlic, cumin, ground coriander, harissa, chickpeas, tomatoes, dried apricots, and black pepper, are all flavors which naturally work very nicely with the sweeter malt flavor and the peppery yeast in a Belgian Blond.

DE KONINCK BOLLEKE

TRY WITH: **CHEESE AND POTATO CROQUETTE**
BREWED IN: **ANTWERP, BELGIUM**
ABV: **5.2%**

In Antwerp, the locals would colloquially order a "bolleke" of the iconic De Koninck Amber Ale, referring to the glass shape—a "small ball" in Brabant dialect—but it was such a common phrase that the brewery made it the name of the beer. It's a classic Belgian Amber, one whose simplicity makes it so good: nutty, lightly caramelized, toasted malts, very clean and balanced, crisply satisfying, with a peppery Czech hop bitterness. When in Antwerp you might have this with fries and mayo, chunks of nutty cheese, or croquettes made with mashed potato and cheese and deep-fried. Dip in mustard for extra oomph.

BRASSERIE DE LA SENNE ZINNEBIR

TRY WITH: **MUSHROOM VOL-AU-VENT OR CARBONARA**
BREWED IN: **BRUSSELS, BELGIUM**
ABV: **5.8%**

This is Brussels's beer and a stalwart for a city of beer lovers. It's a hop-led beer, one which gives orange zest, pear, black pepper, herbs, and some floral hops, then comes the Belgian yeast with an additional peppery crack and some dryness, while the hops which led you in also see you out, being assertive, bitter, and herbal. The malt is in there but you don't really notice it because of the hops and yeast, though when you have this beer with food, it's the malt which is important. Being a beer of Brussels, this is one for the beer café. It's something to drink with a snack, like a toasted sandwich, a slice of quiche, local cheese, cheese croquettes, or try a mushroom vol-au-vent: puff pastry filled with a mushroom, herb, and crème fraiche sauce. A mushroom carbonara made with lots of black pepper is also good.

Mock Coq à la Bière, page 134, made with Belgian Blonde.

LOST ABBEY DEVOTION

TRY WITH: **VEGETABLE BIRYANI**
BREWED IN: **SAN MARCOS, CALIFORNIA, USA**
ABV: **6.0%**

Devotion is a worshipful take on a Belgian Blonde, and it's very classic in its taste, plus an American flourish from a noticeably high hop character. A golden brew, it's got plenty of malt weight but not sweetness, there's a fragrant, floral, lemony, herbaceous hop presence through the middle, with a lasting bitterness and a high carbonation, making it both refreshing and complex. Blondes are often really good with Indian flavors, liking the base spices of ginger, cumin, ground coriander, turmeric, and pepper, while in a biryani you're adding more fragrant ingredients like cinnamon, cardamom, allspice, and bay leaves, plus some dried fruits for sweetness. It's an aromatic dish, and the hop and yeast in the beer bridge right across to the rice. Some roasted cauliflower, or a small cauliflower and root vegetable curry, is a good addition with a Belgian Blonde.

ST STEFANUS BLONDE

TRY WITH: **CAULIFLOWER KORMA OR MAC 'N' CHEESE**
BREWED IN: **GHENT, BELGIUM**
ABV: **7.0%**

There's a lot to work with in a cauliflower korma, especially if you roast the cauliflower first (and you should because it tastes better). It's a curry that's low in chili heat, but layered with spices, using garlic, ginger, cardamom, pepper, and garam masala, then there's the creamy additions of almonds (I use almond butter in mine), honey, and dairy. There's something very comforting about this as a curry, and the rich, smooth, nutty flavors are really nice with a Belgian Blonde that's creamy, toasty, and fruity, like St Stefanus, with an orange zest and pepper dryness at the end to cut through the curry. Belgian Blondes are also great with mac 'n' cheese—see the recipe on page 128 for a Beer Mac 'n' Cheese made with a Belgian Blonde.

BELGIAN TRIPEL AND STRONG GOLDEN ALE

These are food-friendly beer styles and versatile drinks to go with a lot of different dinners. They are similar beers in intensity, both being strong and impactful with alcohol and yeast, though that yeast tends to present itself differently, as does the malt: Tripels are often a little more malt-forward and fuller in body, while the yeast in a Tripel is often more peppery or spicy compared to a fruitier, lighter Strong Golden Ale yeast. They share a high carbonation and a dry, quenching, refreshing finish. Good flavors to go with these beers are ginger, almond, lemon, orange, stone fruits, earthy spices like ground coriander, aniseed-like celery root (celeriac) and fennel, olive oil, and they like some fat and salt to balance the high alcohol content.

BRIDGE: Lemon, black pepper, aniseed vegetables

BALANCE: High fat or cream-based dishes, semi-hard cheese, light citrus

BOOST: Indian spices, citrus cake, Christmas dinner

AVOID: Light salads, heavy desserts

DUVEL

TRY WITH: **PENNE ALLA DUVEL**
BREWED IN: **BREENDONK, BELGIUM**
ABV: **8.5%**

I drink more Duvel than any other beer. I find it a thrilling beer, one that's beautiful gold with a lacy white foam, racy with carbonation, evocative with its aroma of apples and pear schnapps. It's a beer that's remarkably precise and clean, with a dry pepper finish and a spicy warmth of alcohol, and it's all refreshingly light yet powerful and strong. Despite drinking so much of it, I've realized that I rarely have it with food. I developed a dish to emphasize the flavors of Duvel. I called it Penne alla Duvel and it was based on the American-Italian recipe of Penne alla Vodka. It's a tomato-based sauce and I added Duvel-friendly flavors like fennel, fennel seeds, lemon zest, garlic, basil, and pepper, alongside Duvel and some cream, and that worked quite well. I also tried it with many other dishes, focusing on some key flavors which I think are good with Duvel like ginger, coconut, avocado, citrus, and light spice, but never found anything totally perfect. So I have a request: if ever you find the perfect food pairing for Duvel, please please please tell me what it is.

BRASSERIE DUPONT AVEC LES BON VŒUX

TRY WITH: CHRISTMAS OR THANKSGIVING DINNER
BREWED IN: TOURPES, BELGIUM
ABV: 9.5%

There are more Brasserie Dupont beers featured in this book than any other brewery, and I could've easily picked another one or two of theirs to go in here. What makes them so good—for food and on their own—is their superior balance of flavor but also the density of flavor in each brew. There's the malt, which thanks to a direct-fired brewing vessel picks up a caramelized character; a fruity and lightly spicy yeast aroma; and a really snappy and lively carbonation before a very dry finish. Avec les Bon Vœux de la Brasserie Dupont, or "with the best wishes of the Dupont Brewery," is a strong, special Golden Ale. It has a fruity, inviting aroma of stone fruits, apple, and some fragrant spice. The body is full, rich, honey-like, smooth yet spiked with carbonation, and it's strong yet elegant. This style, and specifically this beer, is good with Christmas or Thanksgiving dinner. These are meals with lots of ingredients, flavors, and textures, yet the beer can work with it all.

ALLAGASH TRIPEL

TRY WITH: FENNEL GNOCCHI
BREWED IN: PORTLAND, MAINE, USA
ABV: 9.0%

Like their other Belgian-inspired brews, Allagash's Tripel is a classic take on this classic beer style. It's bright gold, it's fruity in the aroma, with banana, stone fruit, and floral honey. The body is sturdy but not sweet, robustly elegant, then the yeast gives some pepper and a refreshing lemon note. Fennel is a flavor that suits Tripels, especially if it's been roasted. So roast it in olive oil with some garlic, fennel seeds, black pepper, and a pinch of ground coriander. Serve with gnocchi, pasta, or orzo, some Italian-style veggie sausages or meatballs, a little lemon juice and zest, and some Parmesan or Grana Padano. Allagash also brew Curieux, a bourbon barrel-aged Tripel, which is rich with bourbon, honey, and spice, and it's a beer for dessert: ginger cheesecake, apple pastries, or spiced carrot cake.

TRIPEL KARMELIET

TRY WITH: CORIANDER-ROASTED CELERY ROOT (CELERIAC)
BREWED IN: BUGGENHOUT, BELGIUM
ABV: 8.4%

Tripel Karmeliet is a very fruit-forward Tripel, with a lot of orange character—fresh peel, tangy pith, orange oil. That joins with some floral honey, coriander seed, stone fruits, and pepper in a beer with a creamy, sweetish body. Tripels are good with ginger and Indian spices, especially ground coriander, so roast or barbecue celery root (celeriac) in olive oil with lots of ground coriander (ideally toast the whole seeds then grind them yourself, as they taste way better), and the beer's yeast amplifies the celery root (celeriac). You could serve it as a steak or in a sandwich, or mix it into a curry made with coconut, eggplant (aubergine), and the familiar Indian spices with a naan bread on the side.

ST BERNARDUS TRIPEL

TRY WITH: HUMMUS AND FLATBREADS
BREWED IN: WATOU, BELGIUM
ABV: 8.0%

There's a real variety in characteristics among the classic Belgian Tripels, from the potent strength and dryness of Westmalle, to the orangey sweetness of Tripel Karmeliet, to St Bernardus Tripel, which is really fruity to begin, with lemon, orange, pineapple, and banana, then it's like bitter honey and bitter orange, and it's dry, tannic, and high in carbonation, with a coriander-like spiciness. It's good with spiced olive oil cakes, and great with hummus. A little cumin is nice, a squeeze of lemon, rich olive oil, and the beer can work with all of that, complementing some ingredients and balancing others. You could bake some eggplant (aubergine) in oil, garlic, and pepper, then serve it on flatbread with hummus.

BELGIAN BRUNE, DUBBEL, AND QUADRUPEL

These dark, strong Belgian ales share flavors of toasty malt, cocoa, dried fruit, festive spices, and a distinctive fruity yeast. Brunes are generally sweeter and lower in alcohol, stepping up to Dubbels then Quadrupels and Belgian Strong Dark Ales (the last two are similar but the Strong Darks will likely be a little sweeter and richer). Like most stronger Belgian beers they have a robust yet not sweet body and a dry, refreshing finish. Much like most beers brewed with Belgian yeast, they are particularly good with food and surprisingly diverse, plus they have a dexterity to them, so they can work with lighter dishes through to desserts and we can travel the world to get good pairings, from hearty British pies to Italian pasta dishes to Japanese roasted vegetables to chocolate brownies. Complementary flavors include umami-rich foods like mushrooms, soy sauce, tomato, and miso, plus roasted flavors, roasted vegetables, nutty flavors, and fragrant ingredients like ginger, basil, fennel, cinnamon, and star anise.

BRIDGE: Soy sauce, aniseed spices, light chocolate

BALANCE: Baked pasta dishes, rich pies, Moroccan flavors

BOOST: Tomato-based sauces, aged cheeses, roast dinners

AVOID: Light salads, citrus desserts, very sweet food

ROCHEFORT 10

TRY WITH: **MUSHROOM LASAGNA**
BREWED IN: **ROCHEFORT, BELGIUM**
ABV: **11.3%**

Rochefort 10 is a classic Trappist Quad: deep brown-red, evocative aromas of fresh bread, tea cake, chocolate, roasted oranges, and festive spices swirl out of your glass, there's a rum-like richness, figs, brown sugar, and more spice, plus a savory and spicy-floral complexity, as it's brewed with coriander seed. It's one of those beers which sounds sweet when you describe it, but it's not. Instead it's very dry and almost savory, meaning it's a versatile beer with food. I like it with the richness of a mushroom lasagna, where the mushrooms are cooked with garlic and lots of pepper to a deeply meaty, savory depth, then layered up with white sauce and lots of cheese, including Gouda or Comté (you could also mix the mushrooms into a tomato sauce and that works, too). The beer brings fizz and some fruitiness, which is a nice contrast to the dish.

WESTVLETEREN 8

TRY WITH: **SPAGHETTI AND MEATBALLS**
BREWED IN: **WESTVLETEREN, BELGIUM**
ABV: **8.0%**

Brewed at the Abbey Saint-Sixtus, the Westvleteren beers are among the most sought-after Belgian brews, thanks to their scarcity and the long-time allure of Westvleteren 12, the brewery's strongest beer, being regarded as one of the world's best brews. The 8 and the 12 are both dark ales and they brew a Blonde, too. The 8 is red-brown, it's got a teacake and fresh bread quality, sweet dried fruits, aniseed, a peppery dryness, and a density of flavor which helps it stand above other Dubbels. It's a style which I think is perfect for tomato-based sauces. Spaghetti and meatballs is a wonderful match, especially if there's lots of black pepper and fresh basil on it, while eggplant (aubergine) parmigiana is also superb with the beer. I think it's how the yeast works with the herbs, while there's an umami affinity between the malt and the tomato.

TYNT MEADOW ENGLISH TRAPPIST ALE

TRY WITH: **VEG COTTAGE PIE**
BREWED IN: **COALVILLE, ENGLAND**
ABV: **7.4%**

Mount Saint Bernard Abbey brews England's only Trappist beers. Tynt Meadow is their version of a Belgian Dubbel brewed using English ingredients. It's a red-brown brew with an aroma of cherries, raisins, figs, licorice, cocoa, banana, and bitter almond, with a rich body of malts to begin, then a dry bitterness to finish. With a hearty veg cottage pie (you can use the beer in the recipe, too; see page 166), especially one with celery root (celeriac) in the mash, the beer's sweetness and dryness really match the dish. A British mature Cheddar or blue cheese will also work very well with this beer, and perhaps have it with a cream tea—I'd choose this beer over a cup of tea with a scone and clotted cream.

PFRIEM BELGIAN STRONG DARK

TRY WITH: **CHOCOLATE COOKIES OR BROWNIES**
BREWED IN: **HOOD RIVER, OREGON, USA**
ABV: **10.0%**

pFriem's Belgian Strong Dark is doughy with fresh bread and teacakes, there's loads of dried fruit, cacao, roasted banana, cherries, figs, plenty of booze, toffee, a soothing smooth texture, and a long finish. It's a beer which works with some desserts, if they aren't too sweet. While writing this book I got a bit obsessed with the flavors of chocolate with Dubbels and Quads together (the result was a recipe for Dubbel Chocolate Malt Pudding on page 218). The beer is good with cookies, cupcakes, or brownies, where the addition of banana and cinnamon in any of them also works well. If you make your own, add tahini to the recipe, as it's such a good flavor with the beer and chocolate.

CHIMAY RED

TRY WITH: **CHAR SIU BAO BUNS OR MISO EGGPLANT (AUBERGINE)**
BREWED IN: **CHIMAY, BELGIUM**
ABV: **7.0%**

Chimay Red is a lighter-bodied and lighter-tasting Dubbel, one with a flavor of toasted and caramelized malts, roasted nuts, some stone and orchard fruits, aniseed spice, brown sugar, and a dry finish. Those flavors are particularly good with Asian ingredients like miso paste, soy sauce, sugar, five-spice, garlic, and ginger. Mix them together and cook with eggplant (aubergine) or mushrooms, serving them on rice, or use those ingredients to fill fluffy bao buns, and it really enhances the malt and the spice flavor in the beer. Chimay make their own cheeses, so for a more local pairing try that with some good bread.

SAISON AND WILD ALE

Farmhouse Ales, of which the most common is Saison, have developed from an idiosyncratic Belgian beer style into a whole family of beers with enormous diversity. Typically the connecting characteristics are of a very dry beer with an upfront density of malt and a zippy, peppery, fruity yeast profile, while they could be low or high in alcohol, aromatic with hops or funky with wild yeast. Wild Ales are not really like Saisons at all, but I'm putting them here anyway because there are some shared characteristics. These use a wild yeast called *Brettanomyces* which gives aromas ranging from farmyard to tropical fruit, usually with a very dry and snappy finish, sometimes edging into tartness. Saisons and Wild Ales are complex and interesting beers, and they can be very good with a wide range of foods, thanks to their dryness and savory-spicy yeast character.

BRIDGE: Peppery herbs, root vegetables, light citrus

BALANCE: Olive oil, stone fruit desserts, potatoes

BOOST: Thai dishes, creamy Indian curries, ripe and funky cheese

AVOID: Chocolate desserts

SAISON DUPONT

TRY WITH: **TALEGGIO AND POTATO PIZZA**
BREWED IN: **TOURPES, BELGIUM**
ABV: **6.5%**

The classic Saison, Dupont's beer is remarkably complex, the sort of beer which gives you something new every time you drink it. It's often touted as an all-rounder of a food beer which is great with almost everything, and that's something I've written myself, but I don't actually agree with that now. It can be brilliant food beer, but it's a challenging one; it's feisty—high in fizz, bitterness, and spice; there's lots of fruity yeast giving banana, apples, pear schnapps, pineapple peel; it's initially caramelized and sweet but leads to a very dry black pepper finish. Because of all of that I think it's a beer which wants to be balanced by salty, starchy food, with some complementary aromatic

ingredients and the best match I've had (and I've tried a lot of things) is a white pizza (or flatbread or focaccia) topped with sliced potato, taleggio (or use Dupont's own washed-rind cheese), lots of black pepper, some thyme, garlic, good extra virgin olive oil, and black olives. It's going to balance and boost all the best parts of the beer, with the malt sweetness easing through the whole combination.

BURNING SKY PETITE SAISON

TRY WITH: **PEA, BASIL, AND LEMON SPAGHETTI**
BREWED IN: **FIRLE, ENGLAND**
ABV: **3.5%**

Burning Sky specialize in Belgian-style beers, mostly aged in large wooden foudres (barrels). This one demonstrates the breadth of what a Saison can be: it's only 3.5% ABV, it has a firm peppery bitterness, it's aged in wood where it develops a very gentle tartness, and it's dry-hopped for a fresh aroma, where you get elderflower, lemon, and dried orange zest. It's a summer smasher of a beer, best served with something British, fresh and summery—a pea risotto, a salad with peas and zucchini (courgettes), or spaghetti with peas, olive oil, basil, lemon, garlic, and chili flakes, plus Parmesan or feta if you want cheese. The sweet earthiness of the pea works really well with the zingy yeast and hops in the beer.

BOULEVARD BREWING TANK 7

TRY WITH: **SOUTH INDIAN CURRY**
BREWED IN: **KANSAS CITY, MISSOURI, USA**
ABV: **8.5%**

I still vividly remember my first taste of Tank 7, as it burst into my senses with zesty tropical fruit and bright peppery aromas. It was a remarkable flavor experience, combining the upfront American hop aroma with the background of a Belgian brew with its dry spiciness and zinging carbonation, and in combining those qualities it created a new kind of American Saison. It works really well with aromatic ingredients like cilantro (fresh coriander), Thai basil, and lime, so a Vietnamese banh mi or a Thai curry are good. I like South Indian curries which are often prepared with coconut and include bright aromatic ingredients like ginger and tamarind alongside the usual spices, as that's such a good match with all the fruitiness from the yeast and hops.

BRASSERIE SAINT SYLVESTRE 3 MONTS

TRY WITH: **CAMEMBERT AND ASPARAGUS**
BREWED IN: **SAINT-SYLVESTRE-CAPPEL**
ABV: **8.5%**

3 Monts is a classic French beer, brewed in the very north of the country. It's a Bière de Garde, a robust beer which was historically brewed and stored to be drunk mature, not fresh. Today it's best when fresher. It's a bright golden beer with a structured, sturdy base that's initially sweet, bready and toasty, with a hint of yeast fruitiness, some peppery and floral hops, then a bitter finish—it's somewhere between a Belgian Golden Ale and Strong Lager, with just a hint of old rusticity in there. That helps align it with cheese with a bit of funk,

like a ripe Camembert. Use the cheese with some asparagus in a tart, quiche, or omelet. Or it'd be great in and with the Mock Coq à la Bière recipe on page 134.

HILL FARMSTEAD ARTHUR

TRY WITH: **AGED GOAT CHEESE, HONEY, SOURDOUGH**
BREWED IN: **GREENSBORO, VERMONT, USA**
ABV: **6.0%**

Arthur is a remarkable, enticing beer brewed in rural Vermont. It bridges between Saison and Wild Ale in the way that rustic beers like this tend to defy categorization. It's wonderful for its complexity and its lightness, where you get a body of beer that's lean and dry, Champagne-like in its carbonation, aromatic with gentle lemon, lemongrass, stone fruit, and just a little wildness to it with a tart, dry finish. It's the sort of beer you want to consider, to swirl around, to talk about, to share, and that allows time for food. It would work with Thai and Vietnamese salads, but that feels too intense for the beer, and I think you want some local cheeses with it—it's a beer that expresses its place through the yeast and its maturation, and that complements cheese well. An aged goat cheese like Vermont Creamery's Coupole or Bonne Bouche would be ideal, especially with a drizzle of honey and a crack of pepper on sourdough bread.

SLOW SOURS

These sour beers have been brewed and then matured for up to three years. Many are spontaneously fermented, meaning no yeast is added and instead it's naturally inoculated from the air and the environment and barrels around the brewery, so each beer is uniquely of its own place. After fermentation, maturation takes place, usually inside a wooden barrel, and the flavor is going to evolve over time, as it gets drier, more funky, more sour, and more complex. Acidic and umami foods are often best with these beers, plus they tend to like floral, peppery, and briny flavors, and they are versatile by being appetizingly zingy and also making refreshing palate cleansers. Fruit is often added, but rarely does it make these beers sweet.

BRIDGE: Lemon, black pepper, sourdough bread

BALANCE: Creamy desserts and cheese, briny flavors, root vegetables

BOOST: Fresh tomatoes, goat cheese, olives and olive oil

AVOID: Very sweet desserts, spicy food

BOON MARIAGE PARFAIT

TRY WITH: **ORZO, TOMATO, OLIVE, LEMON, FETA**
BREWED IN: **LEMBEEK, BELGIUM**
ABV: **8.0%**

This is a classic Belgian Geuze. When a brewer makes Geuze (or Gueuze) the base brew is called Lambic and it's spontaneously fermented and matured for many years in many different barrels. Then the brewer blends different vintages of Lambic, usually a mix of one, two and three years old. They are bottled and carbonate inside the bottle, where the new blended beer is called Geuze. Boon's Mariage Parfait is a blend of mostly three-year-old Lambic. It's golden yellow, it's lemony, there's funky grapefruit, and an umami aged character. It's electrifying to begin as a fresh jolt of acidity hits your tongue, then it softens right away into oak, stone fruit, light tannins, dried herbs, oranges, and lemon. I designed my own dish to work perfectly with this beer. I mixed orzo (or you could use pasta) with a sauce made from pan-fried

cherry tomatoes with-extra virgin olive oil, sun-dried tomatoes, green olives, salt, black pepper, lemon, dill, basil, and feta. The briny olives were the central flavor, bringing everything together, while the tomato gave umami which matched the beer, and the feta gave a complex acidity (though vegans could skip the cheese and it's still good).

CANTILLON KRIEK 100% LAMBIC

TRY WITH: **GOAT CHEESE, ROAST BEETS (BEETROOT), CARAMELIZED ONION**
BREWED: **BRUSSELS, BELGIUM**
ABV: **5.5%**

This is a Kriek, a spontaneously fermented beer matured with whole cherries. For Cantillon, they add 7oz (200g) of cherries per liter of beer and they add them when the Lambic is already about 20 months old, then they mature together for a few more months, during which time the beer is stained bright red and the yeast in the barrel will consume all the fruit sugars. The beer is very fruity, but it's not sweet; there's tart cherry, tangy apples, and almond, and it has an engagingly acidic finish. Despite the fruit, it's too tart to go with dessert and it needs something savory, creamy, and earthy. Try goat cheese and roasted beets (beetroot) with sweet caramelized onion, in a sandwich, tart, or omelet.

ALLAGASH COOLSHIP RESURGAM

TRY WITH: **SOURDOUGH, CHEESE, HONEY, PEACHES**
BREWED IN: **PORTLAND, MAINE, USA**
ABV: **6.0% (VARIES)**

Allagash were the first American brewery to produce spontaneously fermented beer using their own coolship, a large, flat vessel where the base Lambic wort cools overnight and gets inoculated with wild yeast. The beers are made in the Belgian tradition, meaning it's pale malt, some wheat, hops which are aged instead of fresh, then matured for years and blended. Coolship Resurgam is the classic base Gueuze-style beer, and it has a lemon and stone fruit aroma, some light tropical fruit, wood, tart apples, some funkiness, a moderate and balanced acidity, and a lasting, tannic bitterness. Get some fresh sourdough, top with ricotta or a soft blue cheese, grilled (or better: fermented) peaches, a drizzle of honey, and some salt and pepper. They are all flavors and textures that are great with this kind of sour beer.

BROUWERIJ 3 FONTEINEN OUDE GEUZE

TRY WITH: **CHEESE CROQUETTES OR STRAWBERRY WAFFLES**
BREWED IN: **BEERSEL, BELGIUM**
ABV: **6.0%**

Brewed just outside of Brussels, 3 Fonteinen is one of the best-known Lambic brewers. They have a restaurant, and there you can drink the straight Lambic, which is served flat and is tart, tannic, tropical in a funky kind of way, and gets your mouth watering. Their Oude Geuze is their traditional house beer; it's a blend of one-, two-, and three-year-old Lambics into a beer that's highly effervescent, sharp with lemon, pineapple, unripe stone fruit, then a bracing acidity at the end. They serve a fresh goat cheese salad in their restaurant, which is a good choice, but the fried cheese croquettes are even better and a great beer snack. Some fries and mayo on the side are a nice salty addition. Or make some Belgian waffles and serve with fresh strawberries—Geuze is a surprisingly good match for the tartness of a strawberry.

RODENBACH GRAND CRU

TRY WITH: **ROASTED TOMATO TART**
BREWED IN: **ROESELARE, BELGIUM**
ABV: **6.0%**

The Burgundy of the beer world is how Rodenbach is often described. It's a red-brown brew that's matured in large wooden barrels known as foudres. Different ages of beer are blended, with the regular Rodenbach blended 75/25 young to old, and the Grand Cru 33/67 young to old, making the Grand Cru more complex, more acetic (think balsamic), more vinous and wine-like, and with a fruity apple and cherry aroma. It always makes me think of tomatoes, and a tart made with roasted tomatoes is excellent with the beer (there's a recipe on page 138). A salad dressed with balsamic vinegar makes it even better, as does the addition of Camembert, or a similar creamy, mild cheese.

FAST SOURS

Where some sours can take years to mature, others can be made in a few weeks. They are commonly soured by lactic bacteria (the kind that turns yogurt tangy) or lactic acid (both are suitable for vegans). The beers are often light in body and flavor, so it's typical to have other ingredients added, like hops for extra aroma, or fruits. Berliner Weisse is a version of this beer, noted for its crisp, bright acidity, and there's also Gose, which classically uses coriander seeds and salt in the recipe—modern versions usually add fruit. "Sour" could mean anything from a tiny bit of tartness through to puckering acidity, while the style has become increasingly fruity and strong, with some now more reminiscent of smoothies than beers. Because these beers vary so much, there are no general rules as to what works with them, though bridging to ingredients with a light tartness or fruitiness (citrus fruits, tropical fruits, tangy cheese) is often good, or go with high salt and fat.

AVERY BREWING EL GOSE

TRY WITH: **SWEET POTATO, CORN, BLACK BEANS, AND AVOCADO TACOS**
BREWED IN: **BOULDER, COLORADO, USA**
ABV: **4.5%**

Gose is an unusual historical style that's not so much been resurrected as transformed into something totally modern. The new idea of the style brews a light, refreshing, tart beer with a little salt, which adds a pleasing salinity and softens the sourness. In El Gose, Avery add lime zest and lime alongside the salt, and that's immediately pointing us toward tacos. This is a tortilla-loving all-rounder of a beer, good with everything from guacamole and nachos to a big burrito. The beer's subtle tartness is just like a squeeze of lime, while the salt adds an appetizing savory flavor. I especially like this kind of beer with tacos filled with roasted sweet potato, corn, black beans, and avocado.

BUXTON BREWERY TROLLTUNGA

TRY WITH: **SPANAKOPITA**
BREWED IN: **BUXTON, ENGLAND**
ABV: **6.3%**

A Sour IPA with gooseberries, Trolltunga is a remarkable mix of tart fruit and lightly tart beer with lots of tropical, lemony hops on top. It's got an IPA-like texture and enough malt sweetness to plump up the fruit before a lemon-like tartness comes at the end in place of hop bitterness. It's a fascinating beer to drink, and the acidity and fruitiness makes me think of briny ingredients, which make me think of Greek food: fat olives, olive oil, Greek salad, tzatziki and pitta, and spanakopita, the filo pastry tart packed with feta, dill, mint, and spinach. The acidity in the beer balances the cheese, while the savory, grassy herbs bring out more fruitiness in the hops.

J. WAKEFIELD BREWING DFPF

TRY WITH: COCONUT PANCAKES AND PASSION FRUIT
BREWED IN: MIAMI, FLORIDA, USA
ABV: 7.0%

Florida Weisse has become a new craft beer style which many Floridian brewers make. It's a lightly tart soured ale that's lush with tropical fruits while still maintaining the kind of refreshing balance that you need in the sunshine state. DFPF stands for dragon fruit and passion fruit. It's a bright red color and it's immediately ripe with fruit—the passion fruit is obvious, the dragon fruit comes through like a mix of pomegranate, cherries, and something more elusively exotic. It zings with tropical freshness, with pure fruit and a refreshing tartness, but keeps a crisp malt depth. Have this for breakfast and make some American-style pancakes using coconut milk and serve with toasted coconut, fresh passion fruit, and slices of banana and strawberry.

COLONIAL BREWING CO. SOUTH WEST SOUR

TRY WITH: NOODLE SALAD
BREWED IN: MARGARET RIVER, AUSTRALIA
ABV: 4.6%

Sours are among the most refreshing and quenching beers with their mouth-watering balance of freshness, fizz, and the zip of acidity. In South West Sour, Colonial add a small amount of aromatic hops into the beer, giving the impression of gooseberries, lime, and passion fruit, which is really inviting. You want a nice fresh dish to go with it, and a noodle salad with sweet pickled carrots, cucumber, cilantro (fresh coriander), holy basil, mint, and a salty and sweet peanut and chili dressing is ideal. Usually you'd have lime or vinegar in the dressing, but skip that and let the beer be the acid component, where it'll also bring some of those tropical aromatics. Grill some tofu to go on top or make the DIPA Vietnamese Patties on page 164.

DIPA Vietnamese Patties, page 164.

LOHN BIER CATHARINA SOUR JABUTICABA

TRY WITH: BRAZILIAN BEER SNACKS
BREWED IN: LAURO MÜLLER, BRAZIL
ABV: 4.0%

The Catharina Sour is Brazil's entry into the beer style book. It originated from the state of Santa Catarina in the south of the country, and it's a lightly soured beer brewed with the addition of a fruit, usually something local. Lohn Bier brews a range of these brightly refreshing sours using fruits like butia (fruit from a palm tree), grapes, mango, guarana, and jabuticaba, which tastes somewhere between grape candy, lychee, and blueberry. As it's a uniquely local type of beer, try it with your version of Brazilian snacks like empanadas, veggie coxinha (which are like croquettes and will nicely sweeten the fruit acidity), yuca or cassava fries, or pão de queijo, little cheesy bready balls, which are a great snack with all beers.

FRUIT BEERS

These beers cross over with the Fast Sours and the Slow Sours sections because many of them have a tartness which comes from the fruit and/or the fermentation. Any fruit can be used in a brew, and each will change the foods you might want to have with the beer. These matches are going to be suggestive rather than instructive, and hopefully they'll give an idea as to how flavors and beers can work. Sometimes you'll want to match fruit with fruit, but most of the time you'll use the fruitiness to enhance and play around with something savory. Fresh herbs, fresh fruits, and fatty-creamy ingredients are often good here.

VAULT CITY STRAWBERRY SKIES

TRY WITH: **STRAWBERRIES, MASCARPONE, SHORTBREAD**
BREWED IN: **DUNDEE, SCOTLAND**
ABV: **8.5%**

Vault City specialize in modern fruited sour beers, the sort that you open and immediately smile because of the ridiculousness of the fruitiness. They make a wide range of beers, from juicy session-strength brews through to dessert-like Stouts. Strawberry Skies (there's also a raspberry version, though both are quite rare) is made with enormous amounts of Scottish strawberries plus hibiscus flowers and Madagascan vanilla. The vanilla makes this taste creamy alongside the sweet and just-tart fruit, with the body being full and juicy. I think you need something a little savory, so serve fresh strawberries with mascarpone and a salted shortbread biscuit. You could even roast some strawberries with sugar, vanilla, and a splash of balsamic vinegar (or a little of this beer) to get an even better match.

BROUWERIJ LIEFMANS KRIEK-BRUT

TRY WITH: **CHOCOLATE POT**
BREWED IN: **OUDENAARDE, BELGIUM**
ABV: **6.0%**

When I first had this beer with a dark chocolate pot I realized just how wonderful beer and food could be together—and I realized that it didn't need to be fancy, it didn't need to be complicated, and we didn't need to pick rare and unusual beers to make it wonderful. The flavors of sour-sweet cherry beer are incredible with dark chocolate, whether in a mousse, a brownie, a tart, or as a richer chocolate pot, with the fruity beer enhancing the natural fruitiness in the chocolate. This beer has a base of tart Belgian red ale then the cherries are infused into it in a way which enhances their sweetness, giving cherry pie, cherry juice, and a little nutty quality with a chocolate-loving tartness.

STIEGL RADLER GRAPEFRUIT

TRY WITH: **CITRUS SALAD**
BREWED IN: **SALZBURG, AUSTRIA**
ABV: **2.0%**

I drink a lot of Stiegl Radler and there are always cans of it in the fridge at home for when I just want to be fully refreshed by a glass of fresh grapefruit. Radler is a mix of lager and soda, and this one is a 40/60 blend of Stiegl's Goldbräu lager with a fruit soda made by the brewery and containing mostly grapefruit, plus some orange and lemon. It's a fun and fruity low-alcohol beer, and it can work widely with foods, including lemon crêpes, tofu in ginger and orange sauce, pho and ramen. However, I think it's a beer for light foods, like a salad with bitter leaves, roasted carrots, and beets (beetroot), some grilled orange segments, toasted hazelnuts, couscous or wild rice, and a lemon dressing. While writing this book, I also got a little bit obsessed with drinking Campari Radlers, and they are best with Stiegl: for one large can or bottle, add about 2fl oz (60ml) Campari, perhaps a slice of orange and some ice, too. You can also add Campari to crisp, bitter Pilsner. It's the best beer cocktail you'll ever drink.

NEW GLARUS RASPBERRY TART

TRY WITH: PEANUT BUTTER COOKIE
BREWED IN: NEW GLARUS, WISCONSIN, USA
ABV: 4.0%

Consider this one a deconstructed PBJ. The beer is juicy and jammy and mouth-watering with a little tartness like fruit pips and a light smoothie texture. It's not one of those complex, delicate soured fruit beers; this is an obvious brew that yells raspberries at you, and it's joyful for that reason. Have a peanut butter cookie or a slice of peanut butter cheesecake (or just some peanut butter on bread) with the beer and I think we all know how good the combination will be. Alternative food matches would be a slice of lemon cake, some dark chocolate, some creamy mild cheese, a raspberry almond sponge, a mascarpone-based cheesecake… basically, the sweetness and fruitiness in the beer make it delicious with a lot of different foods.

PASTEUR STREET PASSIONFRUIT WHEAT

TRY WITH: VIETNAMESE SUMMER ROLLS
BREWED IN: HO CHI MINH CITY, VIETNAM
ABV: 4.0%

If there's a more deliciously refreshing beer in the world than this, then I haven't drunk it yet. It's a wheat beer brewed with passion fruit from Da Lat, in the Vietnamese Central Highlands, where a lot of the country's tastiest ingredients grow. The beer is fresh, zingy, tropical, lightly tart, and beautiful—I love it. For an equally refreshing dish, try summer rolls: soft rice paper with a filling of tofu, fresh raw veg like lettuce, carrots, and cucumber, fresh herbs like cilantro (fresh coriander), and a dip made from soy sauce, chili, sugar, and lime. Most of Pasteur Street's beers contain local ingredients, like their Pomelo IPA, which would be great with fried spring rolls.

BRITISH ALE

Here we have Milds, Bitters, and Barley Wines. They are beers which have a depth of British malts and a firm, balanced bitterness. Most are in the amber-to-brown color range, with the specialty malts giving flavors ranging from bread, toast, and caramel, to dried fruits and cacao, while the hops are usually English and in the floral, herbal, stone fruit, and marmalade-citrus range, though modern examples use New World hops alongside the toasty base malts. A lot of these are pub beers, best served and drunk by the pint, so they are often best with pub foods.

BRIDGE: Toasted bread, grilled root vegetables, sausages

BALANCE: Bean chili, creamy curries or risotto, roast dinner

BOOST: Mature cheese, grilled mushrooms, Thai noodles

AVOID: Heavy desserts

CONISTON BREWING CO. NO.9 BARLEY WINE
TRY WITH: **BLUE CHEESE, PEAR, AND HAZELNUT**
BREWED IN: **CONISTON, ENGLAND**
ABV: **8.5%**

No.9 is a pale English Barley Wine, brewed once a year in the Lake District and then matured for almost a year in tank before half is bottled and half is put into casks to serve in the pub. It has a wonderful nutty sherry character; there are stewed apples, bitter almond, and bitter marmalade; it's elegant and complex, and every time you drink it you'll notice something new about it. It's a beer for cheese. Combine pear, blue cheese, and hazelnut in a tart or crostini, or try Eccles cakes with Lancashire cheese for a great sweet-tangy combination with the sherried beer.

HARVEY'S SUSSEX BEST BITTER

TRY WITH: **SAUSAGE, MASH, AND ONION GRAVY**
BREWED IN: **LEWES, ENGLAND**
ABV: **4.0%**

This traditional Best Bitter has been brewed since the 1950s. It's russet-colored and the malt gives toasted grain, toffee, and caramelized dried fruits. The hops are spicy, peppery, tobacco- and tea-like with a lift of light fruit pith in the back. The joy is the balance of the beer, a balance perfected over eight decades of brewing, where you get sweet malts upfront and bitter hops at the back, and it's the sort of beer that has you wanting another, and another, and another… you'll need some belly-filling grub, and a pub classic like (veggie) sausage, mash, and onion gravy is a great choice. The success in the pairing comes from the sweeter malts and the gravy sharing a similar flavor, while the peppery hops spike at the seasoning used in the food. It's also a great beer with a roast dinner.

EMERSON'S BOOKBINDER

TRY WITH: **FRIED NOODLES**
BREWED IN: **DUNEDIN, NEW ZEALAND**
ABV: **3.7%**

This amber-colored Session Ale is inspired by British Bitters and given a Kiwi twist by using local hops. It's got the quintessential quality of making you want to drink more with its nice light base being a little nutty and a little toasty, but not sweet. The hops—NZ Fuggles and Riwaka—are floral, peachy, inviting and they layer through the beer and into a crisply bitter finish. Bitters are really good with spicy Asian noodles, especially if it's got a salty-sweet sauce like a chow mein or pad see ew. Try a freshly hopped Bitter with Thai fried noodles as the salty sauce is great with the malty beer, especially if you use sesame oil, and the hop bitterness balances any of the richer flavors in the noodles, freshening them up.

RHINEGEIST UNCLE

TRY WITH: **CINCY CHILI**
BREWED IN: **CINCINNATI, OHIO, USA**
ABV: **4.2%**

There aren't many Dark Milds brewed anymore, especially not in hop-seeking North America, and that's what makes Rhinegeist's Uncle stand out. It's dark brown and it smells like toasted and lightly roasted malts. It's light-bodied and easy-drinking, with the roasted malts giving it a nutty coffee character. The hops are gentle and nicely balanced, and it's a refreshing dark beer and a refreshing change from all the IPAs. The darker malts naturally align to darker, roasted flavors: barbecue, grilled vegetables, and spicy food. Next to Rhinegeist is a place specializing in Cincy Chili, a thinner-than-normal meat chili (one easily made veggie) made with fragrant spices like cinnamon and allspice, and it's usually served on spaghetti or in a hot dog. Order it veggie '5-way' and it's layered up as spaghetti, chili, onion, beans, and lots of shredded Cheddar. A glass of Uncle is a great choice with it.

DRIFTWOOD NAUGHTY HILDEGARD

TRY WITH: **MUSHROOM, CHEDDAR, AND LEEK RISOTTO**
BREWED IN: **VICTORIA, CANADA**
ABV: **6.5%**

ESB, or Extra Special Bitter, is a stronger version of a Bitter brewed with more malts and more hops. Naughty Hildegard is a rich amber color and the malt brings toast and toffee, but you won't notice that right away because this is definitely a hop-led beer, with Amarillo, Mosaic, and Columbus bringing lots of tangy citrus, grapefruit, pine, and stone fruits, making it more like an IPA. It's a beer which is great with Cheddar, mushrooms, and the sweet-savory flavor of leek and garlic, so combine them all in a risotto or a grilled cheese sandwich, where the hops have an affinity with the allium and the malt likes the mushrooms.

BROWN ALE

Filling the space between Bitters and Porters, Brown Ales vary in their character from nutty and light through to richly malty, with American-style Brown Ales using lots of aromatic hops (some being like Brown IPAs), whereas English-style will be more focused on the malt. In the best examples, the malt will be toasted, a little caramelized, nutty, smooth, roasted but not astringent or coffee-bitter. These beers work well with ingredients like root and cruciferous veg, toasted bread, tomato sauces, aged cheeses, beans, and wholegrains, and stronger versions can work with lighter sweet dishes like cupcakes or cookies.

BRIDGE: Roasted veg, grilled mushrooms, whole grains

BALANCE: Semi-hard cheese, creamy Indian curries, barbecued foods

BOOST: Tomato-based sauces, veg sausages, veg lasagna

AVOID: Light salads, fruit desserts

FIVE POINTS BRICK FIELD BROWN

TRY WITH: **EGGPLANT (AUBERGINE) PARMIGIANA**
BREWED IN: **LONDON, ENGLAND**
ABV: **5.4%**

Brick Field Brown is only available for a few months a year, but it's worth the wait—and it's worth drinking lots of it when you see it, as it's one of the finest Brown Ales you'll drink. An amazing depth of dark malts, roasted nuts, brown sugar, caramel, dark chocolate, but nothing sweet, it has a savory character to it before feisty, bitter, herbal hops cut through. It's a great beer for Italian dishes—pizza, lasagna, or eggplant (aubergine) parmigiana, with layers of grilled eggplant and garlicky marinara sauce and then lots of mozzarella and Parmesan on top. Tomato and cheese both work really well with the dark malts, and the herbal hop bitterness cuts through it at the end.

CIGAR CITY BREWING MADURO

TRY WITH: **VEGGIE ROPA VIEJA OR JAMBALAYA**
BREWED IN: **TAMPA, FLORIDA, USA**
ABV: **5.5%**

Maduro uses oats in the brew for a fuller texture and a nice nutty smoothness. It's got some chocolate, caramel, and coffee character, plus herbal hops, which are all good flavors with earthy spices and tomatoes. The brewery suggest serving this one with ropa vieja, a Cuban dish of beef cooked with tomatoes, onions, bell (sweet) peppers, olive, and spices like cumin, oregano, black pepper, and allspice. Go with black beans and jackfruit to make a veggie version and it's a great match, with the malt in the beer working well with the sweet peppers and onions. An alternative would be a veggie jambalaya, with the veg, beans, and rice all cooked with herbs and spices which nicely complement the beer.

BROOKLYN BROWN ALE

TRY WITH: **CAULIFLOWER CURRY**
BREWED IN: **BROOKLYN, NEW YORK, USA**
ABV: **5.6%**

Brooklyn's Brown Ale is a textbook example of the American version of the style, one that's layered with malts giving it toast, toffee, chocolate, and then some lighter coffee notes, while also being aromatic with American hops which are transformed by those darker malts to have a more herbal, resinous, roasted citrus quality. I really like the flavor of cauliflower with Brown Ales, especially in a nutty and creamy curry like a korma—the nuttiness in the beer and the flavors in the curry come together really nicely, while the hops bring a little zesty citrus. You could also try cauliflower tacos with this beer.

CERVECERIA INSURGENTE BROWN

TRY WITH: **SQUASH AND BEAN CHIPOTLE CHILI**
BREWED IN: **TIJUANA, MEXICO**
ABV: **5.5%**

Insurgente's Brown Ale is a tasty mix of toasty, caramelized, and lightly roasted malts with aromatic American hops adding some of their citrusy qualities and a herbal, peppery bitterness. Brown Ales in general are good with sweet potatoes and squashes, especially if they are roasted. Add some chipotle chili on there for some fruity smokiness, then throw it into a pot with tomatoes, black beans, your typical chili spices, and cook it all together and that's a great match for a hoppy brown ale. Some diced avocado on top is going to add some creaminess which will separate the hops and the chili heat. Squash, black bean, and avocado tacos or tostadas would also be really good.

UERIGE ALTBIER

TRY WITH: **SAUSAGE AND BEAN STEW**
BREWED IN: **DÜSSELDORF, GERMANY**
ABV: **4.7%**

Altbier is an "old beer" style that's the brew of Düsseldorf. It's a brown-colored ale (though no one would ever call it a Brown Ale—it's Altbier) with clean malts, a little toffee, some dried fruits, and a strong bitterness—Uerige in particular is very bitter in a herbal liqueur kind of way. Go to Düsseldorf and you'll drink small glasses of the beer, one after the other, as you move between different beer halls. A local dish there is *Halve Hahn*, which means "half chicken" but it's rye bread with a Gouda-style cheese, served with German mustard—it's great with the beer, as you can imagine. If you're at home then cook up a veggie sausage, tomato, and bean stew and serve it with some rye bread, as the tomato can balance the beer's bitterness.

PORTER AND STOUT

Porter and Stout are brought together because they share similar flavors and their characteristics overlap, where in both we expect a brown-black beer with flavors of chocolate, cacao, coffee, roasted nuts, burnt toast, and perhaps some aniseed or licorice. Porters tend to be a little stronger and sweeter, with more caramel and less coffee-like roast, while Stouts are often drier and more bitter, though there are several sub-categories of Stouts which are sweeter: Oatmeal Stout uses oats to give a smoother texture and usually a less roasted flavor, while Milk Stout uses lactose (so it's not for vegans) for a sweet, creamy flavor. The sweeter versions can be great with spicy food, while the dark malt in all of them aligns them to flavors like soy sauce, roasted foods, smoke, rich sauces, gravy dishes, and root vegetables.

BRIDGE: Mushroom gravy, chocolate cookies, smoked foods

BALANCE: Tomato-based sauce, stews and pies, Szechuan dishes

BOOST: Nut roast, bean chili, barbecue

AVOID: Light salads, heavy desserts

O'HARA'S IRISH STOUT

TRY WITH: **MUSHROOM AND ALE PIE**
BREWED IN: **BAGENALSTOWN, REPUBLIC OF IRELAND**
ABV: **4.3%**

Ireland's most famous export is arguably the Irish Stout. It's the most iconic and recognizable beer: a very dark brown pint with a creamy tan foam on top. O'Hara's Irish Stout is a classic example with lots of roasted malts which give dark chocolate, espresso, licorice, and berries, and it's layered up with bready and toasty malts, giving it great depth and structure for a low-ABV beer. We're drinking this with a mushroom and ale pie, covered in gravy (a nut roast would be just as good). The beer has the job of

refreshing the match because these Stouts are lighter than their appearance suggests, and there's a clean and deep roasted bitterness at the end which refreshes after the savory gravy.

ST-AMBROISE OATMEAL STOUT

TRY WITH: **POUTINE**
BREWED IN: **MONTREAL, CANADA**
ABV: **5.0%**

The texture of this classic Canadian Oatmeal Stout is what makes it so good to drink, as it's very smooth and full-bodied, almost creamy, like silky dark chocolate. It has a great lightness, though, meaning you want to drink a couple, impressed by the cocoa-dusted flavor, the light roast, and chewy oats. We're putting it with a classic Canadian beer food: poutine. Fries, gravy, and cheese curds, and the beer brings sweetness and a cut of bitterness to deal with the gravy, while the squeaky cheese pleases the beer's creaminess. It's a comforting and belly-filling combination.

LEFT HAND MILK STOUT NITRO

TRY WITH: BEAN CHILI
BREWED IN: LONGMONT, COLORADO, USA
ABV: 6.0%

Not one for vegans, Milk Stout is brewed using lactose, or milk sugar. Lactose can't be fermented by the yeast so it remains in the beer and gives it a creamy, full-bodied depth. Historically it's a British style from the pre-war years, and it was seen as a healthful and nutritious drink, one often drunk by nursing mothers. Today it's a style that a lot of brewers make, but none better than Left Hand, especially if you get the Nitro-infused version. Wonderfully smooth, oozing roasted hazelnuts, milk chocolate, coffee, and vanilla cream, it's almost sweet but remains balanced. It's the sort of beer that can cool down spicy food, and it's one of the best things you can have with a bowl of bean chili. A lot of chili recipes contain coffee or chocolate, because they are flavor enhancers, and here the beer adds its roasted and sweet richness to the dish while the sweet creaminess stops it getting too hot.

FULLER'S LONDON PORTER

TRY WITH: BLACK BEAN BURGER
BREWED IN: LONDON, ENGLAND
ABV: 5.4%

London is the home of Porter, the first industrial beer, and one of the first beers to be recognized as a style. There's no linear thread through to today's Porters, and despite its popularity in the early 19th century, the style was overtaken by Milds, Bitters, Pale Ales, and Stouts, and disappeared from pubs in the early 20th century, only to be resurrected by small brewers from the 1970s. Fuller's London Porter is regarded as the textbook modern version: fudgy, cocoa, toasted nuts, low roast but plenty of malt depth, and a light, bitter malt and hop finish. These are flavors which are good with smoke and

Porter Cottage Pie, page 166.

barbecues, so grill up some black bean burgers and make a smoky-spicy barbecue sauce. I doubt they ate bean burgers in Victorian London, but the combination definitely works today.

DESCHUTES BREWERY BLACK BUTTE PORTER

TRY WITH: KUNG PAO TOFU OR MAPO TOFU
BREWED IN: BEND, OREGON, USA
ABV: 5.2%

Black Butte is a classic American Porter, one that nicely demonstrates the lower roast and rounder texture of a Porter. It's got some unsweet cacao, a little coffee, toasted nuts, and lots of smooth malts, while there's also a little freshness from American hops. Porter is a versatile beer food, bringing umami-enhancing dark malts, a bready sweetness, and a smooth texture. It can do most bar foods: mac 'n' cheese, grilled cheese, a veggie burger, bean chili, loaded fries, and so much more. At home, I think it works well with Chinese food, and specifically Szechuan food, like Mapo Tofu or Kung Pao tofu. Porter's mix of sweetness and roasted bitterness can handle the sweet-salty-spicy sauce, and wrap around the tongue-tingling feeling of Szechuan peppercorns.

IMPERIAL STOUT AND BARREL-AGED STOUT

We're into the dessert of beers. Imperial Stouts are strong, rich, luxurious beers which share flavors like chocolate, cacao, coffee, roasted malt, caramel, vanilla, coconut, roasted nuts, licorice, dried fruits, and more. The textures of the beers range from medium to full, and the strengths are often above 10% ABV, so these are beers to go with strong-tasting dishes. To make them even more flavorsome, it's common to see other ingredients added, like vanilla, coffee, and chocolate (which aren't always vegan); barrel-aged Imperial Stouts are usually matured in old bourbon barrels, where they pick up flavor from the wood and the whiskey. Think sweet foods here: cakes, doughnuts, cookies, pies, but also strong cheeses. Lighter Imperial Stouts can work with barbecue dishes.

BRIDGE: Roasted food, chocolate, barbecue

BALANCE: Sweet desserts, hearty stews, coffee

BOOST: Vanilla and coconut, blue cheese, fresh baked goods

AVOID: Light salads, mild cheese, Southeast Asian food

SURLY BREWING CO. DARKNESS

TRY WITH: **PBJ**
BREWED IN: **MINNEAPOLIS, MINNESOTA, USA**
ABV: **12%**

Many Imperial Stouts today are heavily flavored or barrel-aged, so it's nice to return to a classic, straight-up Imperial Stout. Darkness is an intense taste of dark malt, packed with roastiness, dark chocolate, coffee, caramel, and dried fruit; it's powerful with a lasting bitterness which overlaps roasted barley and hops. It has a rich texture but is not sticky on the lips, instead just giving that pure dark malt experience. I love Imperial Stouts like this with a peanut butter and jelly sandwich (my favorite combo is actually almond butter and cherry jam)—simple but always really good. Add some salt to the sandwich, put on far too much peanut butter, then squash it all together. Beer pairings needn't be fancy to be fantastic.

DUGGES COCOA CACAO

TRY WITH: **COFFEE CAKE**
BREWED IN: **LANDVETTER, SWEDEN**
ABV: **11.5%**

A liquid chocolate bar. Literally. There are not many beers with this volume of chocolate flavor in them. It's brewed with creamy oats, cacao, vanilla, and coconut (and it's vegan). It's sweet but not cloying; there's cocoa and cacao, the vanilla and coconut definitely come through but in a way which enhances the overall chocolate flavor, plus there's some bitter roasted coffee in there for a bit of balance. Hold onto the coffee and vanilla parts and put this with a slice of coffee and hazelnut cake. The beer's chocolate sweetness is wonderful with the nutty coffee cake.

BOTTLE LOGIC FUNDAMENTAL OBSERVATION

TRY WITH: **NEW YORK CHEESECAKE OR CRÈME BRÛLÉE**
BREWED IN: **ANAHEIM, CALIFORNIA, USA**
ABV: **14.0%**

Aged in various different bourbon barrels from well-known distillers like Four Roses and Heaven Hill, this impressive Imperial Stout is also packed with Madagascan vanilla, which is an incredible addition of flavor. Vanilla is one of those ingredients which can boost other flavors, and it makes this beer makes taste more chocolatey, more caramely, and richer. The barrel flavor is full-on but in a great way, and it's a thick, oily, luscious beer. Maximize the vanilla and serve a crème brûlée, New York cheesecake, or Basque cheesecake, so that the beer amplifies the creamy vanilla in the dessert.

PÕHJALA ÖÖ

TRY WITH: **MUSHROOM GOULASH**
BREWED IN: **TALLINN, ESTONIA**
ABV: **10.5%**

Öo is an Imperial Baltic Porter, a style local to the Baltic region and especially popular in Poland. Baltic Porter classically has a low roasted malt flavor and hints of caramel and berries, and is often brewed and stored like a lager. Öo is inky black. It's bready, there's cacao, dried fruit, the darkest chocolate you can find, it's boozy and warming, there's some fruitiness in there, savory soy sauce, and sweet espresso. While all that sounds intense it's a beer with a dexterous lightness to it, and you could serve it with a bean chili, or something like a hearty mushroom goulash—the dark malt is a good flavor with mushrooms, tomatoes, and smoked paprika, while noodles or mashed potatoes will handle some of the alcohol.

FIRESTONE WALKER PARABOLA

TRY WITH: **BLUEBERRY PIE**
BREWED IN: **PASO ROBLES, CALIFORNIA, USA**
ABV: **14.0%**

Parabola is an Imperial Stout aged in bourbon barrels for a year before different barrels are blended to get the perfect final brew. It's 14% ABV, so it's big, but it's also remarkably well balanced, complex, and nuanced, subtle in its own powerful way, and not just one of those smack-you-in-the-head kinds of Imperial Stout. Here you get vanilla, bourbon, cherries, cacao, dark chocolate, espresso, and a general oozing comfort and warmth. Try it with a blueberry or cherry pie with whipped cream. The beer's chocolate richness is a nice counter flavor to the sweet fruit.

CUISINES

BRUNCH

I'm not suggesting you open a can of beer with your morning muesli here; instead these are popular brunch dishes which can be enhanced and enjoyed with some good beers. A whole range of beers can work here, from lightly tart ones reminiscent of fruit juice, through to coffee Stouts which kick with caffeine and booze (it's the coffee Stout you want with your muesli, in case you were wondering).

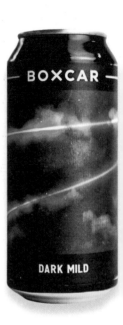

BLUEBERRY PANCAKES

GREAT WITH: **IMPERIAL STOUT**
TRY WITH: **MIKKELLER BEER GEEK BRUNCH**
BREWED IN: **COPENHAGEN, DENMARK**
ABV: **10.9%**

You need a strong, sweet, rich, and well-roasted beer like Mikkeller's Beer Geek Brunch to go with the sweetness of pancakes. This is an oatmeal stout brewed with loads of coffee. It smells like a hazelnut espresso, it's sweet and full-bodied almost like maple syrup, and the coffee roast is deep in the beer along with some berry-like fruitiness and a kick of alcohol. Its sweetness balances the sweetness of blueberry pancakes, with the berry flavor in the beer enhancing the berries in your breakfast—just make sure there's vanilla in there as that seems to be the ingredient which pulls the pairing together. This beer is also really good with a blueberry muffin, if you like drinking strong beer with an afternoon snack.

WELSH RAREBIT

GREAT WITH: **BRITISH ALE, AMBER ALE, ENGLISH IPA**
TRY WITH: **BOXCAR BREWERY DARK MILD**
BREWED IN: **LONDON, ENGLAND**
ABV: **3.6%**

Welsh rarebit is a classic dish for cooking with beer. It's a basic flour and butter roux to begin, then milk goes in, lots of strong Cheddar, some mustard, salt and pepper, a glass of beer, and usually Worcestershire sauce (which contains anchovies, but there are good vegan versions around). It's cooked until thick then layered onto a fat slab of toast and grilled until it bubbles. It's next-level cheese on toast, and dark ales work really well with it. Boxcar's Dark Mild is robustly malty and big in flavor for its brunch-friendly ABV, with flavors of cacao, coffee, toast, bread, and biscuits, plus a refreshing bitterness to cut through the cheese. An English-hopped Amber Ale, with its marmaladey bitterness, also works well.

SHAKSHUKA

GREAT WITH: **PORTER, DARK LAGER, DUNKELWEIZEN**
TRY WITH: **GREAT LAKES BREWING CO. EDMUND FITZGERALD PORTER**
BREWED IN: **CLEVELAND, OHIO, USA**
ABV: **6.0%**

Shakshuka is a dish of eggs (vegans can use tofu) baked in a spiced tomato sauce usually containing garlic, cumin, paprika, and chili, and often topped with feta or a similar tangy cheese. You need a beer that can handle the spice and the slight acidity in the dish, which is why you want something dark and a little roasted. Great Lakes's Edmund Fitzgerald is a classic Porter that's rich with cacao, coffee, and an underlying full-bodied sweetness, all cut with a dry, refreshing finish. A Dunkelweizen—a dark Hefeweizen—also loves tomatoes and spices, and is good with egg.

AVOCADO ON TOAST

GREAT WITH: **PACIFIC PALE ALE, BELGIAN BLONDE, HAZY PALE**
TRY WITH: **BISSELL BROTHERS BABY GENIUS**
BREWED IN: **PORTLAND, MAINE, USA**
ABV: **4.0%**

Avocado on toast has become a brunch favorite all around the world. I think the best versions include spice, from chili or hot sauce, and some tang, perhaps from feta or lemon juice, or just good sourdough. Most often I'll have pickled chili and lots of salt, and that combo is ideal with something light and super-fruity with modern hops, like a Pacific Pale Ale, Hazy Pale, or perhaps the spicy-fruitiness of a Belgian Blonde. Bissell Brothers's Baby Genius, which is hopped with Citra plus Aussie hops, is low on alcohol and big on flavor, with loads of lemon, lime, and ripe tropical fruits, which add their own zestiness to the dish. The beer's texture is also creamy and smooth to match the avocado.

MUSHROOMS ON TOAST

GREAT WITH: **PORTER, BELGIAN DUBBEL, HAZY PALE**
TRY WITH: **ST BERNARDUS PATER 6**
BREWED IN: **WATOU, BELGIUM**
ABV: **6.7%**

There are two ways to approach mushrooms on toast: match the savory flavors of the mushrooms with a dark beer, like a Belgian Dubbel or a Porter, or come at it with fresh hoppy fruitiness and a glass of juice-like Hazy Pale Ale. Both are good, but I prefer the malty, peppery, fruity flavors of a Dubbel, especially if you add a spoonful of brown miso to your mushrooms. St Bernardus's Pater 6 is a lighter Dubbel. It has depth of bread crusts, a little bit of malt sweetness, some fruity coffee, and hints of dried fruit (which is great with miso and mushrooms), and a lively and refreshing fizz at the end.

SOUTHWESTERN SCRAMBLE AND BREAKFAST POTATOES

GREAT WITH: **PACIFIC PALE, SESSION IPA, WITBIER**
TRY WITH: **BENTSPOKE BREWING CO. EASY**
BREWED IN: **CANBERRA, AUSTRALIA**
ABV: **3.2%**

Whether scrambled tofu or eggs, this dish mixes them with onions, bell (sweet) peppers, spices like cumin and garlic powder, perhaps some green veg like kale, plus avocado and hot sauce on top, then serves it up with crispy breakfast potatoes. You want a beer with a little bit of citrusy fruitiness, either from hops or a fruity Belgian yeast. Bentspoke's Easy is a low-ABV refresher, hopped to give it a squeeze of orange, lime zest, and some refreshing tropical fruits. It's very light, nicely crisp, cleanly refreshing, and an ideal brunch brew. A Belgian-style Witbier, with its orange and coriander depth, would also be a good choice with a breakfast scramble.

SANDWICHES

Subs, burgers, bagels, wraps, rolls, naans, hot dogs, focaccia, banh mi—you name a bread with stuff inside of it and it'll almost certainly be something that works brilliantly with beer. It makes sense: the flavor of malt in the beer matches the flavors of the bread, while the hops can provide additional seasoning to match whatever filling you've got.

VADA PAV

GREAT WITH: **PALE LAGER, AMBER LAGER, WEISSBIER**
TRY WITH: **SCHÖNRAMER GOLD**
BREWED IN: **SCHÖNRAM, GERMANY**
ABV: **5.7%**

A vada pav is an Indian street food of spiced mashed potato that's deep-fried and served in soft white bread rolls with a couple of chutneys. There's a restaurant in England called Bundobust who make them, and they're one of my favorite things to eat, ever. I want to put that with a favorite beer style, so I'm going for Schönramer's Gold. It's a stronger-than-usual kind of Helles, just like a Festbier, so it has the malt you expect plus a bit more. It uses a decoction mash so you get that slightly chewy and rich character which offers some honey sweetness, before it dries right out into a herbal, floral bitterness. The sweetness is important with a vada pav, working with the potato and soaking up the spicy sauce, then the bitterness cuts right through at the end. One of the world's best sandwiches and one of the world's best beer styles, and not enough people know about either of them.

FALAFEL WRAP

GREAT WITH: **WITBIER, BELGIAN BLONDE, SAISON**
TRY WITH: **LOST & GROUNDED HOP-HAND FALLACY**
BREWED IN: **BRISTOL, ENGLAND**
ABV: **4.4%**

Grilled flatbread, hummus, falafel, and salad, plus any sauces, are a lot of flavors and textures with a wide mix of different spices and herbs like cumin, cilantro (fresh coriander), mint, dill, parsley, garlic, onion, pepper, and lemon. I personally want something light but robust enough in flavor that it's not overpowered, plus I want some spiciness from the yeast. Think pale and Belgian for the best match, whether a Witbier, Blonde, or Saison. Lost & Grounded's Hop-Hand Fallacy is between a Wit and Saison. It has the ideal interplay of fruitiness and spiciness, boosted by some orange peel and coriander in the recipe. It's a little creamy to begin, but it dries right out into a black pepper finish, with the yeast's spiciness working like an extra herb in the falafel wrap.

TOFU BANH MI

GREAT WITH: **HOPPY LAGER, BELGIAN BLONDE, AMERICAN IPA**
TRY WITH: **HEART OF DARKNESS KURTZ'S INSANE IPA**
BREWED IN: **HO CHI MINH CITY, VIETNAM**
ABV: **7.1%**

The banh mi is one of the world's great sandwiches. The tofu version is cooked with lemongrass, ginger, and garlic, while you'd expect soy sauce, sugar, and chili as a dressing to go inside the crisply light bread, alongside some pickled carrots, cucumber, and lots of fresh, fragrant cilantro (fresh coriander). I like hops with a banh mi, and a Hoppy Lager is great, but it can also handle an American IPA, as the bread will buffer the hop bitterness, while the herbs and spices enhance the citrusy aromas in the hops, and the cucumber and mint cool it all down. Let's pick a Vietnamese-brewed IPA from Heart of Darkness. Kurtz's is golden-colored and is an insane blast of citrus—grapefruit, pomelo, tangerine, and some sticky pine. It's a great beer.

GRILLED CHEESE SANDWICH

GREAT WITH: AMERICAN PALE ALE, AMERICAN IPA, AMBER ALE
TRY WITH: RUSSIAN RIVER BLIND PIG
BREWED IN: WINDSOR, CALIFORNIA, USA
ABV: 6.25%

Grilled cheese and IPA is always a good combination. How could it not be, with all the strong cheese, butter, and bread able to buffer the bitterness and let all the hop fruitiness burst forward? A good grilled cheese sandwich is an individual thing, much like IPA preference. I want white sourdough bread, a mix of mature Cheddar with something like Gruyère, Gouda or red Leicester, and something pungent or sharp like onion, mustard, or pickled chili. With it I want my IPA to be bright, light, and bitter with pithy citrus fruits and zest zinging through it, which is exactly what Blind Pig is like. It's an individual thing, and a comfort thing, giving something uniquely pleasing to everyone who puts together their perfect grilled cheese and their ideal IPA.

VEGAN HOT DOG

GREAT WITH: PALE LAGER, AMBER LAGER, DARK LAGER
TRY WITH: BROOKLYN LAGER
BREWED IN: BROOKLYN, NEW YORK, USA
ABV: 5.2%

Hot dogs go with lagers. Pale lagers, amber ones, brown and black ones, sweet ones, dry ones, strong ones, hoppy ones; sausage, bread, and lager just work, perhaps held together by some long-held Bavarian parentage, and the way in which sausages, breads, and beer spread together around America in the second half of the 19th century. There are now so many great vegan hot dogs that are equal to any meaty version, and with a ball game-style dog I want bready and lightly caramelized malts, a citrusy bitterness (which is good with grilled onions and ketchup or mustard), and clean and refreshing flavors, just like those in Brooklyn Lager.

Porter BBQ Pulled Jackfruit burger, page 170.

PULLED JACKFRUIT BURGER

GREAT WITH: DARK LAGER, AMBER ALE, HAZY IPA
TRY WITH: HOP NATION J JUICE
BREWED IN: FOOTSCRAY, AUSTRALIA
ABV: 7.1%

The texture of jackfruit when it's slow-cooked and then forked apart is remarkably similar to pulled pork. It has a natural tropical fruitiness but isn't sweet, and it soaks up a lot of flavor from the sauce you cook it in. Cook it like pulled pork in a classic barbecue sauce which is sweetly spicy and it's a great match for the tropical, citrusy fruitiness in a Hazy IPA. Hop Nation's J Juice is tropical, zesty, and tangy with citrus, and all that fruitiness plays with the barbecue sauce, wrapping up the smoke, acidity, and umami, and enhancing all the richness, while the key to the match is a cut of juicy acidity and then a noticeable bitterness in the beer.

ITALIAN

For every different plateful of Italian food—from pizza to pasta to risotto—we can find an incredible beer match. Given the use of olive oil, garlic, and fragrant herbs like basil and oregano as foundations for most dishes, I find that European hops and Belgian yeast are often really good flavor bridges to Italian food, while you normally want some richer malts and a crisp, dry finish.

MARINARA PIZZA

GREAT WITH: PALE LAGER, PILSNER, AMBER LAGER
TRY WITH: CAMDEN TOWN BREWERY HELLS LAGER
BREWED IN: LONDON, ENGLAND
ABV: 4.6%

Pizza is my favorite food and marinara is my favorite pizza. Friends mock my cheese-less preference but I stand by it: the combination of tomato sauce, olive oil, and garlic on a dough cooked in a proper pizza oven is perfection which needs no cheese. The simplicity of it requires a simple, clean, and bitter Pale Lager or Pilsner. It's a beer which demands no attention but which adds to your experience in an effortless, casual, crust-chewing-beer-gulping way. Camden's Hells Lager has long been one of my go-to lagers. It has a subtle fresh bread quality from the malt and a fresh lemon and peppery hop finish with a long, deep bitterness which can cut right through the oil and tomato.

SPAGHETTI BOLOGNESE

GREAT WITH: BELGIAN DUBBEL, BRUNE, HAZY DIPA
TRY WITH: BRASSERIE D'CHOUFFE MCCHOUFFE
BREWED IN: ACHOUFFE, BELGIUM
ABV: 8.0%

Bolognese with Belgian Dubbel or Belgian Brune is one of the best beer and food pairings. No matter how you make yours—lentils, mushrooms, veggie mince, or just meat—the flavors you get in dark Belgian beers will boost the dish. Chouffe's McChouffe has caramel and dried fruit flavors, a peppery depth, a little bit of phenol and spice, and some booze to give it structure. The malt and the tomato go together. The seasonings and herbs are really good with the peppery spiciness in the beer. The alcohol strength gives you the intensity you need, plus it has a high carbonation to keep it refreshing. Cooking a Bolognese with a bottle of Brune, Dubbel, or Quad also works really well. An interesting alternative beer would be a Hazy IPA or DIPA, the kind that's more savory, dry, and dank instead of juicy, sweet, and fruity (the sweet ones don't work at all).

Beer Pan Pizza, page 124.

VEGETARIAN LASAGNA

GREAT WITH: **DUBBEL, BELGIAN BLONDE, STRONG LAGER**
TRY WITH: **BRASSERIE DUPONT MOINETTE BRUNE**
BREWED IN: **TOURPES, BELGIUM**
ABV: **8.5%**

Lasagna is one of my favorite foods and my veggie version challenges the one I used to make with meat. I use a load of roasted vegetables in my recipe, things like eggplant (aubergine), mushroom, and zucchini (courgette), and that adds a lot more flavor than a packet of minced meat. With all the veg, plus red lentils, tomato, and cheese (vegan cheese sauce is also good), you need a strong beer, one with toasty malt and still a dryly bitter finish. Belgian Brunes and Dubbels are really good choices. Brasserie Dupont's Moinette Brune has a brioche and dried fruit depth, and the malt sweetness matches that of the roasted veg and tomato sauce. It's almost creamy in texture, and there's a touch of spicy yeast which works with the herbs.

PESTO PASTA

GREAT WITH: **BELGIAN BLONDE, SAISON, PILSNER**
TRY WITH: **ST BERNARDUS EXTRA 4**
BREWED IN: **WATOU, BELGIUM**
ABV: **4.8%**

I decided to do a taste-off to find the best pairing for pesto pasta. That's the kind of exhausting, troublesome research that it takes to write a book like this. I imagined that dry, crisply carbonated beers with some aromatic yeast and perhaps some fruity hops would be good. Tripel was too strong. Hoppy Lager was too aromatic, Saison a little too robust. German Pilsner was good. But the best by far was St Bernardus Extra 4, a light Belgian Blonde. The yeast is peppery and a little clovey, similar to the spiciness of basil, there's some lemony fruitiness to match the lemon in the pesto, and it's really light and refreshing with a lot of fizz. I like to do my research properly, and sometimes (often, actually) that means opening a lot of different beers with my dinner.

PASTA ALLA NORMA

GREAT WITH: **PILSNER, BELGIAN BLONDE, BELGIAN DUBBEL**
TRY WITH: **BIRRIFICIO DEL DUCATO VIÆMILIA**
BREWED IN: **PARMA, ITALY**
ABV: **5.0%**

Viæmilia is an Italian Pilsner. It's a style that took a German-style Pilsner and added more German hops at the end to give more aroma, leaving a dry and bitter beer with herbal, floral, zesty aromas, in a way reminiscent of bitter Italian liqueurs. Those flavors work really well with Pasta alla Norma, a Sicilian dish of fried eggplants (aubergines) with tomato, ricotta, basil, and spaghetti or rigatoni. The beer's hops match the richness of olive oil while being softened by the sweet tomato sauce and the tang of cheese, with the peppery finish lifting it at the end.

RISOTTO MILANESE

GREAT WITH: **BELGIAN BLONDE, SLOW SOUR, AMBER LAGER**
TRY WITH: **BRASSERIE OMER VANDER GHINSTE OMER**
BREWED IN: **BELLEGEM, BELGIUM**
ABV: **8.0%**

Risotto Milanese is a classic recipe from the north of Italy and it's infused with saffron and plenty of butter and Parmesan. It's a dish that's luxurious yet simple, and the saffron makes it special—it also makes it a challenge to pair to. One approach would be to mirror the white wine which would be used in the rice, and pour a Slow Sour or Wild Ale matured in wine barrels, one with oaky complexity and a little tart fruitiness, but low acid. Or try a Belgian Blonde like Omer, which is briskly carbonated, a little peachy and floral (a hop flavor that's great with the saffron), with a fresh cut of crisp carbonation at the end to balance the richness of the dish.

CURRY AND NOODLES

Curries and noodles find their natural matches with cold, simple lager. That kind of beer can cool down any spice—it's refreshing, unchallenging, and just tastes good with the food. So lagers are a first choice, but certainly not the only choice. It's good to consider the use of fats like coconut or dairy, and whether the spices are zesty and herb-packed or earthy and aromatic.

THAI GREEN CURRY

GREAT WITH: **PALE LAGER, HAZY PALE ALE, WHEAT ALE**
TRY WITH: **BEAK BREWERY PARADE IPA**
BREWED IN: **LEWES, ENGLAND**
ABV: **6.0%**

This is one of the world's best-known curries, with zesty lime, lemongrass, ginger or galangal, Thai basil, and cilantro (fresh coriander), there's hot chili, creamy coconut, salty soy (or fish sauce in non-veggie ones), and sugar to sweeten it. It's a dish which can work with a lot of different beers, from an ice-cold Pale Lager, to a Hefeweizen with its creamy texture and hint of spice and citrus, and all the way up to a Hazy Pale Ale or IPA. It's the hazy hoppy beers which I find the most interesting as they can bring their own exotic aroma to this dish. Beak Brewery's Parade IPA is tangy, tropical, zesty, ripe, and really smooth, with some lime lifting it all up.

VEGETABLE JALFREZI

GREAT WITH: **PALE LAGER, PILSNER, WEISSBIER**
TRY WITH: **UTOPIAN BREWING BRITISH PILSNER**
BREWED IN: **CREDITON, ENGLAND**
ABV: **4.4%**

Jalfrezi curry is made with a base of onions, bell (sweet) peppers, chilis, and tomato, and it's often quite hot and rich. It's become one of the most common curries in Britain, and if we eat a curry then invariably we're having a lager. We can upgrade the beer choice with a Utopian Pilsner. It's brewed with all British ingredients, including modern British Jester hops. The beer has a structured malt base, which is a little sweet, and that's what helps it out with a spicy, tomato-based curry; then the hops bring a light gooseberry, elderflower, and stone fruit aroma, which works with the earthy, warming spices in a jalfrezi and adds a little zing of freshness to the match.

PANEER TIKKA MASALA

GREAT WITH: **PILSNER, HOPPY LAGER, SESSION IPA**
TRY WITH: **BREW BY NUMBERS SESSION IPA MOSAIC**
BREWED IN: **LONDON, ENGLAND**
ABV: **4.2%**

Paneer tikka masala is made by marinating paneer in spiced yogurt, roasting it, then adding it to a mildly spiced sauce of tomatoes, garlic, cream, and butter (there's a recipe on page 172). It's a comforting kind of curry, rich with dairy (though you could use tofu and vegan dairy alternatives), and the best match I've found—and I tried seven or eight beers with the curry—was Brew By Numbers's Session IPA Mosaic. It worked because the beer is abundantly fruity with funky Mosaic hops—think pineapple, tropical fruits, and even a tomato vine character—and it has a very clean, very light body with a sharp dryness at the end (sweeter, heavier Session IPAs don't work—it has to be light). The hops teased the spices and then eased through to the dry, refreshing finish. I'd also suggest a dry-hopped Pilsner with a dish like this as you need something lean and dry but also a little aromatic.

STIR-FRIED NOODLES

GREAT WITH: **PALE LAGER, AMBER LAGER, DARK LAGER**
TRY WITH: **YUENGLING TRADITIONAL LAGER**
BREWED IN: **POTTSVILLE, PENNSYLVANIA, USA**
ABV: **4.5%**

Everyone has their own way of cooking stir-fried noodles, right? We all have our preferences—more soy sauce, more chili sauce, sweeter, richer, lighter, rice noodles, egg noodles, buckwheat noodles, different vegetables, different proteins. However you get to sitting down and eating your noodles, I think it's a dish for lager. You want something with a little malt sweetness and a quenching dryness but not too much flavor or hop aroma to interfere, which is why a beer like Yuengling Traditional Lager works. It's a little toasty, clean, slightly citrusy, and refreshingly bitter. Good alternative beers would be a Czech-style Pale Lager or a German Helles or Dunkel.

MASSAMAN CURRY

GREAT WITH: **HEFEWEIZEN, WITBIER, PORTER**
TRY WITH: **LIVE OAK HEFEWEIZEN**
BREWED IN: **AUSTIN, TEXAS, USA**
ABV: **5.3%**

Massaman is a deeply aromatic Thai curry with a spice mix including star anise, allspice, cardamom, cinnamon, cumin, ground coriander, ginger, plus tangy tamarind, creamy coconut, and peanuts (I use peanut butter in mine). It's not a chili-hot curry and it's a hearty, comforting kind of dish that usually includes sweet potatoes in the veggie versions (there's a recipe for a beer-infused one on page 151). I love this curry with Weissbier and Live Oak's HefeWeizen is a textbook Bavarian-style brew. Hazy yellow, a creamy texture which is both satisfying and refreshing, some banana and soft stone fruit, then an allspice finish. It's the smoothness that you want with the curry to begin, bridging to the nuttiness of the dish, then you want the dry spiciness to amplify some of the more aniseed-scented spices in the dish.

PAD THAI

GREAT WITH: **PILSNER, PALE LAGER, BRITISH ALE**
TRY WITH: **OAKHAM JHB**
BREWED IN: **PETERBOROUGH, ENGLAND**
ABV: **4.2%**

Thai food is surprisingly common in British pubs. I don't really know why that is, but I do know that the food is well suited to British Ales. Pad Thai will always be on the menu (though it often contains fish sauce and egg, so watch out) and it's a classic dish: stir-fried rice noodles, garlic, chili, soy sauce, sugar, lime, tamarind, and peanuts. You want something dry and refreshing with the noodles, and a simple Pilsner is fine, but well-hopped British Bitters are a really good choice. Oakham's JHB is 4.2% ABV in bottle (3.8% ABV on cask), it's light gold, lightly aromatic, and a little citrusy, then has a long, dry, and bitter finish which balances all the other tastes in the noodles.

PUB GRUB

Travel around the world and every different culture has different beer foods. They are usually fried or come with bread, and they are most often salty, which is why they taste so good with a cold, refreshing beer. You'll typically find that the local styles naturally work best with the local food, though there are exceptions as the beer world expands its inspirations.

PRETZELS

GREAT WITH: **PALE LAGER, AMBER LAGER, DARK LAGER**
TRY WITH: **DONZOKO BIG FOAM**
BREWED IN: **HARTLEPOOL, ENGLAND**
ABV: **5.0%**

I'm sure pretzels taste great with an IPA, but to me that feels as wrong as having a pizza with a cup of tea. Pretzels go with lager, and they go with all lagers. I think the best pretzels are fat, chewy, and salty, and they are unputdownable as you continue to bite a piece off, vowing that you don't need more, then you drink more beer then you want more bread. It repeats forever. Because all lagers work, you can pick your favorite, and Donzoko's Big Foam is a favorite of mine. It uses English spelt, which gives a little nuttiness, and there's a slight malt sweetness, then an intriguing hop character which is a little lemony, peachy, peppery, and floral. And it's called Big Foam because you're supposed to pour it with a big foam. Best enjoyed with a Big Pretzel.

Lagerbier Pretzels, page 180.

BUFFALO WINGS

GREAT WITH: **PILSNER, PALE LAGER, PORTER**
TRY WITH: **CHUCKANUT BREWERY PILSNER**
BREWED IN: **BELLINGHAM, WASHINGTON, USA**
ABV: **5.0%**

Buffalo wings—whether they're made with tofu, cauliflower, jackfruit, or even chicken—are some intense flavors to put with a beer, and it's the tangy and spicy electric-red hot sauce which we need to match the beer to. You could try and smother it in something dark and roasted, like a sweetish Porter, and that works really well, but I think the better option is to put it with a crisp, bright, clean, and bitter German-style Pilsner, like Chuckanut's Pilsner. Herbal hops are happy with the sharpness and spice, they cut through the tang, and they also poke at the heat a bit. Go with a lighter, crisper lager if you prefer something more refreshing.

LOADED NACHOS

GREAT WITH: **PALE ALE, SESSION IPA, AMBER ALE**
TRY WITH: **SOCIETE THE COACHMAN**
BREWED IN: **SAN DIEGO, CALIFORNIA, USA**
ABV: **4.9%**

No beer is going to taste bad with loaded nachos, but some will be better than others. I'm assuming the basics with this one: nachos, salsa, cheese (or vegan alternative), avocado or guacamole, maybe some chili or jalapeño slices. That's a lot of flavor and I reckon the best choice is going to be something with plenty of hop bitterness and hop aroma. A Session IPA like Societe's The Coachman is ideal: it's pretty light in body but has plenty of depth of flavor and a big whack of refreshing bitterness to cut through the saltiness in the nachos, while the different toppings are going to poke and play with the hops.

MAC 'N' CHEESE

GREAT WITH: **AMBER LAGER, AMBER ALE, BELGIAN BLONDE**
TRY WITH: **BRASSERIE DUPONT MOINETTE BLONDE**
BREWED IN: **TOURPES, BELGIUM**
ABV: **8.5%**

You can go with a lot of different beers with a mac 'n' cheese. The high fat content and the cheesy tang are qualities which can interact positively with most beers, from a crisp, dry Pale Lager to a robust, roasted Stout. My preference is for toasty malt (but not caramely crystal malt) flavor, and one with a fairly high alcohol content. From there you could go hoppy to cut the richness, but I prefer the fruity spice and brisk carbonation of a Belgian brew. I love a Belgian Blonde like Dupont's Moinette. It has honeyed malt, some fruity yeast like peach and apple, peppery spice, and it's bitter-sweet and incredible with cheese. If you're eating a vegan version then Belgian Blondes are good, but I think Amber Lagers or Ales are better.

TO-FISH AND CHIPS

GREAT WITH: **PILSNER, ENGLISH PALE ALE, AMERICAN IPA**
TRY WITH: **ST AUSTELL PROPER JOB**
BREWED IN: **ST AUSTELL, ENGLAND**
ABV: **4.5–5.5%**

Fish and chips is a pub staple around the world, but especially so in Britain, and increasingly more pubs have to-fish and chips on the menu: tofu wrapped in nori seaweed then battered and fried and served with fat, fluffy, crispy chips (the best kind of fried potatoes in the world). I think it's best with a beer which has a balance between a toasty malt sweetness, a refreshing but balancing bitterness, and some citrus hop aroma. That's exactly St Austell's Proper Job. It's a beautiful beer and those qualities lift the batter and freshen it up perfectly. Just one comment: the cask version is 4.5% ABV and uses fish-derived isinglass to make it clear. The bottled version, which is 5.5% ABV, doesn't use this, so grab bottles and your to-fish and chips to go—it tastes better when you eat them by the sea anyway.

BURGER AND FRIES

GREAT WITH: **AMERICAN IPA, AMERICAN PALE ALE, AMBER ALE**
TRY WITH: **EPIC ARMAGEDDON**
BREWED IN: **AUCKLAND, NEW ZEALAND**
ABV: **7.0%**

Most pale hoppy beers are great with a burger. The bread helps, of course, and the patty contributes, but it's the toppings which really bring it together. Cheese, ketchup, mustard or mayo, perhaps a pickle, some onion, and lettuce; those flavors fuse with the fruitiness in the hops, while the malt sweetness acts like some liquid bread. American-style IPAs are my favorite with a burger and fries, and they work really well with Beyond Meat-style burgers, especially with a slice of cheese or vegan cheese. Epic's Armageddon is a proper West Coast-style American IPA with a strong pithy bitterness and lots of pulpy citrus fruit.

MEXICAN

Mexicans drink a lot of beer, and that's good enough evidence to say that beer goes really well with Mexican and Mexican-inspired dishes. One tip is to look at what's served on or with the food, as these will be prominent flavors like fresh lime, salsa, avocado, cilantro (fresh coriander), mild cheese, and onion, and we can match beers to these as much as we can to the fillings like beans and grilled vegetables. If you just want one beer style to go universally with Mexican food, then Amber Lager would be a good choice.

GRILLED VEG STREET TACOS

GREAT WITH: **AMBER LAGER, PALE ALE, FAST SOUR**
TRY WITH: **SIERRA NEVADA OTRA VEZ**
BREWED IN: **CHICO, CALIFORNIA, USA**
ABV: **4.9%**

These are the kind of street tacos that are quickly cooked up and which you top with onion, salsa, and cilantro (fresh coriander). They are loaded with grilled vegetables, maybe some black beans,

and a mild cheese (if you eat it), and the veg takes on a deep savory flavor from its seasoning. A citrusy Pale Ale is good, especially with the addition of cheese and avocado, but a tart and lightly salty Gose is better thanks to being able to share the same flavors as a squeeze of lime. Sierra Nevada's brightly refreshing Otra Vez is brewed with lime and agave, and it's great with most tacos.

BEAN AND AVOCADO TOSTADA

GREAT WITH: **HAZY PALE ALE, HOPPY LAGER, PILSNER**
TRY WITH: **CERVEJARIA EVERBREW BALANCE**
BREWED IN: **SÃO PAULO, BRAZIL**
ABV: **5.2%**

Top a tostada with savory refried black beans, some fresh guacamole, tomato. and spicy salsa, and it's a dish to go with a Hazy Pale Ale, the kind of beer that's juicy and a little tangy with orange, lime, and tropical fruits. Those flavors naturally work with the guac and salsa, while it also adds some fruitiness to the beans, which are rich with umami. EverBrew's Balance is a Hazy Pale Ale with some sweetness from the malt and lots of lush juiciness. A crisp Hoppy Lager would also be a nice choice here.

Four-Beer Taco Feast, page 140.

FRIED AVOCADO TACOS

GREAT WITH: **PILSNER, AMERICAN IPA, AMERICAN DIPA**
TRY WITH: **BEACHWOOD BREWING CITRAHOLIC**
BREWED IN: **LONG BEACH, CALIFORNIA, USA**
ABV: **7.1%**

Let's call this one the veggie take on a Baja fish taco. Not quite the same, but close enough, plus anyone who's ever had deep-fried avocado in a taco will know just how good it is. Like a fish taco, load it up with slaw, lime, salsa, and crema, and have a proper West Coast IPA, one that's bright gold, dry, and bitter and with loads of citrusy hops, like Beachwood's Citraholic. It's a wonderful West Coaster, super-lean and brilliantly fresh with the hops. Those hops and the fried avocado nicely balance each other, while the taco toppings lift it all.

QUESADILLAS

GREAT WITH: **PILSNER, AMERICAN PALE ALE, HAZY IPA**
TRY WITH: **THREES BREWING LOGICAL CONCLUSION**
BREWED IN: **BROOKLYN, NEW YORK, USA**
ABV: **7.0%**

A lot of beers are good with quesadillas, and different additional fillings are going to change the perfect beer pairing. If you're going with a straight just-cheese quesadilla, dipped into guacamole, then I really like Hazy IPA with it. Threes's Logical Conclusion has a light, clean texture for a 7% ABV beer, a refreshing fizz, a nice sweetness, but mostly lots of really good hops—orange, lemon, melon, grapefruit, and a Campari-like bitterness. Put some mushrooms in the quesadilla and you want more malt, like an Amber Ale; add grilled veg and you want an American Pale Ale; put lots of salsa on it and a Pilsner is best; black beans like Dark Lager or Oatmeal Stout. You could happily enjoy a whole menu just pairing beers and quesadillas.

BEAN BURRITO

GREAT WITH: **PALE ALE, DARK LAGER, PORTER**
TRY WITH: **ANCHOR PORTER**
BREWED IN: **SAN FRANCISCO, CALIFORNIA, USA**
ABV: **5.6%**

A big fat bean-filled burrito, stuffed with rice, cheese, and guacamole, is a meal that can work with a lot of different beers. You could pick a hoppy Pale Ale to give citrus bitterness to try and cut through the weight of the food, or you could go with a Porter to match the more savory flavors in the beans. I like the Porter for this one, and Anchor's is a classic: caramel, cocoa, toasted nuts, some nice sweetness, and a dry, clean finish. Because of the bulk of the burrito, the dark beer is able to refresh it, plus it's a good contrast to the avocado. Anchor's Steam would also be a good choice here.

ROAST VEG ENCHILADAS

GREAT WITH: **BELGIAN BRUNE, DUBBEL, STRONG LAGER**
TRY WITH: **UNIBROUE MAUDITE**
BREWED IN: **CHAMBLY, CANADA**
ABV: **8.0%**

Roasted vegetables and black beans are cooked in spices, rolled up in tortillas, then covered in a spiced tomato sauce, some cheese, and then baked like Mexican cannelloni. Enchiladas are a big dish, a belly-filling and comforting dish, which is hearty and spicy. You need a strong beer with plenty of sweeter malts to soften the spice and tomato, but it also needs to have a dry finish and a brisk carbonation to stop it overpowering, so a Belgian Brune or Dubbel is ideal. Try Westmalle's refreshing Dubbel, Chimay's stone-fruit Red, or Unibroue's Maudite, which has some brown sugar, clove, cinnamon, toasty malt, and roast citrus, then a dry finish.

CHEESE

Cheese can give us some of the best matches to beer. Malt provides some sweetness and umami, hops give a balance of bitterness or an additional flavor bridge (fruity, grassy, herbal), carbonation cuts through the fat, and yeast can match up to funky cheeses. Here I'm suggesting style matches instead of naming specific beer brands, because cheese and beer pairings should be flexible and it's good to try different combinations as you'll often be surprised at how they interact.

Mac 'n' Cheese, page 129.

FRESH CHEESE

EXAMPLES: MOZZARELLA, RICOTTA, BURRATA
TRY WITH: PALE LAGER, WEISSBIER, FAST SOURS

Milky, creamy, light cheeses need delicate beers. Pale Lager will bring a soft maltiness while Weissbier will have its own creaminess, also adding a little fruit and spice from the yeast. These cheeses are often eaten with other ingredients, so more often we are trying to match to them instead of the cheese itself, but a creamy-textured light beer is nice.

GOAT CHEESE

EXAMPLES: CHÈVRE, INNIS LOG, HUMBOLDT FOG
TRY WITH: SLOW SOURS, FRUIT BEER, WILD ALE

The distinct goat flavor is something which works well with Slow Sours, like Belgian Gueuze. The beer has a gentle acidity (you don't want a really sour beer), some of its own rural funk, and a very dry finish. Even better is the fruitiness in a raspberry Framboise. Something like Humboldt Fog is more distinctive in taste, a little fruity and floral, and a low-acid Wild Ale is good.

BLOOMY RIND CHEESE

EXAMPLES: BRIE, CAMEMBERT, BRILLAT-SAVARIN
TRY WITH: PILSNER, BELGIAN BLONDE, SAISON

These high-fat soft cheeses want a beer with plenty of carbonation to lift them off the palate. The rind also carries some of its own natural earthy flavor, which is often good with a little herbal hop bitterness, like in a classic Pilsner, or the spiciness of Belgian yeast in a dry Blonde or Saison. Just keep the beers restrained or they will overpower.

SOFT WASHED RIND CHEESE

EXAMPLES: ÉPOISSES, REBLOCHON, TALEGGIO
TRY WITH: SAISON, PILSNER, WILD ALE

The washing of these rinds gives a more distinctive aroma and flavor to otherwise creamy cheeses. These aromas could be fruity, earthy, or mushroom-like, or they could be incredibly pungent like Stinking Bishop (washed in perry). Fruity and peppery Saisons can generally work well. Pilsner will be good with milder cheeses, while stronger ones will enjoy the *Brettanomyces* funkiness of a low-acid Wild Ale.

SHEEP MILK CHEESE

EXAMPLES: BERKSWELL, MANCHEGO, PECORINO
TRY WITH: HOPPY LAGER, PILSNER, AMBER ALE

A little sweet, nutty, salty and tangy, these cheeses like hops and dryness but they want lighter flavors. A herbal Pilsner, a dry-hopped Lager, a Session IPA, or a nutty Amber Ale can all work well with these.

SEMI-HARD CHEESE

EXAMPLES: COMTÉ, GRUYÈRE, MONTEREY JACK
TRY WITH: AMBER ALE, AMBER LAGER, BELGIAN BLONDE

These cheeses have a nutty and buttery taste and a semi-firm texture. They want malt flavor and sweetness from the beer, so look for amber-to-brown brews, while also wanting a bitter finish. Nice malty Amber Lagers and Ales are good here and you don't want too much hop aroma in these. Peppery Belgian yeast can add a nice additional flavor.

AGED SEMI-HARD CHEESE

EXAMPLES: GOUDA, MATURE CHEDDAR
TRY WITH: AMERICAN IPA, PALE BARLEY WINE, OATMEAL STOUT

These stronger cheeses want beers with more malt and more hops. Aged Gouda likes maltiness, so try Amber Ales, Belgian Blondes or Oatmeal Stouts. Mature Cheddar is really good with American IPAs, with the cheese highlighting the hop fruitiness, while English IPAs and pale Barley Wines are also excellent here.

HARD CHEESE

EXAMPLES: PARMESAN, GRANA PADANO
TRY WITH: AMERICAN IPA, HOPPY LAGER, TRIPEL

When you have these cheeses with light-bodied, dry, hoppy IPAs and lagers, and fruity-spicy Tripels, you really notice how fruity the cheeses are, a bit like pineapple or tropical fruits. The salty strength of the cheese can sweeten malts and soften bitterness.

CREAMY BLUE CHEESE

EXAMPLES: ROQUEFORT, GORGONZOLA
TRY WITH: BELGIAN BRUNE, BARLEY WINE, MILK STOUT

These blue cheeses have their vein of funk in the middle and plenty of creamy fat. Belgian Brune and dark Barley Wines can be like a raisiny chutney on the side of the cheese while also bringing plenty of carbonation to cut the richness. A sweeter Stout can add a caramel and chocolate flavor which is really nice here.

STRONG BLUE CHEESE

EXAMPLES: STILTON, STICHELTON, MAYTAG BLUE
TRY WITH: AMERICAN DOUBLE IPA, BARLEY WINE, IMPERIAL STOUT

Strong blue cheeses are really good with stronger beers, and they are versatile. Bitter, orangey Double IPA can be like marmalade on the side. Barley Wine brings a raisin chutney quality. Imperial Stout brings a richness of roast and alcohol to balance the cheese's intensity.

CHOCOLATE DESSERTS

The obvious first thought with chocolate desserts will be dark, rich Imperial Stouts because they share all the roasted and sweet flavors, and they can naturally work really well together (plus I think there's something about the fermented flavors of chocolate and of a strong beer which draw them together). We can also drink more broadly to get some great matches: fruit beers can enhance the chocolate's fruitiness; strong wheat beers and Belgian ales complement banana, dried fruit, and some festive spiciness; barrel-aged beers might give vanilla, coconut, and caramel, which all enhance the chocolate flavors.

CHOCOLATE BROWNIE

GREAT WITH: FRUIT BEER, IMPERIAL STOUT, BELGIAN BRUNE
TRY WITH: NEW GLARUS WISCONSIN BELGIAN RED
BREWED IN: NEW GLARUS, WISCONSIN, USA
ABV: 4.0%

You can go in a few directions with a fudgy chocolate brownie—dark and strong with Imperial Stout, or perhaps some dried fruitiness with a Belgian Brune, or you can go with a sweet cherry beer, which is like putting cherries in the brownie. I recommend cherry beer with a brownie (especially a dark chocolate one) as it's a remarkable booster beer pairing. New Glarus's Wisconsin Belgian Red is brewed with a lot of Montmorency cherries and then aged in oak for a year. It's like sweet-sour cherry juice and it's fun, super-fruity, and super-tasty with the chocolate, which helps to soak up all that cherry sweetness, enhancing the natural fruitiness in the chocolate.

CHOCOLATE CHIP COOKIES

GREAT WITH: BELGIAN QUADRUPEL, COFFEE STOUT, IMPERIAL STOUT
TRY WITH: LA TRAPPE QUADRUPEL OAK AGED
BREWED IN: BERKEL-ENSCHOT, NETHERLANDS
ABV: 11.0%

Lots of beers could work with a chocolate chip cookie, including a roasty coffee Stout or a smooth, strong Imperial Stout, but I like the different flavors that a Belgian Quadrupel brings, with its dried fruit

Dubbel Chocolate Malt Pudding, page 218.

spiciness—you just need a sweeter version of the style. La Trappe make an oak-aged version of their Quadrupel and the wood draws vanilla, toasted nuts, caramel, and more sweet spice into the beer. It's a very complex beer and that's a nice contrast to the simplicity of a cookie.

WHITE CHOCOLATE CHEESECAKE

GREAT WITH: **IMPERIAL STOUT, BARREL-AGED BEERS, FRUIT BEER**
TRY WITH: **REVOLUTION BREWING STRAIGHT JACKET**
BREWED IN: **CHICAGO, ILLINOIS, USA**
ABV: **15.0%**

This is a sweet dessert and you need to go with sweet on sweet to make it work. A barrel-aged beer is the best choice here as we want the oaky, vanilla, and creamy coconut flavors to give us a bridge to the white chocolate. Revolution's Straight Jacket is a bourbon barrel-aged Barley Wine. There's a lot of sweet malt, caramel, maple syrup, vanilla, dried fruits, cinnamon, and spice, and a warming bourbon depth. If you make your own cheesecake then I'd recommend adding some bourbon and maple-roasted apricots or peaches as that'll enhance the match even more.

CHOCOLATE LAVA CAKE

GREAT WITH: **IMPERIAL STOUT, FRUIT BEER**
TRY WITH: **PRAIRIE ARTISAN ALES BOMB!**
BREWED IN: **OKLAHOMA CITY, OKLAHOMA, USA**
ABV: **13.0%**

Bomb! is a much-celebrated Imperial Stout aged on coffee, chocolate, vanilla beans, and ancho chili peppers. Those additional ingredients infuse the rich, chewy, cacao-like brew with more roast, the subtle sweetener of vanilla, and a fruitiness and slight warmth from the chili. It's a complex, intriguing, surprising beer, and it's able to add its own sweet-spicy flavors to a chocolate lava cake, boosting the natural chocolate in there but also giving it more flavor, while that background chili flavor and peppery bite become an exclamation point which makes this a special match. Most intense Imperial Stouts are worth trying with lava cake, but not all of them can add something like Bomb! can.

TIRAMISU

GREAT WITH: **COFFEE STOUT, IMPERIAL STOUT**
TRY WITH: **JACK'S ABBY COFFEE BARREL-AGED FRAMINGHAMMER**
BREWED IN: **FRAMINGHAM, MASSACHUSETTS, USA**
ABV: **11.0%**

I think you want to kick up the caffeine content and go for coffee with coffee with this pairing. Tiramisu is a dessert which feels like it should be easy to get right, but it can be tricky. You need a beer with a thick, luscious body, a high sweetness, and you need it to have a powerful roasted finish as that cuts through the alcohol in the dessert. Jack's Abby's Framinghammer is a Baltic Porter—a strong, dark lager—and they age that base brew in wood with other ingredients. This one goes into barrels with coffee beans and it pours like molasses, with vanilla, mocha, cacao, light espresso, and some subtle bourbon. It's a definite pick-me-up pairing.

CHOCOLATE AND BANANA

GREAT WITH: **IMPERIAL STOUT, DOPPELBOCK, DUNKELWEIZEN**
TRY WITH: **SCHNEIDER WEISSE AVENTINUS EISBOCK**
BREWED IN: **KELHEIM, GERMANY**
ABV: **12.0%**

The combination of banana and chocolate is a good one, whether in banoffee pie, banana breads or cookies, cakes, or baked together as a quick dessert with some cinnamon and salt sprinkled on top. You need a strong beer, and Schneider Weisse's Aventinus Eisbock is really strong. To make it they put it through a freezing process, in which water freezes before alcohol so the ice chunks are removed, making the liquid stronger. You get a rich, boozy, brandy-like wheat beer with dried fruit, cacao, some clove spice, cinnamon, roasted banana, and toasted nuts, before a liqueur-like finish. It's a good beer for any banana and chocolate dessert.

DESSERTS

The sweetness in pudding requires strong flavors in the beer. You can approach it with more sweetness, like an Imperial Stout or sweet Fruit Beer, or you can try and keep it refreshing by pouring a beer with carbonation and a dry, spicy finish from the yeast, like a Tripel or Quadrupel. The stuff on the side—ice cream, whipped cream, custard—will often have an impact, as cream is usually neutral or buffers sweetness, whereas ice cream has a dulling effect on the tongue, meaning only really strong or well-carbonated beers work well with it.

CHERRY PIE

GREAT WITH: DOPPELBOCK, IMPERIAL STOUT, QUADRUPEL
TRY WITH: BRAUEREI SCHLOSS EGGENBURG SAMICHLAUS
BREWED IN: EGGENBERG, AUSTRIA
ABV: 14.0%

Samichlaus is an extraordinary 14% ABV Doppelbock brewed once a year, on 6 December, then aged for almost a year before it's bottled. It pours a deep red and the alcohol content immediately comes through. It's boozy like cherry brandy, there's stewed stone fruit, sherry, almond, dried fruits, a full and sweet richness, and yet still an assertive bitterness. Try it with a big slice of cherry pie, as the cherry and almond notes in the beer are a great match, plus it's one of the few beers able to stand up to the pie's sweetness and strength. Another good beer choice would be a bourbon barrel-aged Imperial Stout.

PEACH COBBLER

GREAT WITH: HAZY DIPA, HAZY IPA, BELGIAN TRIPEL
TRY WITH: MONKISH BIGGIE, BIGGIE, BIGGIE
BREWED IN: TORRANCE, CALIFORNIA, USA
ABV: 10.1%

Peach cobbler, or other similar desserts with hot cooked stone or tropical fruit topped with a sponge or batter, is something to pair to a Hazy DIPA. The sweet, juicy, hot fruit underneath will match some of the sweet, juicy, cold fruitiness in the hops, especially in stronger versions, where the alcohol's presence is able to make the hop character more intense. Go with cream instead of ice cream and go with something extra-strong, like Monkish's Biggie Biggie Biggie, a Triple IPA, which is like a lush glass of peach and mango juice, with some orange Creamsicle (like a Solero or Splice for non-Americans) and a thick, smooth body, reminiscent of actual juice with a slug of booze. The fruit flavors combine and boost each other brilliantly.

APPLE STRUDEL

GREAT WITH: WEIZENBOCK, DOPPELBOCK, QUADRUPEL
TRY WITH: MAHRS BRÄU WEISSER BOCK
BREWED IN: BAMBERG, GERMANY
ABV: 7.2%

Mahrs are best known for their lagers, but their Weisser Bock, a Dunkelweizenbock (that's a strong dark wheat beer), is an annually released favorite in Bamberg. It's got lots of malt sweetness, some toffee, sweet pastry, bitter cacao, dried fruits, stewed stone fruits, and peppery, festive spice. It's a great flavor match to apple strudel, plus it has the characteristically lively carbonation of a Weissbier. With some whipped cream (and a shot of hazelnut liqueur) on the side it's even better.

STICKY TOFFEE PUDDING

GREAT WITH: RED IPA, DOUBLE IPA, BARLEY WINE
TRY WITH: PORT BREWING CO. SHARK ATTACK
BREWED IN: SAN MARCOS, CALIFORNIA, USA
ABV: 9.5%

When you brew an imperial-strength Red Ale, like Port Brewing's Shark Attack, you get a ton of toffee character, lots of caramelized stone fruits, dried fruit, some coffee roast, and a lot of piney, resinous, and bitter marmalade hops. With sticky toffee pudding, the bitter-sweet beer is able to cut through the sticky sweetness to give you some balance. The malt will also pick out the dates and sugar in the cake, while the hops can accent the spices (like ginger and allspice), and there's also some alcohol warmth which further amplifies the spices.

CRÈME BRÛLÉE

GREAT WITH: IMPERIAL STOUT, QUADRUPEL, FRUIT BEER
TRY WITH: ALESMITH BARREL-AGED SPEEDWAY STOUT
BREWED IN: SAN DIEGO, CALIFORNIA, USA
ABV: 12.0%

Crème brûlée is a dessert that you can match to a few different beers. A sweet-sour fruit beer made with cherries or raspberries will be able to work with the creamy dessert and it makes a fun, fresh match. You could go with a Quadrupel, but it'll need to be a sweet American-made one (the American ones are usually always sweeter) with plummy dried fruits and a kick of spice. Or you can go with a barrel-aged Imperial Stout, where the bourbon, vanilla, toffee, mocha, and coconut flavors in the beer are naturally brilliant with the crème brûlée. Alesmith's beer also has some coffee in there for extra roastiness, while it has a really nice full body and a surprising elegance for such a big beer.

LEMON AND ALMOND OLIVE OIL CAKE

GREAT WITH: TRIPEL, DOUBLE IPA, FRUIT BEER
TRY WITH: WESTMALLE TRIPEL
BREWED IN: WESTMALLE, BELGIUM
ABV: 9.5%

An olive oil-based cake with almond and lemon is a lighter dessert or sweet treat which can work nicely with a strong, pale beer like a Tripel. Westmalle Tripel is brewed in a Trappist monastery and it's the classic example of the style. The aroma is all yeast: almond, banana, vanilla, stone fruit, a little spice. The body is taut, lean, with some bitter almonds, bitter honey, a richness of alcohol, and a long, dry, bitter finish. I love the snap of carbonation, dryness, and yeast spice in this, and I think it's a beer which wants a small amount of sweetness. Lemon and almond olive oil cake is a great choice. The beer wants the fat from the oil, while the almond and lemon are shared flavors in the beer, with the beer's bitterness then refreshing the bitter lemon peel. The brewery also suggests strawberry as an ingredient with shared flavors, so you could try a strawberry and lemon cheesecake.

Imperial Stout Coconut Cheesecake, page 217.

1

BREADS AND BRUNCH

A NOTE ON THE RECIPES

Where milk, butter, cream, or other dairy products are listed in the ingredients or method, unless otherwise stated, you can use a vegan alternative. For most of these recipes, I myself used unsweetened almond milk, oat milk, oat cream, and vegan butters.

Use either imperial/cup or metric measurements, don't switch between the two.

This is the easiest bread to make, and it's totally customizable to different flavors and ingredients. I'm giving you the basic recipe, but you can adapt it however you want. For example: you can use all-purpose (plain), wholewheat (wholemeal), spelt, or oat flour, or a combination of different flours; you can choose whatever beer you want; and you can add any additional flavorings you like. This loaf is great fresh and warm, but it makes decent toast the day after. Just remember that soda bread, being unfermented, is naturally a denser loaf. For a simple breakfast loaf, I'd use a mix of wholegrain and spelt flour and put Porter in the recipe. For a sweeter loaf, you could make it with a handful or two of dried fruit, such as apricots, plus a Belgian Dubbel and a teaspoon of cinnamon.

BEER SODA BREAD

Vegan option

Makes 1 loaf

Takes 1 hour

2 cups (250g) flour (see introduction)

1 tablespoon honey or white sugar

½ cup (100g) plain natural yogurt

⅓ cup (100ml) beer

½ teaspoon salt

½ teaspoon baking soda (bicarbonate of soda)

Any other flavorings you want

Preheat the oven to 400°F/200°C/Gas 6 and line a baking sheet with baking parchment.

Mix all the ingredients in a bowl, then combine with your hands into a dough ball.

Place the ball on the baking sheet, score a cross in the top, and bake for 40–45 minutes. Leave to cool for at least 15 minutes before you cut into it.

Crumpets are somewhere between an English muffin and a fat American pancake but with lots of air bubbles in the middle, so they come out light and chewy and then crisp on the outside. I like my crumpets with savory toppings such as butter and salt, melted cheese, or peanut butter, and these taste great with the dark ale used in the recipe—just go for a beer with low roasted bitterness and a bit of sweetness. I add a tablespoon of nutritional yeast to enhance the savory, beery flavor, but if you like your crumpets with a sweet topping, then you can omit the yeast. The crumpets can be eaten straight away or can be left to cool then toasted. It's best to use crumpet rings, but they aren't essential—you can make them by just dropping the batter into the pan as for a pancake.

BEER CRUMPETS

Vegan option

Makes 6–8

Takes 1–1½ hours

Eat it with: Mild or Porter (or a cup of coffee)

½ cup (120ml) milk

1 teaspoon malt extract (or white sugar)

1 teaspoon instant dried yeast

¾ cup (100g) all-purpose (plain) flour and scant ¾ cup (100g) strong white bread flour, or use 1½ cups (200g) all-purpose (plain) flour

⅔ cup (160ml) Mild or Porter at room temperature

1 tablespoon nutritional yeast (optional)

1 teaspoon salt

½ teaspoon baking powder

½ teaspoon baking soda (bicarbonate of soda)

Butter or oil to cook

Warm the milk in a pan or in the microwave until it's hand hot but not boiling. Stir in the malt extract and yeast and mix together to activate the yeast, then leave for 5 minutes.

In a mixing bowl, combine the flours with the beer and whisk together. Then add in the milk-yeast mix and whisk to combine into a thick batter. Cover the bowl with plastic wrap (clingfilm) and leave it in a warm place for 30–90 minutes—you are waiting for the yeast to start bubbling, but the mixture can handle sitting around for a while.

Whisk the nutritional yeast (if using), salt, baking powder, and baking soda (bicarbonate of soda) into the batter. Cover and set aside for 10–15 minutes—when you return, it should have started to bubble a little.

Butter or oil the insides of the crumpet rings, if using. Put a small amount of butter or oil in a large pan over a low heat, and then place the crumpet rings in it. Pour batter into the rings until three-quarters full. (If you are not using rings, pour in about a ladleful of batter for each crumpet.) Cook for around 5 minutes, in which time you'll see bubbles appear in the top of the crumpet. When the crumpets look mostly cooked through, though still a little runny on the top, remove the rings and flip the crumpets over to cook for one more minute.

I consider this a snacking bread. A few bakeries in London make something similar, and they are addictive and delicious things which I end up buying and eating on the walk home. This version contains Witbier, which is great with the briny olive flavor and the sweet tomatoes, and you could add ⅔ cup (75g) of cubed Cheddar cheese (or similar) if you wish. The polenta gives the bread a really nice crispiness.

BEER OLIVE BREAD

Vegan

Makes 4–6 small breads

Takes 5 hours (active cooking time 30 minutes)

Eat it with: Saison, Pilsner, or Pale Ale

3 scant cups (400g) strong white bread flour

1 teaspoon dried yeast

1 cup (250ml) Witbier

1 cup (100g) olives, pitted

Scant ½ cup (50g) sun-dried tomatoes (or Oven-Dried Beer Tomatoes, see page 138)

1 tablespoon olive oil

1½ teaspoons salt

1 teaspoon garlic powder

⅓ cup (50g) polenta, for dusting

Combine the flour, yeast, and beer completely in a bowl and knead into a dough for around 6 minutes until smooth and elastic—it's a high-hydration dough, so might be a bit sticky to begin, but persevere and it'll come together.

Cover the dough and let it rest while you measure out the olives and tomatoes, then fold them in along with the olive oil, salt, and garlic powder. You're adding lot of extra things but just keep on working them until they are well combined and dispersed (you don't need to be delicate here). Put the dough in a bowl, cover with plastic wrap (clingfilm), and place in the refrigerator for 1–2 hours.

Remove the dough from the refrigerator. Line a baking sheet with baking parchment. Dust the countertop with polenta. Divide the dough into 4–6 equal pieces and roll each piece out to about 12in (30cm). Place the dough on the sheet. Cover and refrigerate for 2 hours.

Preheat the oven to 425°F/220°C/Gas 7. Remove the breads from the refrigerator while the oven heats up. Uncover and then bake for 16–20 minutes until crisp and golden.

Soft, chewy, and a little charred, these fat naan breads are great with a curry or to make a wrap. You can use pretty much any beer you like, but something malty and/or low in bitterness is best—I've used Pale Lagers, Witbiers, and Porters.

BEER NAAN BREAD

Vegan option

Makes 4 large naans

Takes approx. 2 hours including proving

Eat it with: depends on what food you serve it with

2 tablespoons (25ml) warm water

1 teaspoon white sugar

1 teaspoon instant yeast

2 cups (250g) all-purpose (plain) flour, plus extra for dusting

3 tablespoons plain natural yogurt

5 tablespoons (75ml) beer

1 tablespoon olive oil

2 teaspoons salt

Combine the warm water, sugar, and yeast and stir to activate—leave for around 5 minutes. Meanwhile, in a large bowl, stir together the flour, yogurt, beer, oil, and salt, and then add the yeast mix and combine into a dough. Knead the dough for 5 minutes, then put it back in the bowl, cover with plastic wrap (clingfilm), and leave in a warm place to prove for 1–2 hours, until the dough has doubled in size.

Place the dough on a clean, floured surface and punch it around a bit, knocking out the air and folding and kneading it for a few minutes. Then divide into four equal pieces.

Set a large skillet (frying pan) on a medium-high heat on the stove-top and while it warms up, roll out the first piece of dough into a large flatbread, about the size of your skillet. Put it into the dry pan and cook for 1–2 minutes—you'll know when it's time to flip it as air bubbles will begin to form. Cook for another minute or two on the other side, then set aside (you can wrap it in aluminum foil to keep warm) while you cook the others.

This is a versatile recipe for wiener (hot dog) or burger buns, or just for dinner rolls. They are light, soft, and really easy to make. I use a Hefeweizen because you want a slightly sweet, slightly creamy beer to go with the milk.

BEER BUNS

Vegan option

Makes 6 rolls

Takes 2 hours

Eat it with: depends on what other food you serve it with

½ cup (120ml) milk

2 tablespoons (30g) butter

2 heaped cups (280g) all-purpose (plain) flour

2 tablespoons cornstarch (cornflour)

1 teaspoon dried yeast

2 teaspoons white sugar

1 teaspoon salt

4 tablespoons (60ml) Hefeweizen

Gently warm the milk and butter in a small pan until the butter melts, but don't let it boil. Take off the heat and allow it to cool to room temperature.

In a large bowl, combine the flour, cornstarch (cornflour), yeast, sugar, and salt, then pour in the milk and butter mixture and the beer. Combine, then knead for a few minutes—a stand mixer is preferable for this, but by hand is also fine. Place in a bowl, cover with plastic wrap (clingfilm), and leave somewhere warm to prove for 1 hour.

Line a baking sheet with baking parchment. Divide the dough into 6 pieces and shape into rolls. Place on the baking sheet, spaced well apart because they'll expand (but if they do end up touching it's fine—they are good as pull-apart rolls), cover loosely with plastic wrap (clingfilm), and leave somewhere warm for 30 minutes.

Preheat the oven to 350°F/180°C/Gas 4. Bake for 15–18 minutes or until lightly golden. Allow to cool before serving.

I use miso in a lot of recipes because when cooking with beer and veg, it adds a fermented flavor, depth, and richness to dishes. I especially like barley miso and how it works with Stout, but you can also make this with a Belgian Brune, a Porter, or a Dark Lager. This is one of the simplest recipes in the book—ideal for brunch, a boozy lunch, or even as a simple appetizer.

MISO STOUT MUSHROOMS ON TOAST

Vegan option

Serves 2

Takes 15 minutes

Eat it with: Stout or Dark Lager

1 shallot or small white onion, diced

1 garlic clove, crushed

2 tablespoons butter (30g) or
   1 tablespoon olive oil

7½ cups (500g) mixed mushrooms,
   chopped up

3 tablespoons Stout or dark beer

1 tablespoon barley miso (or whatever
   miso you like best)

1 tablespoon soy sauce

Black pepper

Chili flakes (optional)

Toast, to serve

Fried or poached egg, to serve (optional)

Chives, to serve (optional)

Soften the shallot and garlic in the butter or oil (butter is definitely better, by the way) for a couple of minutes. Add the mushrooms and cook over a medium-high heat—you want them to release most of their liquid, which will take about 10 minutes.

Meanwhile, in a cup or bowl, stir together the beer, miso, and soy, then add to the pan for about 2 minutes so that it heats up and some of the alcohol is cooked away.

Taste and season well with the black pepper and chili flakes, if using, then serve on hot buttered toast. You could also add an egg on top, if you like, or some chopped chives (but I think most mushroom on toast recipes call for chives just so that the pictures don't look so brown).

If you're hungover—and if you have this book, there's a good chance that at some point you will be—then this will likely already be a go-to morning-after breakfast. My version encourages you to fast-track onto the hair of the dog route. I've cooked this with a smooth Stout and with Belgian Brune and both are great. This recipe is open to adding different spices and extra veg, and while the traditional recipe bakes eggs into it, you can replace the eggs with tofu slices. Before you start cooking this, I recommend making up a quick Beer Soda Bread (see page 108) to go on the side.

STOUT SHAKSHUKA

Vegan option

Serves 2

Takes 45–60 minutes

Eat it with: Stout, Belgian Brune, or Dark Lager

1 white onion, diced

1 tablespoon olive oil

2 bell (sweet) peppers, sliced

2-3 garlic cloves, crushed

½ teaspoon each ground cumin, paprika, cayenne pepper, salt, black pepper, sugar, harissa paste (optional), and as much chili powder as you like

2 tablespoons tomato paste (purée)

2 x 14oz (400g) cans chopped tomatoes

⅓ cup (100ml) Stout or Belgian Brune

4 eggs (or 7oz/200g tofu or smoked tofu)

Feta or Beer Nozzarella (see page 190), to serve

VERY HUNGOVER COOKING INSTRUCTIONS

Put all the ingredients apart from the eggs (or tofu) and cheese into a large skillet (frying pan) and cook for about 45 minutes (try and remember to stir it occasionally).

Make four small wells in the sauce and crack the eggs into them (or place the tofu in), and season them. Put a lid on the pan and cook for 6–10 minutes, depending on how you like your eggs.

Remove from the heat, sprinkle the feta or Beer Nozzarella over it, and serve. If you use the Beer Nozzarella recipe, make it feta-style, since it'll have a tangier flavor which works well here.

MODERATELY HUNGOVER COOKING INSTRUCTIONS

Soften the onion in the oil for a few minutes, then add the pepper and cook for a few more minutes. Add the garlic and the spices and stir into the onions and pepper. After a minute or so add the tomato purée, cook for a couple more minutes then add the chopped tomatoes and the beer.

Bring to a simmer and hold it there for 30–45 minutes, stirring occasionally so that it doesn't stick to the pan. It should end up really thick.

When nearly ready, make four wells in the sauce, crack in the eggs (or place in the tofu), and season them. Put a lid on the pan and cook for 6–10 minutes, depending on how you like your eggs.

Remove from the heat, sprinkle the feta or Beer Nozzarella over it, and serve. If you use the Beer Nozzarella recipe, make it with feta, since it'll have a tangier flavor which works well here.

Use a sweet cherry beer for this recipe as it gives a lovely depth of fruitiness to these fat, fluffy, American-style pancakes. This recipe is also good for waffles if you have a waffle maker and would prefer to use that.

CHERRY BEER PANCAKES

Vegan option

Serves 2

Takes 30 minutes

Eat it with: cherry beer or coffee Imperial Stout

1 cup (125g) all-purpose (plain) flour

1 tablespoon white sugar

2 teaspoons baking powder

6 tablespoons (90ml) cherry beer

3 tablespoons almond milk (or other milk of choice)

1 teaspoon vanilla extract

½ teaspoon salt

Oil or butter, to cook

For the cherry beer sauce

1 heaped cup (200g) cherries, fresh or frozen and pitted (stoned)

4 tablespoons (60ml) cherry beer

2 tablespoons maple syrup (or more if you like it really sweet)

1 teaspoon vanilla extract

½ teaspoon cinnamon

1 teaspoon cornstarch (cornflour)

Put all the pancake ingredients into a large bowl and whisk together. You want a thick batter but you can adjust slightly if necessary by adding more beer or milk to thin it down, or flour to thicken it. Put in the refrigerator for 10 minutes.

Meanwhile, make the cherry sauce. Put the cherries in a pan with the rest of the ingredients apart from the cornstarch (cornflour). Over a medium heat, cook for around 10 minutes or until the cherries are soft. Put the cornstarch into a small cup or bowl and pour a couple of tablespoons of the cherry liquid from the pan into it. Stir it into a thick paste, then put it back into the pan to thicken the sauce.

To fry your pancakes or waffles, take a large pan or waffle maker and add some oil or butter. Pour in the batter and cook for a few minutes on each side, until golden and fluffy. Keep the pancakes warm while you repeat with the rest of the batter. Serve with the cherry sauce on top. You can add some thick yogurt or cream too.

LONDON PORTER BAGELS

Vegan

Makes 8 bagels

Takes 24 hours (active preparation time: 1 hour)

Eat it with: Porter, Mild, or Pale Ale

These are somewhere between a New York bagel and a London one—pleasingly dense and a little chewy. I've used London Porter but any malty beer will taste good, just avoid hop bitterness. The dough is best after a long overnight ferment in the refrigerator, so plan ahead. These are great with Whipped Beer Cheese (opposite).

½ cup (120ml) warm water

4 tablespoons malt extract (or 2 tablespoons packed (soft) light brown sugar)

2 teaspoons dried yeast

2¾ cups (385g) strong white bread flour

2 tablespoons vital wheat gluten (or use more bread flour)

2 teaspoons salt

½ cup (120ml) beer

2 tablespoons polenta

"Everything" bagel seasoning or sesame seeds (optional)

Combine the water, 2 tablespoons of the malt extract (or 1 tablespoon of sugar), and the dried yeast in a cup and stir together to activate the yeast. Leave for a few minutes.

In a large bowl, combine the flour, vital wheat gluten, and salt. Add the beer and stir to combine.

Add the yeast-water mix and stir into a dough. Tip it out onto a clean surface and knead for 6–8 minutes—it starts out quite wet and sticky, so keep working it. Let it rest for 10 minutes, then knead for another 4–6 minutes. You should have a thick, elastic dough.

Divide the dough into 8 equal pieces, about 3oz (80–90g) each. Let them rest on the countertop for 10 minutes. Meanwhile, make some space in the refrigerator then line 2 baking sheets with baking parchment, and sprinkle the polenta over them.

Now shape the bagels. There are videos online showing how to do this, but it's easy. Roll out the dough into a long sausage, around 9–10in (23–25cm) long, and twist it slightly. Wrap it around your hand like it's a knuckle-duster, then squeeze the ends together in your palm. Place on the countertop, smooth it out, and shape it into a neat-looking bagel with a large hole in the middle (the dough will rise and the hole will shrink).

Place the bagel on the polenta-dusted baking parchment, then repeat for all the other bagels, leaving lots of room between them. Cover loosely with plastic wrap (clingfilm) and leave out for 1 hour, then refrigerate for 18–24 hours.

Preheat the oven to 450°F/230°C/Gas 8. Take a large pan and half-fill it with water. Bring it to the boil and add the remaining 2 tablespoons of malt extract (or 1 tablespoon of sugar). Using a spatula, take each bagel and place it in the boiling water, cooking for 20–30 seconds on each side. Remove from the water and place back on the baking sheet, then repeat for the rest of the bagels (you can boil two or three in the same pan at the same time).

Add any seasonings to the top of the bagels, such as Everything seasoning or sesame seeds, if desired. Bake for 16–18 minutes, or until golden.

WHIPPED BEER CHEESE

Whipped Beer Cheese is a vegan cream cheese made using beer.
It's a little creamy and a little tangy with a thick, spreadable
consistency. I recommend using Gueuze, Wild Ale, or Belgian
Witbier for the best flavor, but malty Pale Lagers are also fine.
It's really easy to make and you can eat it as soon as you've blitzed
it up, or you can put it in the refrigerator for a few hours where it'll
get firmer. It'll keep in the refrigerator for a day or two.

Vegan

Serves 2–4

Takes 5 minutes

**Eat it with: Pale Ale, Pilsner,
or Wheat Beer**

7oz (200g) firm tofu

3½ tablespoons (50g) vegan butter, melted

4 tablespoons beer

2–3 tablespoons nutritional yeast

2 tablespoons lemon juice

2 tablespoons apple cider vinegar

1 tablespoon white miso

1 teaspoon tahini (optional but good)

1 teaspoon salt

½ teaspoon onion powder

Put all the ingredients in a high-power
blender and blitz until very smooth.
Taste and add any extra ingredients—
the flavor you're aiming for is like that
of a feta or cream cheese, so if you
want it to be tangier then add more
vinegar or lemon, or add more
nutritional yeast if you want it cheesier.
Scrape into a bowl or container and
refrigerate until needed.

2

MAINS AND
SIDES

This is somewhere between a Roman-style *pizza al taglio*, a Detroit-style pizza, and a topped focaccia. You get a dough that's thick but light, crispy, and chewy, with the best crusts, and capable of holding a lot of toppings—it's an impressive thing to eat. As this recipe replaces most of the liquid with beer, use something that's low in bitterness and preferably with a light sweetness—Pale Lager or malty Amber Lager are ideal. If you follow this recipe up to the point of adding the tomato sauce but skip that and instead sprinkle over some extra olive oil and salt, then you'll have a Beer Focaccia—the proving and cooking times are all the same. This pizza is great hot and fresh, and it also heats up really well the next day—just put a slice into a hot oven for 2–3 minutes and it'll come out perfect.

BEER PAN PIZZA (AND BEER FOCACCIA)

Vegan option

Serves 2

Takes 4 hours

Eat it with: every beer is good with pizza

2 tablespoons (30ml) lukewarm water

1½ teaspoons instant yeast

1 teaspoon white sugar

2¼ cups (300g) Tipo "00" flour (or strong white bread flour)

1 teaspoon salt

¾ cup (210ml) beer

3 tablespoons extra-virgin olive oil (plus 2 more if making focaccia)

2 x Beer Marinara Sauce recipe (see page 127)

Pizza toppings of your choice, such as mozzarella, Beer Nozzarella (see page 190), brick cheese, Monterey Jack, Parmesan or Vegan Parmesan (see page 126), roasted bell (sweet) peppers, vegan pepperoni, olives, etc.

Combine the water with the yeast and sugar in a small cup and stir to combine—this is to start to activate the yeast.

In a large bowl, combine the flour, salt, beer, and 1 tablespoon of the oil. Stir it together into a loose dough then add the water-yeast mix. Knead the dough for 6–8 minutes—it's quite a wet dough, so ideally use a stand mixer, or add a little more flour if it's difficult to work.

Place the dough in a bowl, cover it with plastic wrap (clingfilm), and leave in a warm place for 1–2 hours to rise until dough has doubled in size.

Take a large, deep baking pan (9 x 13in/23 x 33cm) and pour in 2 tablespoons of olive oil. Using your fingers, make sure the whole pan is covered, especially the corners and all up the sides.

With your oily hands, knock back the dough in the bowl to push out some of the bubbles, then lift it into the baking pan, press it down, and gently stretch it out toward the corners of the pan—it might not reach the edges, but it's going to prove for some more time and will stretch itself out. Cover and leave in a warm place for another hour, or place the whole sheet in the refrigerator for up to 24 hours if you want to cook it the next day.

Make the Beer Marinara Sauce by following the recipe on page 127, including ½ teaspoon each of dried oregano, dried basil, and chili flakes.

continued overleaf

About 30 minutes before you want to bake the pizza, preheat the oven to 480°F/250°C/Gas 9.

If the dough has been in the refrigerator, take it out 60 minutes before putting it in the oven, to get back up to room temperature. To prepare the pizza for baking, uncover the dough and, using a little olive oil on your hands, stretch out the dough and press down any large bubbles—try to make it an even surface. You can bake now to make Beer Focaccia, or add your toppings. Feel free to top this in whatever order you like—in a traditional Detroit-style pizza, the cheese goes on the bottom, then the sauce follows, but I usually stick to tomato sauce first, covering in a complete layer all the way to the edges, then adding on any other toppings.

Once topped, bake for 15–20 minutes or until bubbling and golden in color. Allow to cool for just a minute or two then eat while still hot.

VEGAN PARMESAN

Makes 1 small jar

Takes 1 minute

1 cup (120g) cashew nuts

6 tablespoons nutritional yeast

1 teaspoon garlic powder

1 teaspoon onion powder

1 teaspoon salt

I constantly have a little jar of this in my kitchen. It doesn't contain beer, but it's a powerful flavor boost to many meals. The recipe here will keep in a sealed jar in a cool dark place for at least two weeks.

In a high-power blender, blitz all the ingredients together for a few seconds until the mixture has a sand-like consistency. Store in a jar.

This is your basic go-to beer tomato sauce which can work with pasta and pizza. The longer you cook it, the thicker and richer and it will get, so adjust the cooking time accordingly—if you want it really thick (for the Beer Pan Pizza on page 124, for example), cook it for 50–60 minutes, but if you want a simple sauce to go with spaghetti and meatballs, cook it for 20–30 minutes. You can also add other herbs and spices, such as dried oregano and basil. I've made this with a lot of different beers, and most darker, sweeter beers are ideal: a sweeter Stout will give a nice dark malt richness; a malty Brown Ale is a good all-rounder, as is a Belgian Dubbel, which will add a little peppery, spicy depth. A Belgian Sour Red is very good, and I was also surprised by using a Rauchbier as a lot of smoked flavor came through, so if that's something you like then use a smoked beer. I don't recommend Strong Golden Belgian Ales or IPAs. This recipe can easily be scaled up—the amount here is enough for pasta sauce for two people, but you'll want to double or triple it if you're making a large pizza or something like a lasagna.

BEER MARINARA SAUCE

Vegan

Serves 2

Takes 20–60 minutes

1 tablespoon olive oil

1 or 2 garlic cloves, crushed

14oz (400g) tin of tomatoes (whole or chopped)

4 tablespoons (60ml) beer

½ teaspoon white sugar

Salt and black pepper, to taste

2 stalks of basil

Any other herbs or spices dependent on recipe (e.g. chili flakes, dried oregano, dried basil)

Warm the olive oil, then add the garlic for a minute so that it softens but doesn't caramelize.

Add the tomatoes, then the beer, sugar, salt, pepper, and basil, and bring to a simmer.

Simmer gently for 20–60 minutes until it reaches the desired consistency (see introduction). Remove the basil stalks and blend (if you want it smooth) before serving.

BEER MAC 'N' CHEESE

Vegan and veggie

Serves 2

Takes 45 minutes

Eat it with: Belgian Blonde, Brown Ale, American IPA

Beer works so well in mac 'n' cheese and it's one of the most popular recipes I've written. Here I've provided an updated vegetarian version, and also developed a vegan version (which took quite a few attempts to perfect), which I now prefer to eat. The cheese flavor in the vegan dish is really good and it's one of those recipes where the beer definitely adds its own flavor and richness. I favor using a Belgian Blonde (I often use Leffe, as it's cheap and widely available) in both versions of this dish, as the beer adds a little bit of a peppery flavor, but you can also use a malty lager.

VEGETARIAN BEER MAC 'N' CHEESE

1¼–2 cups (100–150g) pasta (depending on your appetite)

3 tablespoons (40g) butter

3 tablespoons all purpose (plain) flour

¾ cup (200ml) whole milk (or I've used oat milk and it's good)

⅔ cup (150ml) beer

1 teaspoon Dijon mustard

1¼–1¾ cups (150–200g) cheese of your choice (a mix of Cheddar, Gruyère, Parmesan, and even some low-moisture Mozzarella works—and always add more than you think is a reasonable amount), grated

Salt and white pepper

Preheat the oven to 400°F/200°C/Gas 6.

Cook the pasta, draining it while it still has a bit of hardness to it (it'll continue cooking in the cheese sauce and soak up the cheese flavor instead of water).

In a large pan, melt the butter and when it bubbles and starts to turn golden add the flour and stir into a thick paste. Stir for a minute or two to cook the flour, then gradually add the milk, stirring or whisking so there are no lumps. When most of the milk has been added and you have a thick sauce, add the beer, the mustard, then the rest of the milk, and cook for a minute. Add the cheese, reserving a handful or so, then cook for another minute or until melted. Season to taste.

Pour the drained pasta into the cheese, then pour it all into a large baking dish. Top with the remaining cheese and bake for 20–30 minutes until it's golden and bubbling. Let it sit for a few minutes before you serve it.

VEGAN BEER MAC 'N' CHEESE

1¼–2 cups (100–150g) pasta (depending on your appetite)

3 tablespoons (40g) vegan butter

½ cup (60g) cashew nuts

1¼ cup (300ml) unsweetened vegan milk

4 tablespoons nutritional yeast

1½ tablespoons white miso

1½ tablespoons apple cider vinegar

1 tablespoon tahini

1 teaspoon Dijon mustard

1 teaspoon salt

½ teaspoon onion powder

½ teaspoon garlic powder

⅔ cup (150ml) beer

Vegan Parmesan, to serve (see page 126)

Whereas the cheese version needs to be baked, this one also tastes good straight from the pan. If you want to bake it, preheat the oven to 400°F/200°C/Gas 6.

Cook the pasta, draining it while it still has a bit of hardness to it (it'll continue cooking in the cheese sauce and soak up the cheese flavor instead of water).

Put all the sauce ingredients, apart from the beer, in a high-powered blender and blitz until thick and smooth. (A lot of recipes suggest soaking the cashew nuts but I don't think that's essential if you have a good enough blender; if you do want to soak them, combine the cashew nuts and vegan milk and refrigerate for at least 4 hours before blending.) Taste the mixture and adjust the seasoning, adding more of anything you think it needs.

Pour the mixture into a pan, add the beer, and gently warm it up while the pasta cooks.

When the pasta is ready, drain it and mix into the cheese sauce. Either serve straight from the pan or bake it for 15–20 minutes until golden brown. Serve with Vegan Parmesan.

The love child of two of my favorite dishes. You can make this veggie or vegan, but I prefer the vegan option—I think that the vegan sauce works really well with cauliflower.

CAULIFLOWER CHEESE LASAGNA

Vegan and veggie

Serves 4

Takes 45–60 minutes

Eat it with: Belgian Blonde, Brune

2 x quantity of cheese sauce, vegan or veggie (see page 129)

1 head cauliflower, chopped into florets

1 head broccoli, chopped into florets

½ leek, sliced into rings

8-12 dried lasagna sheets

Preheat the oven to 350°F/180°C/Gas 4.

Make the cheese sauce, doubling the quantities of whichever version of the Beer Mac and Cheese recipe you're using. You can also optionally roast the stems of the cauliflower at 400°F/200°C/Gas 6 for 30 minutes and add them into the sauce.

Boil the cauliflower, broccoli, and leek in salted water for about two minutes, then drain.

In a large lasagna dish, create a layer of the cauliflower, broccoli, and leek, pour over some sauce, then put a few dried lasagna sheets on top to cover. Repeat for three layers and top with one final layer of cheese sauce and some Parmesan (vegan or regular).

Cover with aluminum foil and bake for 30 minutes. Uncover and bake for another 10 minutes.

CAULIFLOWER CHEESE

Alternatively, if you want to skip the lasagna part, just follow the other steps, mixing the vegetables into the cheese sauce and then baking for 15–20 minutes until the mixture is bubbling and golden on top.

BEER CHICK'N

It took me a lot of mistakes until I finally managed to make great seitan, the ancient "wheat meat" vegan protein source, made using wheat gluten. I persisted because I loved the idea that I could make a meaty meat-replacement which used beer as one of the ingredients. This is a meatless version of a chicken breast or pork loin. It's a great base protein to be used in numerous dishes, like Beer Chick'n Tenders (page 132), Mock Coq à la Bière (page 134), and Vegan Schnitzel (page 144). I've had the best results with a malty Pale Lager like a German Helles, and ideally, you'll want the beer to be flat, so leave it out for a little while before cooking with it. The key to getting the texture really meaty (and not oddly spongy) is to knead it a lot, so be prepared for that. You can find the vital wheat gluten online or in organic shops. This recipe can easily be doubled up in quantity.

Vegan

Serves 4/makes approx. 14oz (400g)

Takes 45–60 minutes

2 cups (260g) vital wheat gluten

3 tablespoons chickpea/gram flour
(you can't replace this with all-purpose/plain flour so if you can't get chickpea/gram then use oat flour)

7oz (200g) firm tofu

1 cup (240ml) beer (flat, not fizzy)

3 tablespoons nutritional yeast

2 tablespoons white miso

1 tablespoon apple cider vinegar

1 tablespoon soy sauce

2 teaspoons salt

½ teaspoon onion powder

½ teaspoon garlic powder

Combine the vital wheat gluten and chickpea/gram flour in a bowl and set aside. Then, in a high-power blender, mix the rest of the ingredients. Pour the wet mixture into the flour mixture and stir together with a fork. When it looks like a dough, start kneading it (it'll come together and seem to snap into a new consistency), then continue kneading it for at least 10 minutes and ideally 15 minutes. Punch it, elbow it, slap it around, and just keep on going as it gets firmer and firmer. Be rough with it, it's fine.

To cook it, you'll ideally need a steamer, but you can poach it. You can cook it as one large piece or you can divide it into smaller "steaks". Either way, wrap it very tightly in baking parchment (baking parchment) and then aluminum foil, and steam smaller pieces for 30–35 minutes, and larger ones for 50 minutes. (To poach, wrap it in foil and then plastic wrap/clingfilm, then place in gently simmering water for 50 minutes.)

Allow to cool, then refrigerate for a few hours (or a few days), until you're ready to use it. When you want to cook it, it's fine to be fried, grilled, baked, or boiled.

These spicy Beer Chick'n Tenders have a beer batter as well as using beer in the wheat meat, and you get something that's nicely chewy in the middle and crispy on the outside.

BEER CHICK'N TENDERS

Vegan

Serves 4

Takes 15 minutes

Serve with: cold Pale Lager, Hazy Pale Ale, or Saison

Beer Chick'n (see page 131)
Vegetable oil

For the batter

½ cup (60g) chickpea/gram flour

½ cup (120ml) beer (Pale Lager is ideal)

½ teaspoon salt

For the seasoned flour

3 tablespoons all-purpose (plain) flour

½ tablespoon cornstarch (cornflour)

1½ teaspoons salt

1 teaspoon black or white pepper

1 teaspoon cayenne pepper (or less if you don't want so much spice)

½ teaspoon chili powder

½ teaspoon sweet paprika

½ teaspoon onion powder

½ teaspoon garlic powder

Pinch of allspice

You can deep-fry or bake these tenders—frying obviously tastes better, but sometimes we need to consider our health. If baking, preheat the oven to 425°F/220°C/Gas 7, put a few tablespoons of oil on a large baking sheet and place in the oven to heat up—allow at least 10 minutes for this. If deep-frying, heat the recommended amount of vegetable oil for your fryer to around 350°F/180°C.

Have two large shallow bowls in front of you. In one, whisk the batter ingredients–the batter should be thick and able to coat a piece of Beer Chick'n. In the other bowl, combine the flour and seasoning ingredients.

Shape the Beer Chick'n into tenders (or nuggets or "popcorn"). Dip each piece into the seasoned flour, then cover in the batter, then put back into the seasoned flour. Remove from the flour and put them on a plate.

If baking, place the tenders on the warmed baking sheet and cook for 20–30 minutes or until deep golden brown, turning halfway. If deep frying, cook for 3–4 minutes on each side, or until deep golden brown (you'll need to do this in batches, so keep the already-fried tenders warm while you cook the rest).

PREFER BREADCRUMBS?

If you want these to be more like chicken nuggets, then set up three bowls: one with just a couple of tablespoons of all-purpose (plain) flour, one with the batter mix, and the third with breadcrumbs (golden or panko). Dip the tenders in the flour, then the batter, then the breadcrumbs, and bake or fry as above.

MOCK COQ À LA BIÈRE

Vegan option

Serves 4

Takes 90–120 minutes

Eat it with: Belgian Blonde

6 large shallots, thickly sliced

2 tablespoons (30g) butter

1 tablespoon olive oil

4 garlic cloves, crushed

2 carrots, peeled and sliced

6 cups (400g) king oyster mushrooms, tops off (but still cook them) and bases "pulled" into strips

10 cups (600g) mixed mushrooms (wild mushrooms such as oyster are best)

1 cup (250ml) hot vegetable stock

1 bottle of Belgian Blonde

2 tablespoons malt extract, honey, or agave syrup

1 tablespoon white or barley miso

1 tablespoon Dijon mustard

2 bay leaves

14oz (400g) Beer Chick'n (see page 131) or alternative protein of your choice

¾ cup (200ml) cream

1 tablespoon white wine vinegar or apple cider vinegar

Salt and black pepper

Coq à la Bière is a classic *cuisine à la bière* recipe from Belgium and northern France. and this is my veggie take on it. The first time I cooked it I just used king oyster mushrooms and "pulled" them like sliced pieces of chicken breast, but I thought it needed more substance and some protein. You could add a can or two of butter beans, but I prefer using Beer Chick'n (see page 131)—proper Mock Coq. I use a sweetish Belgian Blonde in this recipe and Leffe works well, as does a French Bière de Garde— just avoid bitterness as it can come through too strong in this recipe. This tastes better the day after you cook it, so if you have the time and the organization then make it in advance. Serve it with Brewers' Fondant Potatoes (see page 136) or the potato dish of your choice, such as mash, and some green veg. Cooking time will vary based on your pan and the mushrooms you use, and it should be thick and rich.

In a large pan with a lid, soften the shallots in the butter and oil for five minutes. Add the garlic and carrots and cook for a couple of minutes, then add the mushrooms a handful at a time.

When all the mushrooms are in and have been stirred through, add the stock followed straight away by the beer, then all the rest of the ingredients apart from the Chick'n, cream, and vinegar. Bring to a boil, then lower to a simmer and put the lid on the pan. Cook for around 45 minutes, stirring occasionally.

Remove the lid, add the Chick'n, and keep the lid off as it continues to simmer. Cook for another 20–30 minutes, then add the cream and cook for another 10–20 minutes. It's ready when the sauce is rich and thick.

Take off the heat, add the vinegar, then season to taste. Let it sit for at least 15 minutes before you serve (it'll stay hot for ages).

BREWERS' FONDANT POTATOES

I've got a great Belgian book published in the 1950s which has over 300 recipes for cooking with beer. In it is a recipe for something called "Brewers' Potatoes," which bakes potatoes in Lambic. I used that as inspiration for this dish and combined it with a traditional fondant potato recipe. The result is one of the best potato dishes I've cooked. I like it on the side of Mock Coq à la Bière (see page 134)

Vegan option

Serves 2

Takes 1 hour

Eat it with: Belgian Blonde, Brune

3 tablespoons (45g) butter

1 tablespoon olive oil

18oz (500g) potatoes, such as Maris Piper or Yukon Gold

2 or 3 whole garlic cloves

2 or 3 shallots, peeled and quartered

2 or 3 springs of thyme

2 or 3 bay leaves

¾–1¼ cups (200-300ml) Gueuze or Wild Ale (but not one with fruit in it)

Vegetable stock (optional)

Salt and pepper

Preheat the oven to 350°F/180°C/Gas 4. Prepare the potatoes by peeling them and slicing off each end so that they look like mini barrels and can stand up—ideally they should all be roughly the same height.

Put the butter and oil in a large Dutch oven or deep ovenproof pan and warm it on the hob. When hot, put the potatoes in with one of the cut sides down and cook on a medium heat until golden brown. Then flip them over and cook the other cut side for a few minutes. Sprinkle around the garlic, shallots, thyme, and bay leaves, before pouring in the beer until it comes about halfway up the potatoes—be careful, as it could be quite fizzy and may bubble up. Add plenty of salt (this recipe can handle a lot of salt) and some pepper.

Bake in the oven for 30–45 minutes or until the potatoes are soft through to the middle. If the pan gets too dry before it's cooked then you can add more beer or a little vegetable stock, but it should end up as a mostly dry pan only at the end.

The Lambic or Gueuze adds some acidity and some richness to the sweetly caramelized onions in this tarte tatin. You could add some goat cheese or Beer Nozzarella (see page 190 and follow the feta instructions) on top of the tart when you serve it. And if you want to make this into a more substantial meal, then the Brewers' Fondant Potatoes (see opposite) are a great side dish.

LAMBIC SHALLOT TARTE TATIN

Vegan option

Serves 4

Takes 30–45 minutes

Eat it with: Lambic, Belgian Blonde, Belgian Dubbel

6-8 whole garlic cloves, peeled

1 pack of (vegan) puff pastry (10½–12oz/300–350g)

2 tablespoons (30g) butter

2 tablespoons packed (soft) light brown sugar

5 cups (500g) shallots (banana or round), peeled and halved

3 thyme sprigs

Salt and black pepper

½ cup (120ml) Lambic or Gueuze

Goat cheese or Beer Nozzarella (see page 190) to serve (optional)

Salad leaves, to serve

For the Lambic salad dressing

2 tablespoons Lambic or Gueuze

2 tablespoons extra-virgin olive oil

1 tablespoon balsamic vinegar

1 teaspoon honey

Salt and pepper

Preheat the oven to 400°F/200°C/Gas 6.

Put the garlic cloves into a pan of boiling water for 10 minutes.

Roll out the puff pastry and cut it to slightly larger than the 8–9in (20–23cm) ovenproof skillet (frying pan) that you're going to use. Cover the pastry with paper towels and set aside.

Melt the butter in the ovenproof skillet (frying pan) over a medium heat, then add the sugar, stirring until the sugar dissolves. Add the shallots and cook for about 5 minutes, so that they soften and turn a golden color but don't burn. Remove the garlic from the water and add to the shallots along with the thyme, salt, and pepper, then pour in the beer and bring to a simmer. Simmer for 2 minutes.

Place the pastry over the shallots, pushing it down so that it's all inside the pan, and make two small slits in the middle of the pastry. Bake in the oven for 25–30 minutes.

Meanwhile, mix all the salad dressing ingredients together.

Allow to cool for 5 minutes before turning it out onto a board, so that the pastry is underneath. Add some goat cheese or feta-style Beer Nozzarella on top, if desired, and serve with the salad leaves and the Lambic salad dressing.

To me, Belgian Reds have a flavor reminiscent of tomatoes—it's the combination of sweet-sourness and an umami-like depth. This tart uses that beer to emphasize the flavors in the tomatoes, but a Pale Lager also works well. Feel free to add more toppings to this: slices of mozzarella, Parmesan, olives, artichokes, pesto, whatever—think of it like a pizza. The instructions are for one large tart, but you could make four small ones

RED TOMATO TART WITH OVEN-DRIED BEER TOMATOES

For the oven-dried beer tomatoes

2 cups (300g) cherry tomatoes, halved

2 tablespoons beer (Belgian Red or Pale Lager)

2 tablespoons extra-virgin olive oil

1 teaspoon white sugar

½ teaspoon salt

Black pepper

For the tomato sauce

14oz (400g) can chopped tomatoes or passata

1 tablespoon olive oil

3 garlic cloves, crushed

4 tablespoons (60ml) Belgian Red or Pale Lager

1 tablespoon balsamic vinegar (use 2 tablespoons if using Pale Lager)

½ teaspoon onion powder

½ teaspoon chili flakes (optional)

Salt and black pepper

Handful of fresh basil leaves

1 tablespoon nutritional yeast

1 pack (vegan) puff pastry (10½–12oz/300–350g)

Heaped ½ cup (100g) cherry tomatoes, halved

Fresh basil leaves, to serve

Vegan option

Serves 4

Takes 2½–3 hours

Eat it with: Pilsner, Belgian Red, Belgian Dubbel

Start a couple of hours in advance by making the oven-dried tomatoes. Set the oven to 250°F/120°C/Gas ½ and line a baking sheet with baking parchment. In a bowl, combine all the other ingredients and mix together with your hands.

Spread the tomatoes cut side up on the baking sheet and roast for 1½ hours. Set aside and allow to cool.

To make the tomato sauce, put all the ingredients into a pan and bring to a simmer. Allow to reduce to a thick sauce—this should take 30–45 minutes (and can be done in advance).

Preheat the oven to 400°F/200°C/Gas 6. Roll out the pastry onto a large baking sheet (using baking parchment if it doesn't come with the pastry). Score a small border about ½in (1cm) inside the edge of the pastry and, inside that border, prick the pastry all over with a fork. Bake the pastry for 8–10 minutes then remove from the oven.

Spread the tomato sauce out over the tart, then top with the halved cherry tomatoes, open side up, and scatter over the roast tomatoes, plus any additional ingredients you wish to put on the tart. Bake for 20 minutes or until the pastry is golden and crisp. Allow to cool for a few minutes before adding any other toppings, such as fresh basil leaves or grated parmesan, and serving warm.

FOUR-BEER TACO FEAST

Vegan option

Serves 4

Takes 1½ hours (plus some marinating time)

Eat it with: Pale Lager, Amber Lager, Dark Lager, or IPA

TOP TIP

If you want to be extra-organized, cook in the following order: Mushroom Al Pastor (because it needs to be marinated), Lager Tomato Salsa, Jackfruit Carnitas, Black Beans, IPA Slaw, and IPA-Battered Avocado.

Visit Mexico and you'll find three kinds of lager everywhere you go: Pale Lager, Amber (or Vienna) Lager, and Dark Lager, with the amber and dark ones often drunk with food. With that in mind, and then hopping across the border into California where the main beer is an IPA, I designed four taco toppings, one for each of the beers, and brought them together in a big feast. There are a lot of individual elements here, but if you're organized nothing is difficult to cook, plus most of it can be made in advance and kept warm or reheated. To serve, you'll want loads of corn tacos, some limes, diced white onion, cilantro (fresh coriander), avocado, and any additional hot sauces you like. And, of course, any of these can be eaten on their own and not as part of a feast.

LAGER TOMATO SALSA

2 heaped cups (350g) cherry tomatoes

1 teaspoon white sugar

2 teaspoons salt

1 tablespoon ancho or chipotle chili flakes/powder

2 whole garlic cloves, peeled

1 white onion, peeled

4-8 fresh chilis

1 tablespoon oil

Juice of ½ lime

2 tablespoons Lager (Pale, Amber, or Dark are all fine here)

Handful of fresh cilantro (fresh coriander), finely chopped (optional)

Preheat the oven to 325°F/170°C/Gas 3. Put 1½ cups (250g) tomatoes, the white sugar, salt, chili flakes/powder, garlic, half the onion, the chili, and the oil on a large roasting sheet and cook for 30–40 minutes, until everything is soft but not burnt.

Remove from the oven and allow to cool for 30 minutes. Then put into a blender with all the remaining ingredients (including the rest of the fresh tomatoes and onion) and pulse until thick and well mixed together. Season to taste. Set aside and, when cold, refrigerate until needed. It will keep for a couple of days.

DARK LAGER MUSHROOM AL PASTOR

⅔ cup (150ml) Dark Lager

½ cup (75ml) fresh orange or
pineapple juice

3 tablespoons soy sauce

1 teaspoon chipotle chili powder
(or smoked paprika)

1 teaspoon ancho, habanero, or regular
chili flakes

1 teaspoon ground cumin

1 teaspoon garlic powder (or
2 cloves, crushed)

½ teaspoon ground cinnamon

1 tablespoon oil

Salt and black pepper

10-13 cups (600g-800g) large flat
mushrooms, sliced

Fresh or canned pineapple

To serve: corn tacos, diced onion, lime,
cilantro (fresh coriander), and salsa

"Al Pastor" is used creatively here and it's a recipe seeking to get that meaty, roasted flavor you find in a classic al pastor, which cooks on a spit and gets juicy and delicious (the old meat-eater in me is getting hungry at the thought…). Serve these like street tacos with diced onion, lime, cilantro (fresh coriander), and salsa.

In a large container, mix everything together apart from the mushrooms and pineapple. Try the mix and adjust to taste. Then add all the mushrooms, making sure they're all covered, and leave to marinate for 1–4 hours.

Preheat the oven to 400°F/200°C/Gas 6, place everything on a baking sheet (reserving a few tablespoons of the marinade), and roast for about 1 hour or until it's thick and dry and a little crisp. You might want to turn the oven up at the end (which can overlap with the Carnitas recipe, should you follow that step).

Put a few pieces of pineapple and the rest of the marinade into a separate small roasting tin, and bake for 15–20 minutes. Put this on top of the tacos when you serve them.

PALE LAGER JACKFRUIT CARNITAS

1 white onion, diced

3-4 fresh chilis, diced (jalapeños, if you
can get them)

2 garlic cloves, crushed

1 tablespoon oil

2 x 14oz (400g) cans young jackfruit (not
in syrup), drained

1 teaspoon ground cumin

⅓ cup (80ml) hot water

4 tablespoons soy sauce

Scant ¾ cup (180ml) Pale Lager

Salt and black pepper

To serve: corn tacos, diced white
onion, lime, cilantro (fresh coriander),
and salsa/hot sauce

As with the Al Pastor, these "Carnitas" are pretty loosely inspired by the classic recipe. They are best served simply with diced onion, lime, cilantro (fresh coriander), and salsa.

In a large pan over a low to medium heat, soften the onion, chilis, and garlic in the oil for a few minutes, then add the rest of the ingredients, starting with the jackfruit and ending with the beer. Bring to a simmer then hold there for 45–60 minutes, until all the liquid has reduced and the sauce is thick—it should end up dry in the pan, but not stuck to the bottom. Season to taste.

As an optional extra step to get more texture and flavor, once cooked, pour half of this mixture on a baking sheet and cook at 425°F/220°C/Gas 7 for 20–30 minutes to get it crispy. Then reheat the other half and combine.

IPA SLAW AND IPA-BATTERED AVOCADO

For the slaw

Vegan Beer Mayo (see page 179, but use IPA and
fresh orange juice instead of lemon juice)

¼ white cabbage, very finely chopped

1 carrot, grated

½ small white onion, grated or very finely diced

Juice of 1 lime

Pinch of ground cumin

Pinch of garlic powder

½ teaspoon salt

Handful of cilantro (fresh coriander)

For the battered avocado

Vegetable oil, to deep-fry

1 heaped cup (140g) all-purpose (plain) flour

1 cup (250ml) IPA

1 teaspoon salt

½ teaspoon garlic powder

4–6 ripe avocados

To serve: corn tacos, lime, salsa, and hot sauce

**Inspired by fish tacos, this version uses a
sliced avocado instead. Top with the slaw
and extra hot sauce. For this dish, choose
an IPA that's more fruity than bitter.**

First, make the IPA Slaw. Start by making the Beer Mayo.
Then mix all the other ingredients in a separate bowl,
add 2–4 tablespoons of Beer Mayo, and mix it all
together. Taste and add more salt or lime if necessary.
Keep refrigerated until ready to serve.

For the battered avocado, prepare a large pan for deep-
frying. Add the oil so that it's 2in (5cm) deep in the pan.
Heat to about 350°F/180°C.

In a large bowl, combine the flour, beer, salt, and garlic and
mix into a thick batter. Cut the avocados in half, remove
the stone, scoop the flesh out of the skin, and slice each
avocado half into 2 or 3 slices.

Dip the slices in the batter and then put them into the hot
oil for a couple of minutes or until golden, flipping them
over during the cooking. Put onto paper towels to dry off
any excess oil.

AMBER LAGER BLACK BEANS

½ white onion, finely diced

2 garlic cloves, crushed

1 tablespoon oil

1 teaspoon chili powder, fresh or dried

1 teaspoon ground cumin

½ teaspoon chipotle flakes or
smoked paprika

2 x 14oz (400g) cans black beans, drained

6 tablespoons (100ml) Amber Lager

Salt and black pepper

To serve: corn tacos, sliced avocado,
sweetcorn, lime juice, salsa, and feta
(optional)

**This cooks down into a thick, rich mixture
with a deep flavor that's lightened up by
the taco toppings.**

In a pan, cook the onion and garlic in the oil for 5–7
minutes or until soft. Add the spices, then the beans and
the beer. Stir to combine then gently cook down for about
30 minutes until it's all soft and thick. Season to taste.

VEGAN SCHNITZEL AND POTATO SALAD

Vegan option

Serves 4

Takes 90 minutes, plus extra
to make Beer Chick'n

Eat it with: a big glass of great
lager

For the potato salad

1¾lb (800g) potatoes, such as Maris Piper
   or Yukon Gold, peeled and sliced into
   ½in (1cm) rounds

3 tablespoons white wine vinegar

¾ cup (200ml) vegetable stock

1 small red onion, finely diced

½ cucumber, sliced in half, seeds removed,
   cut into fine slices (optional)

2 tablespoons lager

2 tablespoons vegetable oil (I use
   rapeseed)

1 tablespoon German (or Dijon) mustard

Salt and black pepper

For the vegan Schnitzel

1¾lb (800g) extra-firm tofu or Beer
   Chick'n recipe (see page 131) sliced
   into 4–8 "steaks" before steaming/
   poaching

10 tablespoons all-purpose
   (plain) flour

1 tablespoon nutritional yeast (if
   using tofu)

½ cup (120ml) lager

1 teaspoon Dijon or German mustard

2 tablespoons soy sauce

1 cup (75g) dried breadcrumbs

Oil and vegan butter to cook

Salt and black pepper

A schnitzel is one of the ultimate German or Austrian beer foods, and I wanted to make a vegan-friendly version. There are two options for the schnitzel: one is made simply with firm tofu, while the other, which is much closer to the meat version, uses the Beer Chick'n on page 131. If you're using Beer Chick'n, you need to start making it a few hours in advance, or make it the day before and leave in the refrigerator until needed. It's served with a classic beer-hall potato salad, meaning it has a savory-tangy flavor (unlike the American mayo-heavy version) and it's best served at room temperature, so you can make the salad before focusing on cooking the schnitzel.

Boil the potatoes in salted water until soft but not falling apart. Then drain and tip them onto a baking sheet and spread them out so that they can air-dry. Sprinkle 2 tablespoons of the vinegar over the top.

In a small pan, heat the stock and the onion. Bring to a simmer and allow the liquid to reduce in volume by about half.

Meanwhile, if you're using the cucumber, sprinkle over a little salt, leave it for a few minutes, then squeeze as much moisture out of it as you can.

When the stock has reduced, remove it from the heat and add the lager, oil, mustard, and remaining vinegar, then season with salt and pepper.

Put the potatoes in a large bowl, add the cucumber (if using), then pour the stock over. Leave to infuse and cool for 30–60 minutes.

If you're using tofu, drain it and slice into ½in (1cm) thick "steaks." Wrap up the tofu with several pieces of kitchen paper or a kitchen towel, then place something heavy on top, such as a book or bowl. Repeat a few minutes later. This will draw out the moisture in the tofu and to make it as dry as possible. If you're using Beer Chick'n, you want 4 to 8 "steaks," each about ½in (1cm) thick

To cook the schnitzel, it's the same approach whether you're using tofu or Beer Chick'n. Set up three bowls or plates in a row.

In the first, put 2 tablespoons of the flour plus the nutritional yeast (if using), and some salt and pepper. In the second, stir together the rest of the flour, the beer, and more salt and pepper, and the mustard and soy, until you have a thick batter. Put the breadcrumbs in the third bowl. Put two large skillets (frying pans)—you'll need a couple, or you will have to fry in batches and keep them warm—on a medium heat with a tablespoon of oil and a tablespoon (15g) of butter in each.

Working quickly, take a piece of tofu or Beer Chick'n and coat it in the flour. Then coat it in the batter and then cover in breadcrumbs. Put in the skillet (frying pan) and repeat for all the other pieces. Fry for 2–3 minutes on each side and until golden brown and warm through to the middle. Alternatively, you can bake these on an oiled baking sheet for 25–30 minutes at 400°F/200°C/Gas 6, or until golden brown.

Check the seasoning of the potato salad (you may want more vinegar or salt), then serve with the schnitzel.

Some cooks find making risotto really calming and relaxing, as they slowly stir and it becomes rich and creamy. I find it stresses me out as it always takes longer than planned, so I drink a beer while I cook. Classic risotto recipes use wine to deglaze the pan before the stock goes in; don't do that with beer, as it'll kick out too much bitterness. Instead, deglaze with stock (or white vermouth), then add the beer after the second ladleful of stock. Tripels vary a lot in flavor and character—you'll want one which is more sweet and fruity (like Tripel Karmeliet) rather than brisk and dry (like Westmalle Tripel).

TRIPEL FENNEL RISOTTO

Vegan option

Serves 2

Takes 45 minutes

Eat it with: Belgian Tripel, Belgian Blonde, or American IPA

2 fennel bulbs

2 tablespoons olive oil

2 tablespoons (30g) butter

½ small leek, chopped

2 garlic cloves, crushed

1 teaspoon fennel seeds, plus an extra pinch

½ teaspoon ground coriander (ideally freshly toasted and ground, as this will be more orangey and fragrant)

4 cups (1 liter) vegetable stock

1 heaped cup (200g) risotto rice

¼ cup (50ml) white vermouth (optional)

½ cup (120ml) Tripel

Salt and white pepper

Juice of ½ lemon

Parmesan or Vegan Parmesan (see page 126), to serve

Start by opening the beer and, after measuring out the beer you need to cook with, pour yourself a glass to drink while you cook.

Finely dice one of the fennel bulbs, reserving any fennel tops, then soften in a large pan (with a lid) with half of the olive oil and half of the butter. Cook with the lid on for 5–10 minutes, until the fennel is soft, then add the leek, garlic, 1 teaspoon of fennel seeds, and ground coriander. Stir it all together and allow it to soften and sweeten for another 5–10 minutes.

Prepare the vegetable stock and preheat the oven to 400°F/200°C/Gas 6. Take the other fennel bulb and cut it into quarters, top to bottom. Place on a baking sheet with the remaining olive oil, a pinch of fennel seeds, and some salt. Roast for 20–30 minutes, until golden and soft.

When the fennel and leeks in the pan are soft, add the risotto rice and stir for a couple of minutes, then add the vermouth (or a ladle of stock). Cook off the alcohol for a minute, then start adding the stock, a ladle or two at a time, stirring constantly. After the second ladle, add most of the beer, reserving a few tablespoons. Keep adding stock until the risotto is almost done. Most rice packets say 15–20 minutes for this, but it'll probably be closer to 30 minutes. And you might need more vegetable stock (and another bottle of beer to drink while you stir).

When you add the final ladle of stock, also add the last of the beer, stirring for a final few minutes. Take off the heat, add the remaining butter, a squeeze of lemon juice, the salt, white pepper, and Parmesan. Put the lid on the pan and leave for a few minutes, then check the seasoning, adding more of whatever you think it needs, and serve with the roasted fennel on top, garnished with some fennel fronds. You'll also probably need to open another beer now.

DUBBEL DRUNKEN NOODLES

Vegan

Serves 2

Takes 30 minutes

Eat it with: Dubbel, Dunkelweizen, or Pale Lager

7oz (200g) dried wide rice noodles

2 tablespoons sesame oil

7oz (200g) firm tofu, cubed

½ white onion, sliced

3 garlic cloves, crushed

Fresh bird's eye chilis, to taste (it should be very spicy)

1 medium carrot, peeled and julienned into thin strips

5½oz (150g) mixed vegetables of your choice: broccoli, bell (sweet) peppers, etc., sliced or chopped

6 tablespoons soy sauce

2 tablespoons packed (soft) light brown sugar or maple syrup

1 teaspoon cornstarch (cornflour)

4 tablespoons Dubbel

2 scallions (spring onions), finely sliced

1 cup (20g) fresh Thai basil or holy basil leaves, chopped

Sriracha (or other hot sauce), to serve (optional, if you want it even hotter and more garlicky)

There are a few theories about how *pad kee mao*, or drunken noodles, got their name. One is that they are popular when people have had a few too many beers; one suggests that the dish is so spicy that people drink extra beer while they eat, and so get drunk; while another supposes that the soy, garlic, and chili in the dish are enough to pick you up the next day. Either way, this is a great dish that's salty, sweet, and spicy, made extra delicious by the use of Thai basil or holy basil. Don't even bother making this dish then if you haven't got the proper basil— the regular kind just isn't the same. I use a Belgian Dubbel in this as it gives some of its own spiciness and a subtle sweetness, plus these beers are typically low in bitterness so can handle being stir-fried. You could alternatively use a Dunkel (Dark Lager) or Dunkelweizen (a dark wheat beer).

Cook the rice noodles according to the packet instructions then drain.

In a large wok, heat the sesame oil and fry the tofu. After a couple of minutes, add the onion, cook for one minute then add the garlic and chilis, followed by the carrots and other vegetables. Cook for 3–5 minutes.

Add the soy and sugar or syrup to the pan. In a cup, stir the cornstarch (cornflour) with the beer and then add to the pan and stir through. Add the scallions (spring onions) and the Thai or holy basil and cook for one minute. Mix in the noodles and stir to coat them in the sauce.

Check the seasoning, then serve with Sriracha or other hot sauce, if desired.

Stout and miso combine in this recipe and they are made richer by adding tahini, which enhances the flavor of the sesame oil. This is great served on plain white rice with steamed or stir-fried green veg. If you want to include some protein, you can make more marinade (about 50% more would be enough) and use it to cover some tofu, which can be cooked alongside the eggplant (aubergine) for the final 20 minutes of roasting time.

MISO STOUT EGGPLANT

Vegan

Serves 2

Takes 45–60 minutes

Eat it with: Stout, Dubbel, or Dark Lager

2 eggplants (aubergines)

4 tablespoons Stout

3 tablespoons barley or brown rice miso

3 tablespoons maple syrup, honey, or agave syrup

5 tablespoons soy sauce

2 tablespoons black vinegar or rice vinegar

1 tablespoon tahini

1 teaspoon sesame oil

½ teaspoon garlic powder

½ teaspoon chili flakes

To serve: cooked rice, steamed or stir-fried greens (spinach, broccoli, or kale), diced scallions (spring onions), and sesame seeds

Preheat the oven to 350°F/180°C/Gas 4. Line a deep-sided baking sheet with baking parchment. Slice the eggplants (aubergines) down the middle from top to bottom and score the flesh. Place them flesh-side up on the sheet.

In a bowl or jug, mix together all the other ingredients. Taste and adjust the seasoning as needed—it should be rich, salty, and a little sweet.

Cover the flesh of the eggplant with most of the sauce, trying to get it into the scored grooves, but reserving 4–6 tablespoons for later. Then cover in aluminum foil and bake for 25–30 minutes.

Remove from the oven, take off the foil, and pour the rest of the sauce over the eggplants, then bake for another 20 minutes, or until bubbling and golden.

Serve with rice and greens, and sprinkle over some diced scallions (spring onions) and sesame seeds.

THAI RED AND WEISS CURRY

Vegan

Serves 4

Takes 30 minutes

Eat it with: wheat beer, Hazy IPA, or Pale Lager

For the curry paste

4–8 fresh red chilis (according to your spice preference)

1 tablespoon dried red chili flakes

4 garlic cloves, peeled

1in (2.5cm) piece of fresh ginger or galangal, peeled

2 sticks of lemongrass or 2 teaspoons of lemongrass paste

Juice and zest of ½ lime

3 or 4 dried kefir lime leaves (optional)

2 shallots or ½ white onion

2 tablespoons soy sauce

2 tablespoons white sugar

2 tablespoons vegetable oil

1 teaspoon coriander seeds (or ½ teaspoon ground coriander)

For the curry

2 x 14oz (400ml) cans full-fat coconut milk

14–21oz (400–600g) protein of choice

14oz (400g) vegetables of your choice (see introduction)

Scant ¾ cup (180ml) Weissbier or Witbier

¾ cup (15g) Thai basil leaves, chopped (omit if you can't get it—don't replace with regular basil)

4 tablespoons (10g) fresh cilantro (coriander), finely chopped

2–4 fresh red chilis, diced

Lime juice

Salt or soy

Cooked rice, to serve

The flavors of Weissbier and Witbier are both great with Thai food, where they can bring their own creaminess and a little hint of spice, with the alcohol adding a richness to the sauce. You can use a store-bought Thai red curry paste if you prefer, but I'm giving the recipe if you want to make your own—you can make the paste in advance if you wish, as it will keep for a few days covered in the refrigerator. Add whatever protein you prefer (I use tofu) and your favored vegetables—broccoli, bell (sweet) peppers, eggplant (aubergine), etc. My preference is to roast some diced eggplant in oil for 30 minutes, then add it to the curry so that it soaks up the sauce and turns really soft.

To make the curry paste, simply blend all the ingredients, adding just enough water to allow it to form into a thick paste. Use immediately or keep it covered in the refrigerator for a few days.

To make the curry, fry the curry paste in a large wok for a couple of minutes. Add the coconut milk and bring to a gentle simmer. Add the protein, vegetables, and beer and increase to a medium-high heat. (If you're using chicken-style pieces which take 10–15 minutes to cook, then put these in and cook for 5 minutes before you add the veg and the beer.) Cook until the vegetables and protein are ready (8–12 minutes, depending on how crunchy you like your veg.)

Remove from the heat, add the herbs, fresh chili, and lime, then season with salt or soy sauce. Serve with rice.

The combination of peanut butter, sweet potato, and coconut makes this a properly comforting and hearty curry which is also spicy and aromatic. The Porter—or any sweeter dark ale, such as a Belgian Brune or Oatmeal Stout; just avoid one that's really roasted and bitter—adds its own richness, plus underlying warmth from the alcohol. The paste needs a lot of ingredients, but you just put them all in a blender and blitz it up. I like this with a Dunkelweizen—a dark German wheat beer—as it's refreshing and cuts through the stronger flavors.

PORTER PEANUT BUTTER MASSAMAN CURRY

For the curry paste

3-5 fresh red chilis

4 garlic cloves

2 sticks of lemongrass or 2 teaspoons lemongrass paste

1in (2.5cm) piece of fresh ginger or galangal, peeled

3 peeled shallots or 1 small white onion

Handful of cilantro (fresh coriander) stalks (optional)

4 tablespoons peanut butter

1 teaspoon ground cinnamon

Seeds from 2 cardamom pods

1 teaspoon ground cumin

1 teaspoon ground coriander

1 teaspoon five spice powder

Pinch of allspice

2 tablespoons tamarind paste

Juice and zest of ½ lime

2 tablespoons brown sugar or coconut sugar

4 tablespoons soy sauce

2 tablespoons vegetable oil

For the curry

2 sweet potatoes, peeled and cubed

1 tablespoon coconut or vegetable oil

2 x 14oz (400ml) cans of full fat coconut milk

14-21oz (400-600g) tofu (or other protein)

Optional extra vegetables: red bell (sweet) peppers, green beans, broccoli, etc., chopped or sliced

Scant ¾ cup (180ml) Porter

Salt or soy sauce, to taste

Cilantro, (fresh coriander) to serve (optional)

Cooked rice, to serve

Vegan

Serves 4

Takes 30 minutes

Eat it with: Dunkelweizen, Dark Lager, or Porter

Preheat the oven to 400°F/200°C/Gas 6 and roast the sweet potatoes in the oil for 20–30 minutes, until soft. When cooked, remove from the oven and reserve until needed.

Make the curry paste by blitzing all the ingredients in a blender, adding just enough water to make it a thick paste.

In a large pan or wok, fry the curry paste for 1–2 minutes. Add the coconut milk and bring to a simmer, then add the tofu, the roasted sweet potato, and any other vegetables, plus the beer. Bring to a simmer and cook for 5–10 minutes, until all the vegetables are soft. Season to taste—you may want more lime, more chili, or more salt, and you may want to sprinkle some cilantro (fresh coriander) on top. Serve with rice.

WEISSBIER DOSA WITH SPICED POTATOES AND SAMBAR KETCHUP

Vegan

Serves 2 (and makes 6 dosa)

Takes 45–60 minutes

Eat it with: Weissbier, Belgian Blonde, or Pale Lager

This is a great Indian chickpea flour pancake wrapped around spicy potatoes. It's often served with a sambar, a spicy lentil and vegetable dish, and the version here takes the flavors of the sambar and thickens it up into a spicy beer ketchup. This makes a great brunch, lunch, or lighter dinner, and you should make more than you think you need as this is addictively delicious.

For the sambar ketchup

1 white onion, finely diced

1 tablespoon rapeseed or vegetable oil

2 garlic cloves, crushed

1in (2.5cm) piece of fresh ginger, peeled and finely chopped

2 fresh red chilis, finely chopped

½ teaspoon each ground chili, cumin seeds, ground coriander, ground cardamom, ground cinnamon, and allspice

¼ teaspoon fennel seeds

1 teaspoon salt

1 tablespoon tomato paste (purée)

¼ cup (50g) red lentils, rinsed in cold water

2 tablespoons tamarind paste

2 tablespoons apple cider vinegar

3 tablespoons packed (soft) brown sugar

14oz (400g) can tomatoes (chopped or whole)

½ cup (120ml) Weissbier

Start by making the Sambar Ketchup, which can be made up to a week in advance and kept covered in the refrigerator. Soften the onion in the oil for a few minutes, then add the garlic, ginger, and chili. Add all the spices and stir together for a minute, then add the rest of the ingredients in order and simmer until thick but pourable: around 30–40 minutes. You may want to add more beer (or water) if it gets too dry. When cooked, season to taste—it should be sharp, sweet, and spicy. Blend until smooth.

continued overleaf

For the spiced potatoes

14oz (400g) new potatoes

1 teaspoon salt

1 tablespoon coconut oil or olive oil

½ teaspoon black mustard seeds

10 dried curry leaves

½ teaspoon cumin seeds

½ white onion, finely sliced

2 fresh green chilis, finely chopped (or ½ teaspoon dried chili powder, or to taste)

1 garlic clove, crushed

½ teaspoon ground coriander

½ teaspoon ground turmeric

Black pepper, to taste (I like lots)

For the Weissbier dosa

Heaped ¾ cup (100g) chickpea/ gram flour

6 tablespoons (50g) all-purpose (plain) flour

½ teaspoon salt

½ teaspoon baking soda (bicarbonate of soda)

¾ cup (200ml) Weissbier

Coconut or vegetable oil, to fry

Boil the potatoes in salted water until soft—around 15 minutes— then drain.

While the potatoes are boiling, make the Weissbier dosa batter by simply combining everything, apart from the oil, in a bowl and whisking together—it should be the consistency of heavy (double) cream, so add more beer or water to achieve that if needed.

In a large pan, heat the oil and add the mustard seeds, curry leaves, and cumin seeds, frying until they all pop and sizzle. Then add the onion, chili, and garlic and fry to soften the onion, being careful that it doesn't burn—this should take around 10 minutes. Add the ground coriander and turmeric, then add the potatoes, using a fork to crush them open and mix them into the spicy onion mix. Cook for 5–10 minutes while you fry the dosa.

Add a little oil to a large skillet (frying pan) over a medium heat. Take a ladle of the batter and add enough to the pan to form a thin layer, then fry for a minute or two before flipping it over and cooking for another 30–60 seconds. Wrap in aluminum foil to keep warm while you repeat with the rest of the dosa batter.

To serve, take a dosa and place a large spoonful of potatoes in the middle Add some sambar ketchup, then wrap it up and eat.

BEER RIBS

Vegan

Serves 4

Takes 1¼–1½ hours

Eat it with: American IPA, Porter, or Amber Lager

2 cups (280g) vital wheat gluten

4 tablespoons chickpea/ gram flour

1 cup (160g) cooked black beans or chickpeas

1 tablespoon Marmite or soy sauce

1 cup (250ml) Rauchbier, Porter, or Stout

6 tablespoons ketchup

6 tablespoons soy sauce

4 tablespoons barley or rice miso

4 tablespoons maple syrup or packed (soft) brown sugar

2 tablespoons liquid smoke

2 tablespoons Sriracha (optional, if you want it spicy)

2 tablespoons olive or vegetable oil

2 tablespoons apple cider vinegar

3 teaspoons salt (smoked, if you have it)

2 teaspoons Dijon or American mustard

1 teaspoon cayenne pepper

1 teaspoon sweet or smoked paprika

1 teaspoon garlic powder

1 teaspoon onion powder

These seitan ("wheat meat" vegan protein) beer ribs are tender, yet have a great meaty texture. Like other seitan recipes, these ribs are great for this book because they are made with beer (you can't do that with pork ribs!) and then served in a beer sauce. I've used a smoky Rauchbier (some smoky flavor comes through, but not a lot), and Porter and Stout both taste good. You can make the seitan ribs a day in advance and they can be cooked on the barbecue or in the oven.

Combine the vital wheat gluten and chickpea flour in a bowl and set aside.

In a high-speed blender, blend the black beans or chickpeas, the Marmite or soy sauce, and half of all the rest of the ingredients (put the other half into a pitcher for later) into a thick sauce. Pour the sauce into the dry ingredients and stir to combine.

When it forms a dough, tip it out onto a clean work surface and knead vigorously for at least 10 minutes. The kneading is really important to get the firm texture. Punch it, beat it up, do whatever you like, just keep on kneading it. Form it into the shape of one large rack of ribs or two smaller racks, depending on the size of your pan.

Half-fill a large pan with boiling water and bring to a simmer. Tightly wrap the seitan ribs in aluminum foil, then in plastic wrap (clingfilm), and poach for 50 minutes. Drain, allow to cool, then unwrap and refrigerate until you're ready to cook it.

To cook the seitan, either prepare a barbecue or preheat the oven to 350°F/180°C/Gas 4. Mix the remaining wet ingredients and season to taste. Score lines down the seitan so that it looks more like a rack of ribs.

To barbecue, pour the sauce over the seitan and marinate until needed, then cook for 10 minutes, turning frequently, and basting with more sauce. Serve with any leftover sauce.

To oven-cook, fry the seitan for a minute or two on either side in an ovenproof skillet (frying pan), then pour in most of the sauce, reserving a few spoonfuls, and let it bubble. Place in the oven for 20–30 minutes, turning after 10 minutes. Cook until the sauce is sticky and thick but not burnt. Pour the remaining sauce over the ribs when you remove them from the oven.

BEER PICKLES

Vegan

Makes 3 jars

Takes 15 minutes

Pickling liquor

1⅓ cups (340ml) water

1⅓ cups (340ml) apple cider vinegar

½ heaped cup (120g) white sugar

4 teaspoons (20g) salt

¾ cup (210ml) beer

Additional vegetables and spices
(see the recipes below)

Witbier Pickled Carrots

Pickling liquor

6 cups (750g) carrots, peeled and sliced
into batons

Slice of lemon peel

1 teaspoon toasted coriander seeds

½ teaspoon black peppercorns

½ teaspoon fennel seeds

¼ teaspoon cumin seeds

IPA Pickled Chilis

Pickling liquor

14–18oz (400–500g) fresh chilis, sliced

6 whole garlic cloves, peeled

½ teaspoon coriander seeds

½ teaspoon black peppercorns

1 star anise

Saison Dill Pickles

Pickling liquor

16–20 baby cucumbers

6 fronds fresh dill

3 whole garlic cloves, peeled

1 teaspoon yellow mustard seeds

½ teaspoon coriander seeds

½ teaspoon black peppercorns

These are quick non-fermented pickles and, like a lot of recipes in this book, it's possible to adapt it to different beers and vegetables. Here is a basic pickling liquor with a few suggested additions. The liquor recipe will give you three 12oz (280ml) jars, but it's easy to scale up and down. Each vegetable recipe is also for enough to fill three jars. Ideally, leave the pickles for a week before you eat them and they'll keep in the refrigerator (they'll improve, in fact) for a few months.

For the pickling liquor, bring the water, vinegar, sugar, and salt to a gentle boil and simmer for a couple of minutes to allow the sugar to dissolve. Remove from the heat and leave to cool.

Prepare your vegetables and any spices and place them in your jars, packing in as many as possible and evenly distributing herbs, garlic, spices, etc.

When the hot liquid mixture has cooled, stir the beer into it and then pour the whole mixture into the jars with the vegetables, filling the jars to the top. Put the lids on, then refrigerate.

CHICKFU BURGER AND SAMBAR KETCHUP

Vegan option

Makes 4 big burgers

Takes 45 minutes (plus cooling time)

Eat it with: Pale Lager, Witbier, or Hazy IPA

For the Chickfu

1 onion, very finely diced

1 tablespoon olive oil or vegetable oil

2 garlic cloves, crushed

1 or 2 fresh chilis, finely diced

1 tablespoon tomato paste (purée)

1 teaspoon salt

1 teaspoon ground turmeric

1 teaspoon ground coriander

1½ teaspoon ground cumin

½ teaspoon ground black pepper

¼ teaspoon ground cardamom (or cinnamon)

1½ scant cups (350ml) light vegetable stock, or water with 1 teaspoon salt

1 tablespoon nutritional yeast

1 tablespoon miso (white or brown)

1½ cups (180g) chickpea/gram flour

1½ scant cups (350ml) Hefeweizen, poured out into a large bowl at least 15 minutes in advance to make it go flat (stir it to reduce the carbonation)

To make the burgers

½ cup (60g) chickpea/gram flour

½ cup (120ml) Pale Lager or Weissbier

½ teaspoon salt

1 cup (50g) panko breadcrumbs

Sambar Ketchup, to serve (see page 152)

Beer Buns, to serve (see page 114)

This is inspired by a *vada pav* (a fried ball of spiced potato in a soft bun), but I use a kind of tofu made with chickpea flour, hence Chickfu. The burger is crisp on the outside, soft and spiced in the middle, and really satisfying. I serve it with the Sambar Ketchup on page 152 and in the Beer Buns on page 114.

To make the Chickfu, in a large pan, soften the onion in the oil for 3–4 minutes (it should be really soft but not brown/caramelized). Add the garlic and chili and cook for a minute or two, then add the tomato paste (purée), followed by the spices and seasonings. Cook for a minute, then add all the stock plus the nutritional yeast and miso. Bring to a simmer over a medium heat.

In a bowl, combine the chickpea/gram flour and the Hefeweizen and whisk into a smooth batter. Pour it into the pan with the spicy stock and whisk so there are no lumps. Stir with a wooden spoon until it becomes really thick—6–10 minutes. Line a dish or container (a loaf pan is good) with baking parchment. Pour the mixture into the prepared dish, allow to cool, then cover and refrigerate for at least two hours or overnight.

If you're making the ketchup, do that now, then make the Beer Buns.

To finish the Chickfu burgers, preheat the oven to 400°F/200°C/Gas 6. Grease or line a baking sheet with baking parchment. Line up two bowls in front of you: in one, combine the chickpea/gram flour, beer, and salt and whisk until it's a thick batter. In the other, put the breadcrumbs. Remove the Chickfu from the refrigerator and slice into four (or more) burger shapes (they could be square). Dip each piece in the batter then the breadcrumbs, ensuring it's totally coated, then place on the prepared baking sheet. Repeat for all the burgers (and with any leftover pieces, which will be great little snacks). Bake for 25–30 minutes until golden and really crispy.

This recipe is inspired by the Italian American dish of sausages cooked with peppers and onions. I use my favorite store-bought vegan sausages, chopped into meatballs, but you can make your own by following the Wurst recipe on page 162 and adding some fennel seeds and 2 tablespoons tomato paste (purée). The sauce is sweet, sticky, spicy, and savory, and the Pilsner adds a little bitterness to cut through it.

SAUSAGE AND PEPPER PILSNER PASTA

Vegan

Serves 2

Takes 45 minutes

Eat it with: Dark Lager, Dubbel, or Porter

4-6 sausages of your choice

2 tablespoons olive oil

1 large white onion, thickly sliced

2 tablespoons soft brown or superfine (caster) sugar

1 teaspoon salt

3 garlic cloves, crushed

2 tablespoons tomato paste (purée)

¼ teaspoon fennel seeds

¼ teaspoon dried basil

¼–½ teaspoon dried chili flakes (to taste)

Black pepper

3 bell (sweet) peppers (red and green), finely sliced

3 tablespoons balsamic or red wine vinegar

¼ cup (50ml) water

6 tablespoons (90ml) Pilsner

Your preferred pasta, to serve (I like rigatoni)

In a large pan with a lid, fry the sausages in 1 tablespoon of olive oil. When the sausages are cooked, remove from the pan and set aside.

Add the rest of the oil to the pan and fry the onion, sugar, and 1 teaspoon salt over a medium heat until it begins to soften. Then add the garlic, tomato paste (purée), fennel seeds, dried basil, chili flakes, and some black pepper, and cook for 2 minutes.

Add the peppers and stir to combine, then pour in the vinegar, water, and finally the beer. Bring to a simmer then put the lid on the pan and cook for around 20 minutes.

After 20 minutes, cook the pasta according to the packet instructions. Chop the sausages into "meatballs," and add to the peppers and onions. Continue cooking until the mixture is thick and sticky—at least another 10 minutes.

Drain the pasta, reserving some of the water. When the peppers are really soft, season to taste, then stir the pasta into the sauce with some of the cooking water. Serve immediately.

VEGAN BEER SAUSAGES: AMERICAN HOT DOG, GERMAN WURST AND BRITISH BANGERS

Vegan

Makes 6–8 sausages

Takes 1¼–1½ hours

Eat it with: the beer you used in the recipe

I set myself the challenge of recreating three classic sausages, all using beer, and all being vegan (my personal favorite is the American hot dog, which is remarkably close to the original). They are made with vital wheat gluten and the process for making each of them is the same, with just the wet ingredients changing. While the recipes look long, all you need to do is combine all the wet ingredients, blend them, and mix them into the dry ingredients. They can be made in advance and cooked on the barbecue, and you can easily double the recipe if you want to make more. There's a Beer Bun recipe on page 114 for hot dog rolls.

continued overleaf

1 cup (140g) vital wheat gluten

1 heaped tablespoon chickpea/
  gram flour

For the American hot dogs

4oz (120g) smoked tofu

½ cup (120ml) American Lager

3 tablespoons soy sauce

2 tablespoons olive oil or rapeseed oil

3 tablespoons miso paste (barley or rice)

2 tablespoons tomato ketchup

2 tablespoons American mustard (or
  1 tablespoon Dijon mustard)

2 tablespoons nutritional yeast

1 teaspoon salt

¾ teaspoon garlic powder

¾ teaspoon onion powder

¾ teaspoon white pepper

¾ teaspoon smoked paprika

½ teaspoon ground coriander

For the German Wurst

4oz (120g) firm tofu (or ¾ cup (100g)
  cooked white beans)

½ cup (120ml) German Helles Lager

2 tablespoons olive oil or rapeseed oil

3 tablespoons miso paste (white
  or barley)

3 tablespoons nutritional yeast

1 tablespoon German or Dijon mustard

1 tablespoon white wine vinegar

1 teaspoon salt

1 teaspoon bouillon powder or
  1 crumbled bouillon (stock) cube

¾ teaspoon onion powder

¾ teaspoon white pepper

½ teaspoon marjoram

½ teaspoon mace (optional)

For the British Bangers

¼ heaped cup (80g) cooked
    haricot beans

½ cup (120ml) British Ale, such as Porter

2 tablespoons olive oil or rapeseed oil

3 tablespoons soy sauce

2 tablespoons miso paste (barley or rice)

2 tablespoons tomato paste (purée)

2 tablespoons Marmite (or 2 tablespoons
    nutritional yeast and 2 tablespoons
    soy sauce)

½ teaspoon mustard powder (or
    1 teaspoon English/Dijon mustard)

1 teaspoon salt

1 teaspoon garlic powder

1 teaspoon onion powder

¾ teaspoon white pepper

¾ teaspoon black pepper

½ teaspoon marjoram

½ teaspoon mace

Pinch of nutmeg

Pinch of other dried herbs, such as sage
    or thyme (optional)

Combine the vital wheat gluten and chickpea/gram flour in a large bowl. Then put all the ingredients for your chosen sausage recipe in a high-speed blender and blitz them.

Pour the wet mixture into the dry and stir together. When it becomes a scruffy dough, tip it out onto a clean surface and knead it until it comes together. Continue kneading for at least 10 minutes. You can be as rough as you like. Punch it, hammer it with your fists, do whatever, just do it for a long time—the longer you do it, the firmer and meatier the sausages will be.

Leave the dough to rest for a minute while you half-fill a large pan with boiling water. Hold it at a gentle simmer. Divide the dough into 6–8 even pieces and roll them out some more, shaping them into sausages. Tightly wrap up each sausage in aluminum, twisting at both ends of the sausage to hold it in place. Then wrap each one tightly in plastic wrap (clingfilm). When done, place all the sausages into the simmering water. Cook for 50 minutes, turning them occasionally.

Drain the sausages and allow to cool. Then unwrap them and refrigerate in a covered container until needed.

To cook, fry or barbecue the sausages for around 10 minutes or bake for 15 minutes at 400°F/200°C/Gas 6. Serve the American hot dog with ketchup, mustard, and fried onions. Serve the German Wurst with currywurst sauce (see below) or German mustard and some fries. Serve the British banger with breakfast, in a sausage sandwich, or with mashed potato and gravy.

CURRYWURST SAUCE

14oz (400g) tomato passata

4 tablespoons tomato ketchup

2 tablespoons curry powder (mild,
    medium, or hot), plus extra to serve

1 teaspoon salt

1 teaspoon white wine vinegar

1 teaspoon sweet or smoked paprika

1 teaspoon onion powder

Cayenne pepper, to taste

This is a quick version of the classic sauce.

Combine all the ingredients in a small pan over a medium heat, then simmer and allow the sauce to reduce until thickened. Season to taste and serve over the Wurst with an extra sprinkling of curry powder.

These fragrant and meaty little patties can be used in a Vietnamese salad, or you can have them in a banh mi roll (or use the Beer Bun recipe on page 114, and shape into larger rolls). They are great with a Hazy DIPA on the side—just choose something really aromatic and a little sweet with low bitterness.

DIPA VIETNAMESE PATTIES

Vegan

Serves 2

Takes 1¼ hours

Eat it with: Hazy DIPA, Pale Lager, or Witbier

1 cup (140g) vital wheat gluten

1 heaped tablespoon chickpea/gram flour

4oz (120g) tofu

4 tablespoons (60ml) Hazy DIPA

3 tablespoons (40ml) water or light vegetable stock

4 tablespoons soy sauce

4 tablespoons miso paste (barley or rice)

2 tablespoons olive oil or rapeseed oil

2 tablespoons nutritional yeast

1 tablespoon Sriracha

1 tablespoon superfine (caster) sugar or maple syrup

2 garlic cloves

2 fresh chilis (or to taste)

2 scallions (spring onions), diced

1 small stick lemongrass, outer layer removed

Handful of cilantro (fresh coriander) leaves (optional)

1 teaspoon ground turmeric

1 teaspoon salt

¾ teaspoon white pepper

Zest of ½ lime

For the dressing

4 tablespoons soy sauce

3 tablespoons water

2 tablespoons caster sugar

1 tablespoon miso paste

1 tablespoon Hazy DIPA (optional)

1 tablespoon rice or white wine vinegar

Juice of 1 lime

1 red chili, finely diced

1 garlic clove, crushed

To serve

Cooked rice noodles or a banh mi roll

Julienne carrots

Finely sliced cucumber

Iceberg lettuce

Cilantro (fresh coriander), mint, and Thai basil

Salted peanuts

Sriracha or other hot sauce (optional)

Combine the vital wheat gluten and chickpea/gram flour in a large bowl. Combine the rest of the patty ingredients in a high-speed blender and blitz. Pour the wet mixture into the dry and stir together. When it becomes a scruffy dough, tip it out onto a clean surface and knead it until it comes together. Continue kneading for at least 10 minutes—punch it, hammer it with your fists, do whatever you need to.

Leave the dough to rest for a minute while you half-fill a large pan with boiling water. Hold at a gentle simmer on the hob. Roll up the dough into one large, fat log or sausage, about 2¼in (6cm) thick. Tightly wrap it a couple of times in aluminum foil, twisting at both ends to hold it in place. Then wrap it tightly in plastic wrap (clingfilm). When done, place into the simmering water. Cook for 1 hour, turning occasionally.

Drain and allow to cool, then unwrap and refrigerate until needed. Before cooking, slice into smaller patties, about 1in (2.5cm) thick. You can fry or barbecue the patties in around 10 minutes, or bake for 15 minutes at 400°F/200°C/Gas 6.

To make the dressing, just stir all the ingredients together. Season to taste.

To serve in a banh mi roll: pour over some of the dressing, then top with the vegetables, salad, herbs, peanuts, and hot sauce. To serve in a noodle bowl: place the noodles on the bottom of a deep bowl, put the patties on one side in the bowl, then the salad and herbs on the other, pour over some dressing, and stir to combine when you eat.

PORTER COTTAGE PIE AND BEER-GLAZED CARROTS

Vegan option

Serves 4–6

Takes 2 hours

Eat it with: Porter, Stout, or Dubbel

This cottage pie, made with mushrooms, chestnuts, and lentils, is better than any meat version that I've ever cooked, and I think it's a dish that's completed by having the beer-glazed carrots on the side—the pie filling is rich and savory, and the carrots add some sweetness to it. I like a mix of potatoes and celery root (celeriac) on top, but you can do either on its own. Use a rich Porter with lots of malt flavor.

continued overleaf

For the pie filling

1 white onion, diced

2 garlic cloves, crushed

1 small leek, sliced into thin rings

2 tablespoons oil or butter

1 carrot, finely cubed

2 tablespoons tomato paste (purée)

9–12 cups (600–800g) finely diced
    mushrooms (I like a mix of different
    types)

½ cup (10g) dried mushrooms,
    rinsed clean

1 tablespoon brown miso paste
    (or soy sauce)

1 tablespoon Marmite (or soy sauce)

⅔ cup (150ml) vegetable stock

1 bottle or can of Porter

¾ cup (100g) cooked chestnuts,
    roughly chopped

14oz (400g) can green lentils, drained

Salt and pepper

For the mash topping

2¼lb (1kg) total of celery root (celeriac)
    and/or potatoes, peeled and diced

1–2 tablespoons Dijon mustard

1½ tablespoons (20g) butter

Splash of milk

Salt and white pepper

For the beer-glazed carrots

1¼–1¾lb (600–800g) carrots, peeled and
    sliced lengthways in half or quarters

2 tablespoons (30g) butter

2 whole garlic cloves

3 thyme sprigs

Salt and pepper

2 tablespoons honey or agave syrup

First make the pie filling. In a large pan with a lid, soften the onion, crushed garlic, and leek in oil or butter for a few minutes. Add the carrot, then the tomato paste (purée) and cook for 2 minutes. Add the fresh mushrooms and stir to combine, followed by the dried mushrooms. Put the lid on the pan and cook for a few minutes. Add the miso, Marmite, and stock. Open the beer, pour out 4 tablespoons (60ml) and set aside, then pour the rest of the bottle or can into the pan. Add the chestnuts and green lentils. Bring to a simmer, then lower the heat and cook, with the lid on, for 45 minutes, stirring regularly. Remove the lid and continue cooking until it reduces into a thick filling—another 10–20 minutes.

Boil the celery root (celeriac) and potatoes in salted water until soft. Drain, then add the rest of the topping ingredients and mash until smooth. Season to taste—I like a lot of Dijon mustard in this recipe. Set aside until needed.

Preheat the oven to 400°F/200°C/Gas 6. For the carrots, place the carrots, butter, reserved Porter, garlic, thyme, and seasoning on a large deep baking sheet. When the pie filling is thick, season to taste, then pour it into a large baking dish. Top with the mash. Place in the oven and cook until golden brown on top (around 45 minutes). Add the carrots to the oven at the same time. After 30–35 minutes, pour the honey over the carrots, shake to combine, then cook for 5–10 minutes more. Allow the pie to rest for a few minutes before serving.

This is the beer version of the Thai dish of "son-in-law eggs," which is fried boiled eggs served with a sweet, sour, salty sauce and lots of aromatic herbs. It's really tasty, really quick to make, and great with beer. Although it's an egg recipe, vegans can use tofu and just fry that instead—it's equally good.

STOUT, SOY, AND TAMARIND EGGS

Vegan option

Serves 2

Takes 15 minutes

Eat it with: Porter, Stout, or Dunkelweizen

White rice

4 eggs (or 1 block of tofu)

4 tablespoons Stout, Porter, or Dark Lager

2 tablespoons palm sugar or packed (soft) brown sugar

1 tablespoon brown miso

1 tablespoon tamarind paste

2 tablespoons soy sauce

4 tablespoons vegetable oil

To serve

Fresh Thai or holy basil

Cilantro (fresh coriander)

1 fresh red chili, finely chopped

Crispy fried shallots

Cook the rice according to the packet instructions and soft-boil the eggs (or boil to your preference). Open the beer, pour out 4 tablespoons into a small pan, then pour the rest of the beer into a glass and start drinking it. When the eggs are cooked, allow them to cool, then peel and place on some paper towels.

Put the sugar, miso, tamarind paste, and soy into the pan with the beer. Bring to a gentle simmer until the sugar has dissolved. Meanwhile, heat the oil in a small pan. When hot, fry the whole boiled eggs (or tofu) until golden and crispy on the outside—it'll only take a minute or two.

Cut the eggs in half. Serve on the rice, pour the sauce over, and cover with the herbs, chili, and fried shallots. Drink the rest of the beer with your dinner.

PORTER BBQ PULLED JACKFRUIT

Vegan

Serves 2–4

Takes 45 minutes

Serve with: Hazy Pale, hoppy Lager, or Porter

½ white onion, sliced

2 garlic cloves, crushed

Vegetable oil

14oz (400g) can jackfruit, drained

½ teaspoon ground cumin

½ teaspoon chili powder (more if you like it spicy)

½ teaspoon smoked paprika

2 tablespoons tomato paste (purée)

2 tablespoons brown sugar (or 3 tablespoons maple syrup)

3 tablespoons tomato ketchup

3 tablespoons soy sauce

1 tablespoon liquid smoke (optional)

1 tablespoon vegan Worcestershire sauce (optional)

1 tablespoon apple cider vinegar

1 teaspoon Dijon mustard

⅓ cup (100ml) water or vegetable stock

Scant ¾ cup (180ml) Porter, Dubbel, or Dark Lager

Salt and pepper

When you cook young jackfruit, it can be torn apart and takes on a very similar texture to pulled pork. (You can do a similar thing with king oyster mushrooms—a mix of mushrooms and jackfruit would be good in this recipe.) The jackfruit is also able to soak up a lot of sauce and flavor, making it an ideal pulled pork substitute. Serve this as you would pulled pork: in a bun, with slaw and some hot sauce (try the Beer Buns recipe on page 114 and the IPA Slaw on page 143). I use Porter, but you could use a Belgian Dubbel or Dark Lager. As usual with dishes like this, it is better the next day, so plan ahead if you can.

Soften the onion and garlic in some oil for a couple of minutes. Add the jackfruit and break it apart—the easiest way to do this is by using a potato masher. Add the spices, tomato paste (purée), and sugar and cook for a few minutes, then add everything else, saving the beer till last.

Bring to a simmer and hold it there until the sauce reduces and gets really thick, which should take around 30 minutes (make sure you stir it a few times). Check the seasoning and then it's ready. If possible, let it cool and refrigerate to serve the next day. Reheat in a pan on the hob over a medium heat for 5–10 minutes, or in the oven at 400°F/200°C/Gas 6 for 20 minutes to get it crispy.

PANEER TIKKA WEISSBIER MASALA

Vegan option
Serves 4
Takes 30–45 minutes (plus marinating time)
Eat it with: Pilsner, Session IPA, or Weissbier

Here is a recipe for a paneer tikka served in a Weissbier masala, a creamy and mild curry that's perfect with the cheese. The paneer recipe is also great on its own, served in naan bread. Vegans could use tofu instead of paneer and use vegan alternatives to the other ingredients (I've made it with soy yogurt, vegan butter, and oat cream, and it's good).

For the paneer tikka

½ cup (100ml) natural yogurt

1 tablespoon chickpea/gram flour (optional)

1 tablespoon vegetable oil

2 garlic cloves, crushed

1in (2.5cm) piece of fresh ginger, peeled and grated

1 tablespoon garam masala

1 teaspoon chili powder

1½ teaspoons salt

½ teaspoon ground turmeric

Juice of ½ lemon

3½ cups (400g) paneer (or tofu), cubed

2 red bell (sweet) peppers, diced

For the Weissbier masala

2 tablespoons (30g) butter

1 white onion, diced

2 garlic cloves, crushed

1in (2.5cm) piece of fresh ginger, peeled and grated

1 teaspoon ground cumin

1 teaspoon ground coriander

1 teaspoon ground turmeric

1 teaspoon garam masala

Pinch of cinnamon

Pinch of allspice

1–2 tablespoons superfine (caster) sugar

4 large tomatoes, diced

⅓ cup (100ml) cream

⅔ cup (150ml) Weissbier

2 tablespoons smooth almond or cashew nut butter

Salt and pepper, to taste

To serve

Cooked rice

Naan breads (such as Beer Naan Bread, see page 112)

First, make the paneer tikka. Stir together the yogurt and chickpea/gram flour (if using) to combine without lumps, then add the rest of the marinade ingredients apart from the paneer (or tofu) and peppers. When combined into a thick marinade, add the paneer and peppers and ensure they're all properly covered. Place in a sealed container in the refrigerator for 4–24 hours.

To cook the paneer, preheat the oven to 400°F/200°C/Gas 6. Line a baking sheet with baking parchment and place the paneer and peppers on top. Cook for about 15 minutes, turning halfway through, until the paneer is golden and crisp. (You could also put them on skewers and cook them on the barbecue for about 10 minutes.)

Now make the Weissbier masala. In a pan with a lid, cook the onion in the butter over a medium heat until very soft but not golden—about 6–8 minutes. Add the garlic and ginger, then all the spices, stirring together for a minute. Add the sugar and tomatoes and cook with the lid on until the tomatoes are very soft.

Remove from the heat and blend into a thick sauce using a hand blender, adding a small amount of cream if it's too thick to blend. Put it back on the heat and add the cream, then the beer and the nut butter. Simmer for 5 minutes, then add the cooked paneer and peppers and cook for 1 more minute. Season to taste. Remove from the heat and leave for a minute or two before serving with the rice and naan breads.

3

BEER SNACKS

This is the dirty kind of vegan, not the wholesome green, low-carb, gluten-free, sugar-free, fun-free kind. This is tofu deep-fried in beer, peanuts, and potato chips. It's disgusting in the most delicious of ways, and something for all the tofu-dissenters who think it's boring. Avoid using a beer that's very bitter, or anything with fruit in it—good choices include most Lagers, Amber Ales, and Porters. You could serve it with Imperial Stout Ketchup (see page 178) and/or Vegan Beer Mayo (see page 179).

BEER-AND-PEANUT-BATTERED TOFU

Vegan

Serves 2–4

Takes 15 minutes

Eat it with: any beer you like

14oz (400g) extra-firm tofu or smoked tofu

3 tablespoons all-purpose (plain) flour

¾ cup (90g) chickpea/gram flour (or all-purpose/plain flour)

Scant ¾ cup (180ml) beer

½ cup (50g) roasted salted peanuts, crushed

½ cup (50g) potato chips (crisps), crushed (salted or spicy are best)

Oil, for deep-frying

Cut the tofu into large rectangles, roughly 2 x 2in (5 x 5cm), and ¾in (2cm) thick. Wrap in paper towels or a kitchen towel and press it beneath a heavy weight—I put a chopping board on top then a bowl or pan to press it down. Leave for 5 minutes, then unwrap and rewrap in fresh paper or towel, and press for another 5 minutes. You want the tofu to be as dry as possible.

While the tofu is being pressed, line up three plates or bowls. In the first, put the all-purpose (plain) flour. In the second, mix the chickpea/gram flour and the beer to make the beer batter. In the third, mix the crushed peanuts and potato chips.

In a large pan, heat the oil to 325–350°F (170–180°C). While it warms up, unwrap the tofu and pat it as dry as possible. Working with one piece at a time, and keeping one hand as clean as possible (keep it out of the batter), dip each piece of tofu in the flour, making sure it's all lightly dusted, then put it into the beer batter, coating it all, then cover it in peanuts and potato chips. Repeat with a few more pieces, then fry them in small batches for 2–4 minutes, or until golden brown. Remove from the oil and drain on kitchen paper. Repeat for the rest of the tofu. Eat immediately.

IMPERIAL STOUT KETCHUP

Vegan

Makes 2 x 12oz (280ml) jars

Takes 1½ hours

1 tablespoon olive oil or rapeseed oil

1 white onion, diced

1 garlic clove, crushed

2 tablespoons tomato paste (purée)

¼ cup (50g) packed (soft) brown sugar

¼ cup (65ml) vinegar (malt, red wine, or cider)

1 teaspoon onion powder

1 teaspoon salt

½ teaspoon ground black pepper

Pinch of allspice

Pinch of ground cinnamon

Pinch of cayenne pepper

2 x 14oz (400g) cans whole peeled tomatoes

⅓ cup (100ml) Imperial Stout

I love Imperial Stout in this recipe as it adds an umami-like richness and some of its own natural sweetness. However, you can make this ketchup with any Stout or even a Belgian Quadrupel—just avoid a hop-bitter beer or one with too much roasted bitterness. The ketchup will keep in the refrigerator for a few months.

Soften the onion in the oil for a few minutes, then add the garlic and tomato paste (purée). Cook for a couple of minutes. Add the rest of the ingredients, saving the beer till last. Bring to a simmer, then let it bubble for around 1 hour or until really thick and rich. Taste and adjust the seasoning (the flavor will mellow when you refrigerate it), then allow to cool before blending to make it smooth and pouring into the clean jars.

VEGAN BEER MAYO

This is a surprising and excellent vegan mayo. I've made it with many beers, and sweeter, smoother dark ales or light and spicy Belgian ales are best, while IPAs and very bitter beers don't work very well (though they can be fine if used in something like the IPA Slaw on page 143). Feel free to add extra flavors to this, such as chili powder or hot sauce, garlic, or dried spices or herbs. This mayo will keep for a few days in the refrigerator, but it's best eaten fresh.

Vegan

Makes a 12oz (280ml) jar

Takes 5 minutes

12oz (350g) silken tofu

3 tablespoons beer

1 tablespoon lemon juice

1 tablespoon apple cider vinegar

1 teaspoon salt

1 teaspoon nutritional yeast

½ teaspoon Dijon mustard

½ teaspoon onion powder

Pinch of white sugar

Put everything in a high-speed blender and mix until thick and smooth. Season to taste, then pour into a clean jar, put the lid on, and refrigerate.

DRUNK EGGS

This is a beer-marinated version of a ramen egg, replacing the mirin with a dark beer, ideally a Porter, Dark Lager, or Dubbel. You can eat it on its own as a snack, put it in some noodles, or serve with fried rice.

Not vegan

Makes 6

Takes 20–30 mins (plus 24–48 hours marinating time)

Eat it with: Porter, Dark Lager, or Amber Lager

6 eggs

⅓ cup (100ml) soy sauce

⅓ cup (100ml) dashi, vegetable stock, or water

3 tablespoons superfine (caster) sugar

2 tablespoons rice vinegar

1 star anise

1 garlic clove, peeled

1 teaspoon chili flakes (optional)

100ml Porter

Boil the eggs for 6–8 minutes, depending on whether you want the yolk soft-set or hard. Remove from the water and let cool, then peel.

In a small pan, heat up all the rest of the ingredients apart from the beer, bring up to a simmer, then remove from the heat and allow to cool. When cooled to room temperature, pour into a large bowl or container (or even a freezer bag), and add the eggs and the beer. Marinate in the fridge for 24–48 hours, turning occasionally.

These classic crisp and chewy pretzels are made using a lot of Pale Lager, and that gives them a deeper flavor and color. Choose a lager with low bitterness, such as a classic Munich Helles, a Franconian Amber Lager, or even just a mainstream lager. For authentic pretzels, you should boil them in a solution of baking soda and water before baking, and it's worth including this step for the best results. They are best the day you make them, but can be reheated the next day in a warm oven for 5 minutes.

LAGERBIER PRETZELS

Vegan option

Makes 8 pretzels

Takes 3 hours (active cooking time 30–45 minutes)

Eat it with: any lager you love

2 tablespoons (30ml) warm water

1 teaspoon instant yeast

2 tablespooons (25g) butter, melted

2 tablespoons malt extract
(or 1 tablespoon packed (soft) light brown sugar)

3¼ cups (450g) strong white bread flour

1 teaspoon salt

¾ cup (210ml) lager at room temperature

8½ cups (2 liters) water

4 tablespoons baking soda (bicarbonate of soda)

Salt flakes

Combine the warm water, yeast, butter, and malt extract (or sugar) and leave for a couple of minutes.

Put the flour and salt in a large bowl and stir in the lager and then the yeast mix. Combine and knead, either with a stand mixer or with your hands on a lightly floured surface. You want a soft, smooth dough, and that will take about 10 minutes. Place in a floured bowl, cover, and leave for 1 hour.

Line two large baking sheets with baking parchment, and clear some space in your refrigerator (or in a cool space).

Knock back the dough and divide into 8 equal pieces. It's now time to roll the dough. This might sound a little confusing, but it's pretty easy—search online for some videos to help if you're unsure. Working one at a time (while keeping the other pieces covered), roll out a dough ball until it's thin and roughly 20in (50cm) long. Take the two end pieces, hold them up in front of you like a large U shape, wrap the ends twice around each other, then join them with the fatter central part of the pretzel. Place on the baking sheet and cover with a damp towel. Repeat for all the pretzels, then place in the refrigerator or a cool space for 1 hour.

Preheat the oven to 425°F/220°C/Gas 7. Mix the water and baking soda (bicarbonate of soda) in a large pan over a high heat and bring to a boil (add the baking soda before it starts to boil or it can get a bit lively). Once lightly boiling, take one pretzel at a time and place into the water, giving it 30 seconds on each side, then remove, allow to air-dry briefly (about 10 seconds), then place back on the baking sheet. Repeat for all the pretzels.

Score the fat part of the pretzels with a very sharp knife, then sprinkle with plenty of salt flakes. Bake in the preheated oven for 10–15 minutes until the pretzels have turned a deep golden brown.

OBATZDA

Obatzda is a traditional beer-hall and beer-garden snack in Bavaria and Franconia. It combines cheese and butter with lager, spices, and onion, and you eat it with bread. Here is a classic cheese version, along with a vegan version—it took me four attempts, but I finally got it right and it's great. I recommend serving this with Lagerbier Pretzels (page 180), but it's good with any bread you like—a slice of German-style rye bread would be the most authentic. The recipes make one large serving, which is enough to share between a few people. Use a Pale Lager or Amber Lager that's low in bitterness and ideally with a little malt sweetness. It should be eaten the day you make it, but can be made a few hours in advance and refrigerated until needed. The vegan version is better made in advance, as it becomes firmer in the refrigerator.

Vegan option
Makes one large serving to share
Takes 5 minutes
Eat it with: your favorite lagers

CLASSIC OBATZDA

9oz (250g) Camembert or Brie

½ cup (100g) soft cream cheese

7 tablespoons (100g) butter

6 tablespoons (90ml) lager

½ teaspoon sweet paprika

½ teaspoon salt

¼ white onion, finely diced

½ red onion, sliced into thin rings, to serve

Chives, to serve (optional)

Mash everything, apart from the red onion and chives, together with a fork until it's a thick, scoopable, and spreadable consistency. Taste it and adjust the seasoning to your preference.

Refrigerate until needed, and top with red onion rings and chive,s to serve.

VEGAN OBATZDA

7oz (200g) firm tofu

¼ cup (30g) cashew nuts

7 tablespoons (100g) vegan butter (not margarine)

¼ cup (50g) vegan cream cheese (or 3 tablespoons vegan cream)

6 tablespoons (90ml) lager

3 tablespoons nutritional yeast

2 tablespoon white wine vinegar (or apple cider vinegar)

1 tablespoon white miso

1 teaspoon salt

½ teaspoon sweet paprika

½ teaspoon onion powder

¼ white onion, finely diced

½ red onion, sliced into thin rings, to serve

Chives, to serve (optional)

In a high-powered blender, combine everything apart from the red onion and chives. When thick and smooth, taste it and adjust the seasoning to your preference—it should be rich, creamy, thick, and savory. Stir in the white onion.

Refrigerate until needed, and top with red onion rings and chives, to serve.

These are somewhere between garlic focaccia, dough balls, pull-apart bread, and skillet pizza, and they are incredible beer snacks. I designed them with American IPAs in mind, where those American hops cut through the richness and love the flavor of garlic. The pizza balls are good on their own, or you could make a batch of Beer Marinara Sauce (see page 127) to dip them into. Most beers work in the dough for this recipe, but I recommend a malty lager for the best flavor.

GARLIC PIZZA BALLS

Vegan option

Serves 4 as a snack

Takes 4 hours (active cooking time 30–45 minutes)

Eat it with: Pale Ale or American IPA

1 teaspoon instant yeast

1 teaspoon white sugar

2 tablespoons (30ml) warm water

1½ scant cups (200g) Tipo "00" flour or strong bread flour, plus extra for dusting

1 teaspoon salt

1 teaspoon dried garlic

3 tablespoons extra-virgin olive oil

6 tablespoons (90ml) beer

For the garlic butter

4 tablespoons (60g) butter

2–3 garlic cloves, crushed

½ teaspoon each salt, garlic powder, onion powder, white pepper, and chili flakes

Combine the yeast, sugar, and warm water in a cup and stir together. Leave for a couple of minutes. Meanwhile, in a large bowl, combine the flour, salt, dried garlic, and 1 tablespoon of the oil. Stir in the beer to create a thick dough, then add the water-yeast mix and combine. Knead on a lightly floured surface for around 5 minutes until you have a soft and elastic dough. Place in an oiled bowl, cover, and leave in a warm place to rise for 1–2 hours.

Put the remaining 2 tablespoons of oil in a large ovenproof skillet (frying pan). Knock back the dough and give it a quick knead. Divide it into 10–12 pieces and roll into balls, then place them in the skillet with enough space between them to allow them to prove and increase in size. Cover loosely with plastic wrap (clingfilm) and leave to prove for 1–2 hours—they are ready when all the dough balls are touching and roughly double in size.

About 30 minutes before cooking, preheat the oven to 475°F/250°C/Gas 9 (or as hot as it goes—you can cook these in a pizza oven if you have one). Make the garlic butter by gently melting the butter with the garlic and seasoning in a small pan. Once melted, remove from the heat.

Uncover the skillet and put it over a high heat on the stovetop. Add about half of the garlic butter and as soon as it starts to sizzle, place the skillet in the oven for 10–12 minutes, until the dough balls are golden brown. When done, remove the (very hot) skillet and pour over the rest of the garlic butter. Serve hot, with cold beer.

A filthy plateful of fries loaded with spicy jackfruit and topped with pickled chilis, diced onion, and American mustard. This is a dish you know you should stop eating but just can't—or won't. It should sear with the vinegar heat of chili and mustard, crunch with onion, and be spicy with the jackfruit. You can replace the jackfruit with a mixture of cooked beans or vegan mince, if you prefer, but I think jackfruit works well to soak up all the flavors in the dish. I use Imperial Stout because it's big and rich and bold, but you could use a regular Porter or Stout.

IMPERIAL JACKFRUIT DIRTY FRIES

Vegan

Serves 4 as a snack

Takes 1–1¼ hours

Eat it with: American Amber Ale, Pale Ale, or American IPA

1 white onion, diced

1 tablespoon oil

2 garlic cloves, crushed

2 tablespoons tomato paste (purée)

½ teaspoon each ground cumin, cinnamon, paprika, cayenne pepper, dried chili (more if you like it hot), and white sugar

2 x 14oz (400g) cans young jackfruit (not in syrup), drained

10½oz (300g) passata

Scant ¾ cup (180ml) dark beer

4 tablespoons soy sauce

1 tablespoon barley or brown rice miso

1 tablespoon cacao powder (optional)

Salt and pepper

To serve

Fries

½ white onion, finely diced

American mustard

Ketchup (or Imperial Stout Ketchup, see page 178)

Pickled jalapeños (or IPA Pickled Chilis, see page 156)

American cheese (optional)

In a large pan over a medium heat, soften the onion in the oil for around 5 minutes, then add the garlic and the tomato paste (purée) and cook for a couple of minutes. Add the spices and sugar and stir, then add the jackfruit and break it apart with a wooden spoon or potato masher. Cook for a few minutes.

Add the passata and stir for 1 minute, until it starts bubbling, then add the beer and stir. Add the soy sauce, miso, and cacao powder and bring to a simmer. Let simmer for 45–60 minutes until it's really thick and becoming dry in the pan. Season to taste—it can handle a lot of seasoning, so you might want more salt and more chili.

Cook the fries however you like (I slice potatoes, pour over some oil, salt, pepper, and garlic powder, then bake at 400°F/200°C/Gas 6 for around 45 minutes).

To serve, smother the fries in the jackfruit sauce, then top with the diced white onion, the rest of the condiments, and some American cheese, if you wish (the Beer Nozzarella on page 190 could work here if you want to make your own). Then get dirty.

I won't pretend these are "wings" like a lot of vegan recipes do, but they are kind of inspired by them. What you get here are nuggets of cauliflower which are crispy, chewy, spicy, sweet, and addictive. They are a great beer snack, or you could serve them with rice, steamed green veg, and tofu as a main (make extra Korean sauce and bake the tofu in that). I cook this with a Stout or Porter, but you could use a Pale Lager or Dark Lager. If you wanted to make Buffalo Cauliflower Bites, follow the first part of the recipe, then make a sauce from loads of hot sauce, such as Frank's, and some butter, then smother the cauliflower bites and bake as below.

KOREAN CAULIFLOWER BITES

Vegan

Serves 2–4

Takes 45 minutes

Best with: Pale Lager, Dark Lager, or Double IPA

¾ cup (100g) all-purpose (plain) flour or chickpea/gram flour

⅔ cup (150ml) beer

½ teaspoon each salt, black pepper, garlic powder, and chili powder (ideally gochugaru)

1 cauliflower, cut into large florets

2 or 3 scallions (spring onions), finely diced, to serve

Toasted sesame seeds, to serve

For the Korean sauce

3 tablespoons gochujang (Korean red chili paste)

6 tablespoons beer

3 tablespoons maple or agave syrup

3 tablespoons rice wine vinegar

2 tablespoons sesame oil

2 tablespoons soy sauce

1 tablespoon tahini (optional)

1 teaspoon chili powder (ideally gochugaru)

½ teaspoon garlic powder

Preheat the oven to 425°F/220°C/Gas 7. Line two large baking sheets with baking parchment.

In a large bowl, combine the flour, beer, and seasoning and stir into a batter. Add the cauliflower florets to the batter, making sure they are all covered, then spread them out on the baking sheet, ensuring they aren't touching each other. Bake for 15 minutes.

Meanwhile, make the sauce in a large bowl by stirring together all the ingredients.

After 15 minutes, remove the cauliflower from the oven and turn the temperature down to 400°F/200°C/Gas 6. Put the cauliflower into the bowl of sauce and make sure that the bites are thoroughly covered.

Put the bites back on the baking sheets and cook for another 15–25 minutes or until they're sticky, rich, thick, and starting to turn dark brown. Remove from the oven, scatter over scallions (spring onions) and sesame seeds, and eat while they're hot.

BEER NOZZARELLA

Vegan

Makes 1 block of cheese

Takes 15 minutes (plus setting time)

Eat it with: Pale Lager, Dark Lager, or Double IPA

¼ cup cashew nuts

⅔ cup (150ml) beer

⅓ cup (100ml) oat milk

7 tablespoons (100g) butter (or flavorless coconut oil)

2 tablespoons apple cider vinegar

4 tablespoons nutritional yeast

1 tablespoon white miso

1½ teaspoons salt

3 tablespoons tapioca starch

1½ tablespoons agar-agar powder

This "Nozzarella" has a taste between mozzarella and something nutty like Edam. Why bother? Because it's a great cheese alternative and it's made with beer. It's good on its own and in quesadillas (see page 192), or fried, as in Czech Fried Beer Cheese (opposite) and Beer Cheese Fries (below). It needs a couple of special ingredients to help it become firm and stretchy, otherwise it's simple. I typically use a Pale Lager that's low in bitterness. If you want to make something more like feta, just use 1 less tablespoon of nutritional yeast, add an extra 2 tablespoons of vinegar, and use a Gueuze or other funky Wild Ale.

Put everything apart from the tapioca starch and agar-agar powder in a high-powered blender and blitz until thick and smooth. Taste it and adjust the seasoning—you can add more of anything you want here to get the desired taste for what you're serving it with. When you're happy with it, add the tapioca starch and agar-agar and blend for another few seconds.

Transfer the mixture to a small pan over a medium heat and stir constantly as it warms up. Within a minute or two it'll look like it's getting stuck and lumpy at the bottom, but keep on stirring and it'll become a sticky, thick, stringy, paste-like consistency as you cook it for 6–8 minutes.

Transfer to a bowl, container, or loaf tin, cover, and refrigerate for at least 4 hours to get firmer. It will keep in the refrigerator for a day or two.

BEER CHEESE FRIES

Vegan

Serves 2–4 as a snack

Takes 30 minutes

Eat it with: any beer

This is the vegan version of mozzarella sticks. This cheese will be quite soft when cooked, and has a flavor and texture that remind me of cheese croquettes. You can bake these, if you want, but they don't hold their texture so well (they do still taste great though)—just bake at 425°F/220°C/Gas 7 for about 15 minutes or until deep golden brown. Serve with some Beer Marinara Sauce (see page 127) to dip them into.

Beer Nozzarella (opposite, and use an American lager or Amber Ale in the recipe)

Beer Marinara Sauce (see page 127)

Vegetable oil, for deep-frying

2 tablespoons all-purpose (plain) flour

½ cup (60g) chickpea/gram flour (or all-purpose/plain flour)

½ cup (120ml) American lager or Amber ale

1 teaspoon salt

2 cups (75g) panko breadcrumbs

½ teaspoon onion powder

½ teaspoon garlic powder

½ teaspoon chili powder

heaped ¼ teaspoon dried oregano

½ teaspoon pepper

Make the cheese at least 4 hours in advance. About 1 hour before you want to cook, slice the cheese into sticks and place them on a tray in the freezer, making sure they are spaced apart so they don't freeze together.

Make the Beer Marinara Sauce.

When ready to cook, heat the vegetable oil to about 350°F/180°C in a large pan for deep-frying. Line up three plates or bowls. In the first, put the all-purpose (plain) flour. In the second, mix the chickpea/gram flour, beer, and half the salt to make a batter. In the third, put the breadcrumbs and the rest of the seasoning. Take a Beer Nozzarella stick and dip it in the flour, then the batter, then cover in the breadcrumbs. Repeat for the rest of the sticks.

Deep-fry the sticks for a few minutes until golden brown. Serve with the Beer Marinara Sauce.

CZECH FRIED BEER CHEESE

Vegan

Serves 2

Takes 30 minutes

Eat it with: Czech Lager or Pale Ale

Beer Nozzarella (opposite, and use a Pale Czech Lager in the recipe)

2 tablespoons all-purpose (plain) flour

3 tablespoons chickpea/gram flour (or all-purpose/plain flour)

½ cup (120ml) Pale Czech Lager

½ teaspoon onion powder

½ teaspoon garlic powder

½ teaspoon salt

Pinch of marjoram (optional)

⅔ cup (50g) breadcrumbs (golden breadcrumbs are classic, but you could use panko for more crunch)

Vegetable or rapeseed oil, to fry

Fries, to serve

Smažený sýr is a traditional Czech beer snack and, often, one of the few vegetarian options on a menu. It's breaded and fried cheese, usually an Edam style. It'll be served with fries and tartare sauce (it's not health food) and it's great with a cold Czech lager. This version uses the Beer Nozzarella opposite, and you could also serve this in a bread roll.

Make the cheese at least 4 hours in advance. About 1 hour before you want to cook, slice the cheese into rectangles or small "steaks" roughly ¾in (2cm) thick and place them in the freezer, making sure they are spaced apart so they don't freeze together.

Line up three plates or bowls. In the first, put the all-purpose (plain) flour. In the second, mix the chickpea/gram flour, beer, and seasoning into a batter with a consistency of light (single) cream. In the third, put the breadcrumbs. Take a piece of Beer Nozzarella and dip it in the flour, then the batter, then the breadcrumbs. Repeat for the rest of the cheese.

Put several tablespoons of oil in a large, deep skillet (frying pan) over a medium-high heat. Shallow-fry the cheese pieces in batches until golden brown, flipping halfway through—it should be cooked within a couple of minutes. Place on some paper towels to remove any excess oil before serving with fries.

Use the Beer Nozzarella recipe on page 190 in these quesadillas, which use tortillas made with lager. These tortillas also make great wraps, they can be used as a quicker, no-ferment alternative to Beer Naan Breads (see page 112), and if you have too many you can slice them up and bake them to make nachos. You can make the tortillas a few hours or a day in advance, store them wrapped in plastic wrap (clingfilm) or aluminum foil, and then reheat them.

LAGER TORTILLA QUESADILLAS

Vegan option

Serves 4

Takes 1 hour

Eat it with: Amber Ale, Pale Ale, or IPA

For the tortillas

2¼ cups (300g) all-purpose (plain) flour

2 teaspoons salt

3 tablespoons vegetable or rapeseed oil

6 tablespoons (90ml) boiling water

6 tablespoons (90ml) lager at room temperature

For the quesadillas

Beer Nozzarella (or regular cheese)

Any extra fillings you like: diced onion, sweetcorn, black beans, grilled vegetables, pickled chili, sliced avocado, etc.

Salsa and fresh lime, to serve

First, make the tortillas. Combine all the ingredients in a bowl and, making sure it's not too hot to touch, knead for five minutes on a lightly floured surface. Place in a clean bowl, cover with or wrap in plastic wrap (clingfilm) and leave for 15 minutes.

Divide the dough into 8 equal pieces. On a floured surface, roll out the balls with a rolling pin until they are as flat and round as possible.

Heat a large pan on the stovetop over a medium-high heat, then place a piece of rolled-out dough into it. Cook for a minute or so, until bubbles appear on the surface, then flip it over and cook on the other side for another minute. While the tortilla is cooking, roll out the next one. When it's done, place on a clean kitchen towel or inside some aluminum foil. Repeat with the rest of the dough.

Have everything set up in front of you to make the quesadillas. Place a tortilla in a large, dry skillet (frying pan) over a medium heat. Cover one half of it with the cheese and whatever fillings you like—my favorite is diced white onion and IPA Pickled Chilis (see page 156), but also great are black beans, sweetcorn, and roasted vegetables. Fold over the tortilla to create a half-moon shape. Fry for a couple of minutes then flip over and cook on the other side for a few more minutes. Eat immediately with salsa and fresh lime, or keep it warm while you make some more—you can cook two quesadillas in the same pan.

IPA BHAJI BAKES & MANGO IPA CHUTNEY

Vegan

Makes 8

Takes 40 minutes

Eat it with: Hazy Pale Ale, Hazy IPA, or Pilsner

For the chutney

1 fresh mango, peeled and diced (about ⅔ cup/200g)

1 garlic clove, crushed

½in (1cm) piece of fresh ginger, peeled and grated

3 tablespoons superfine (caster) sugar

Pinch of cumin seeds

Pinch of chili flakes

1 teaspoon salt

Juice of ½ lime

4 tablespoons (60ml) white wine vinegar or apple cider vinegar

2 tablespoons (30ml) Hazy IPA

For the bhajis

3 tablespoons vegetable oil

Heaped ¾ cup (100g) chickpea/gram flour

4–6 tablespoons (60–90ml) Hazy IPA

1 teaspoon salt

½ teaspoon each ground cumin, ground coriander, ground turmeric, chili powder or cayenne pepper, and black pepper

Pinch of cinnamon

Pinch of fennel seeds, crushed

1 large carrot, grated (about ¾ cup/100g)

1 large (or 2 small) cooked beets (beetroot), grated (about ¾ cup/100g)

1 large (or 2 small) white onions, cut into rings

These are similar to onion bhajis, but they have a more bread-like texture, as they're baked instead of fried, plus they use carrots and beets (beetroot) as well as the onions. I use a sweeter Hazy IPA in this recipe, but you could replace that with a Pale Lager or Wheat Beer. The chutney is a quick one designed as a dipping sauce for the bhajis and it also uses the beer—I recommend making it a few hours in advance and serving it cold, but you can serve it warm if you prefer. The bhajis taste good hot or cold, and will keep for a day or two in a sealed container in the refrigerator.

First, make the chutney. Put the mango, garlic, ginger, and sugar in a pan over a medium heat and cook until the sugar dissolves. Add the rest of the ingredients, saving the beer till last, then simmer until it's thick and sticky, and the mango is very soft. Set aside to cool.

Preheat the oven to 400°F/200°C/Gas 6 and line a large baking sheet with baking parchment and 2 tablespoons of the oil. In a large bowl, combine the flour, 1 tablespoon of oil, and enough beer for it to form a thick batter. Stir in the spices and seasoning.

Squeeze out excess water from the carrot and beets (beetroot) and add to the batter along with the onion. Stir into a thick mix, adding more beer if necessary—it should be thick enough to shape with your hands into balls.

Shape the mixture into 8 balls and place on the baking sheet. Bake for 30 minutes, or until golden brown and properly cooked through.

STOUT MUSHROOM BAO

Vegan

Makes 8–10 bao

**Takes 3+ hours
(active cooking time
30–45 minutes)**

**Eat it with: Stout,
Belgian Dubbel, or
Dark Lager**

For the bao dough

½ cup (125ml) warm water

1 teaspoon white sugar

1 teaspoon instant yeast

1 teaspoon vegetable or rapeseed oil

2 cups (250g) all-purpose (plain) flour

½ teaspoon salt

For the Stout mushroom filling

½ white onion, diced

1 tablespoon sesame oil

2 garlic cloves, crushed

7½ cups (500g) mushrooms, finely chopped

1 carrot, very finely diced into small cubes

1 tablespoon vegetable or rapeseed oil

3 tablespoons soy sauce

2 tablespoons black (Chinkiang) vinegar

2 tablespoons packed (soft) brown sugar

1 tablespoon crunchy peanut or almond butter

½ teaspoon Chinese five spice

4 tablespoons (60ml) Stout or Dark Ale

1 tablespoon cornstarch (cornflour)

Inspired by *char siu bao*, these have a rich filling made with mushrooms and Stout, though you could use any sweeter dark beer. The bao aren't the easiest things to fold up on your first attempt, so you might want to find a video online to give you some tips— having a few scruffy bao is part of the fun, though. You'll need a bamboo steamer to make these.

Start by making the dough. Combine the water, sugar, yeast, and oil in a mixing pitcher (jug) and leave for a few minutes. Put the flour and salt in a large bowl, then add the wet ingredients and combine into a dough. Knead on a lightly floured surface for about 5 minutes, or until it's nice and smooth. Put it back in the bowl, cover with plastic wrap (clingfilm), and leave to rise in a warm place for 1–2 hours.

While the dough is proving, make the filling. Soften the onion in the sesame oil for a couple of minutes, then add the garlic, mushrooms, and carrot. Stir around the pan and increase the heat to allow the mushrooms to soften and release their water—the final mix should be dry, and you're going to be adding a lot of liquid, so this whole process will take some time.

After around 10–15 minutes, add the remaining ingredients, apart from the cornstarch (cornflour), and continue to cook until you have a rich and dry mixture—about another 15 minutes. Put the cornstarch into a bowl, pour in some of the liquid from the pan and stir into a thick paste, then add it to the mushrooms and cook for another couple of minutes, until it's really thick. Keep warn until needed.

Cut out 10 pieces of baking parchment (each piece should be about 3 x 3in/7.5 x 7.5cm).

Take the dough and knead for a few seconds. Divide the dough into 8–10 even pieces. One at a time, roll out the dough pieces into an oval, about 5in (13cm) across and ⅛in (3mm) thick.Place each bao on a piece of baking parchment, brush over a little oil and fold it in half. Repeat for all the bao, covering the made ones with a kitchen towel so they don't dry out. Set aside for 15 minutes after you finish shaping the final bun.

When the dough has risen, prepare the steamer by half-filling a large pan (which your steamer baskets will fit in) with water and bringing it to a boil. When the water is boiling, place 2 or 3 bao in each basket (they'll expand), and steam for 6–8 minutes. Repeat until all the bao are cooked.

Open up the bao and fill with the mushrooms (which you might want to reheat first.) Serve on their own or with some crispy chili oil on the side.

4

BAKING AND DESSERTS

RASPBERRY BEER DOUGHNUTS

Vegan option

Makes 6–8

Takes 2+ hours (active
cooking time is 15–30
minutes)

Eat it with: raspberry beer or
Imperial Stout

For the doughnuts

¼ cup (50ml) milk

3½ tablespoons (50g) butter

2 tablespoons malt extract or superfine
(caster) sugar

1 teaspoon dried yeast

1 cup (125g) all-purpose (plain) flour
and 1 scant cup (125g) strong bread
flour (or 2 cups/250g all-purpose/
plain flour)

⅓ cup (100ml) raspberry beer

1 teaspoon vanilla extract

¾ teaspoon salt

Vegetable oil, to deep-fry

Superfine (caster) sugar (optional)

For the jam

1½ cups (200g) fresh raspberries

6 tablespoons white sugar

4 tablespoons (60ml) raspberry beer

1 teaspoon vanilla extract

Juice of ½ lemon

1 tablespoon cornstarch (cornflour)

For the glaze

1 scant cup (125g) confectioners'
(icing) sugar

3–4 tablespoons raspberry beer

1 teaspoon vanilla extract

Do you like your doughnuts round, covered in sugar, and filled with jam? Or are you a glazed ring doughnut fan? Would you go with a double whammy of glazed and filled with jam? Whatever way you prefer, there are options for you here with these beer doughnuts. The ring doughnuts are lighter in texture and are great dipped in raspberry jam, while it's hard to beat a big, fat sugary doughnut that's filled with loads of jam. I've tried these fried and baked, and the fried ones are definitely better. They are still good when baked, but more bready. Just bake at 400°F/200°C/Gas 6 for about 15 minutes.

For the doughnuts, heat the milk, butter, and malt extract or sugar in a small pan gently so that the butter melts. Allow to cool to hand-temperature, then add the dried yeast. Stir to combine and leave for about 5 minutes.

In a large bowl, mix together the flour, beer, vanilla extract, and salt, then add the milk mixture. Combine into a dough and then knead for about 5 minutes—a stand mixer will help here as it's quite a wet dough, but you can do it by hand (you might need to add a little extra flour, but the more flour you add, the breadier the doughnut will be). Place in a bowl, cover with plastic wrap (clingfilm), and leave to rise in a warm place for 1–2 hours, until the dough has doubled in size.

continued overleaf

When the dough has risen, knock it back and roll it out on a lightly floured surface into a rectangle about ⅝in (1.5cm) thick. Line a deep baking sheet with 6–8 squares of baking parchment, each a bit bigger than the doughnuts will be. Using a doughnut or cookie cutter (or just a small beer glass), cut out as many dough rounds as you can, then, if you want a ring doughnut, cut out a smaller hole roughly 1¼in (3cm) across in the middle (this will close up a bit as the dough expands during proving and cooking).

Place one doughnut on each piece of baking parchment on the baking sheet. Roll up the leftover dough and make extra doughnuts (or make some smaller doughnut "holes"). Cover the baking sheet with plastic wrap (clingfilm) or a clean towel and leave to rise in a warm place for 45–60 minutes, until the doughnuts are doubled in size.

If filling with jam, make it now. Put all the jam ingredients, apart from the cornstarch (cornflour), in a small pan over a medium heat. Bring to a simmer and cook for around 15 minutes until you have a thick, jam-like consistency, stirring regularly so it doesn't stick to the pan. When it's almost done, put the cornstarch in a small bowl and pour in a tablespoon or two of the jam liquid, stir to a thick paste, then add it back to the main mixture and cook for one more minute. Pour into a clean bowl and allow to cool and thicken.

When the doughnuts are ready to be cooked, get your deep-fryer or pan ready and heat the oil to 350°F/180°C. If you're glazing the doughnuts, prepare the glaze while the oil heats up. Place the confectioners' (icing) sugar in a jug or bowl and mix the beer and vanilla extract in until it's the right consistency to stick to a doughnut—so not too runny, but runny enough to pour. If you want to sugar-coat the doughnuts, prepare a bowl with some sugar in.

Transfer two or three doughnuts from the sheet into the fryer, trying not to push any air out of them as you do so (that's why they're on baking parchment). Cook for a couple of minutes on each side, or until golden. Remove from the oil and place on paper towels to remove any excess oil. Repeat for the other doughnuts.

If glazing the doughnuts, do so while they are still warm: dip them in the glaze, then set on a wire rack and pour extra glaze over them—the glaze will get firmer as it cools. Similarly, sugar-coat them by rolling them in the sugar while still warm. If you want to fill them with jam, let them cool first. Then push a chopstick or the handle end of a teaspoon into each doughnut and fill it with jam using a piping bag.

I couldn't resist this one. It's a classic—even basic—lemon drizzle cake, but it's made with a lager, playing on the idea of a shandy or Radler (a mix of lager and lemonade), while the top also adds some more beer, riffing on a British pub order of a "lager top," meaning a pint of lager with a dash of lemonade in it. I like to have some of the beer's bitterness come through in the flavor, as it cuts against the sweetness. I also add a lot of lemon juice and zest, because I like that it brings a more mature flavor. I made a version of this cake using an American IPA and a mix of orange and grapefruit juice and zest, and it was pretty good, with a strong citrusy bitterness—worth a try if that's your kind of thing. The cake will keep in an airtight container for a few days.

SHANDY CAKE WITH A LAGER TOP

Vegan

Serves 8

Takes 45 minutes

Eat it with: a bitter Pilsner or Belgian Tripel

2⅔ cups (350g) self-rising (self-raising) flour

2 tablespoons cornstarch (cornflour)

1 cup (200g) superfine (caster) sugar

1 teaspoon baking powder

5 tablespoons (75ml) lemon juice (about 3 lemons)

Zest of 1 lemon

⅔ cup (150ml) olive oil

1 cup (250ml) lager

For the lager top

Heaped ½ cup (100g) superfine (caster) sugar

2 tablespoons (30ml) lager

4 tablespoons (60ml) lemon juice (2–3 lemons)

Zest of ½ lemon

Preheat the oven to 350°F/180°C/Gas 4 and line a 1lb/8 x 4in (20.5 x 10cm) loaf pan with baking parchment.

In a large bowl, mix all the cake ingredients into a batter, then pour the batter into the pan (I told you it was basic). Bake for 30–40 minutes, or until golden brown and a skewer inserted in the middle comes out clean.

While the cake is still in the pan, and still warm, combine the lager top ingredients. Using a skewer, poke some holes in the top of the cake, then pour over the topping mix. Allow the cake to cool before removing from the pan and serving.

These use Quadrupel in the dough and to infuse flavor into some raisins (I'm a raisin-in-my-cinnamon-roll kinda guy). It makes a slab of cake that's great to eat warm on its own or with custard or cream, but is also great the next day when sticky and chewy. I find the rolls a little too sweet to drink with a Quadrupel, but they work well with a barrel-aged Stout.

QUADRUPEL CINNAMON ROLLS

Vegan option

Makes 10–12

Takes 4 hours (active cooking time 30 minutes)

Eat it with: barrel-aged Imperial Stout

Scant ¾ cup (180ml) Quadrupel plus 3 tablespoons (45ml)

⅓ cup (50g) raisins

¼ cup (60ml) milk

¾ cup (160g) butter, plus extra for greasing

3 tablespoons malt extract (or 2 tablespoons white sugar)

1 teaspoon dried instant yeast

3 cups (400g) all-purpose (plain) flour

½ teaspoon salt

½ cup (100g) packed (soft) light brown sugar

1 tablespoon ground cinnamon

In a cup or bowl, soak the raisins in 3 tablespoons of beer and set aside.

Warm the milk, ¼ cup (60g) of the butter, and the malt extract or white sugar in a pan over a low heat until the butter has melted. Remove from the heat, cool to blood temperature, and add the yeast. Stir to combine.

In a large bowl, combine the flour, salt, milk-yeast mix, and beer. Knead into a smooth dough—this should take around 10 minutes and can be done in a stand mixer or by hand on a lightly floured surface. Add more flour or liquid (beer or milk) if the dough is too wet or too dry. Place the dough in a bowl, cover with plastic wrap (clingfilm), and leave in a warm place to prove for 1–2 hours, until doubled in size.

After the proving time, butter a large baking dish, around 12 x 12in (30 x 30cm). Then, in a bowl, cream together the packed (soft) brown sugar (reserving 2 tablespoons) and the remaining butter. Add the ground cinnamon.

Knock back the dough, knead for a few seconds, then place on a lightly floured surface. Roll out into a large rectangle roughly 14in (35cm) long and ¼in (6mm) deep. Spread the sugar-butter-cinnamon mix over the dough, leaving a small gap at the edges. Take the raisins and squeeze out the beer, then spread the fruit over the top of the cinnamon mix.

Starting from the long side of the rectangle of dough, roll it up as tightly as possible, ensuring you don't lose any filling. Cut the roll into 10–12 even pieces and press them into the buttered dish, cut side down, leaving some space between them. Sprinkle the remaining 2 tablespoons of brown sugar over the top. Cover loosely with plastic wrap and leave to prove in a warm place for 30–60 minutes—they will be ready when all the dough has expanded to squash the rolls together.

Preheat the oven to 350°F/180°C/Gas 4. When the oven is hot, uncover the rolls and bake for 20–25 minutes. Leave to cool slightly before eating.

Malt loaf is a squidgy and sticky bread/cake that's loaded with dried fruit and made with malt extract. A lot of recipes call for the fruit to be soaked in black tea, but I'm soaking mine in beer to enhance the malt flavors. I use a Dark Mild which is sweetly malty and biscuity, but any dark, sweeter ale or lager will work well in this (avoid hop or roast bitterness, though). This loaf was better the day after I made it and stays good—improves, even—for a few days in an airtight container. It's common to eat it with butter spread on top. It's also good toasted, with almond butter.

MILD MALT LOAF

Vegan

Serves 6–8

Takes 1 hour 10 minutes

Eat it with: barley wine, Belgian Quadrupel, or a cup of tea

⅔ cup (150ml) Dark Mild or other dark beer, plus 1 tablespoon

1½ cups (200g) dark dried fruit (such as raisins and/or sultanas)

2 cups (250g) all-purpose (plain) flour (or a mix of all-purpose/plain, wholewheat/wholemeal, and spelt)

½ cup (100g) packed (soft) dark brown sugar

1 teaspoon baking powder

½ teaspoon baking soda (bicarbonate of soda)

½ teaspoon salt

9 tablespoons (135ml) malt extract (yes, nine tablespoons)

Preheat the oven to 350°F/180°C/Gas 4. Line a 1lb/8 x 4in (20.5 x 10cm) loaf pan with baking parchment. Soak the dried fruit in ⅔ cup (150ml) beer for a few minutes while you weigh out all the other ingredients.

In a bowl, combine the other ingredients, apart from the malt extract, then add the beer and dried fruit mixture and 8 tablespoons of malt extract and stir with a wooden spoon. Pour the batter into the loaf pan and bake for 55–60 minutes, until a skewer inserted into the middle comes out clean.

In a small bowl, stir together the remaining tablespoons of beer and malt extract and pour over the loaf to glaze. Allow the cake to cool slightly before turning it out of the pan, and ideally wait until it's at room temperature before you eat it (it really does get better, so wait if you can).

QUAD MUG CAKE AND OATMEAL RAISIN COOKIES

When you open a Belgian Quadrupel and pour it out into your glass, you usually leave behind a small amount of beer in the bottom of the bottle, as it contains some yeast sediment. This got me thinking about what I could do with that beer, rather than pouring it away, and that's where these two recipes come from. The Mug Cake is the easiest cake in the world—eat it immediately, either on its own or with cream or ice cream. The cookies are the thick and chewy type. Neither really tastes much of the beer, but that's not the point here.

QUAD MUG CAKE

Vegan option

Serves 1 (or 2 if you want to share it)

Takes 5 minutes

Eat it with: the Quad you made it with

1 tablespoon (15g) butter or flavorless coconut oil

1 tablespoon packed (soft) brown sugar

1 tablespoon maple syrup or malt extract

3 tablespoons all-purpose (plain) flour

3 tablespoons Quadrupel

1 tablespoon raisins or sultanas

¼ teaspoon baking powder

¼ teaspoon ground cinnamon

Pinch of salt

Put the butter or coconut oil in a large microwaveable mug. Put in the microwave for 10–15 seconds, until it melts. Remove the mug from the microwave and stir all the other ingredients into it, making sure they're all combined.

Put it back in the microwave on high power for 1½–2 minutes. Eat.

QUAD OATMEAL RAISIN COOKIES

Vegan option

Makes 10–12

Takes 20 minutes

Eat it with: Quadrupel, Imperial or Oatmeal Stout

⅓ cup (50g) raisins

3 tablespoons (45ml) beer

½ cup (120g) butter

⅔ cup (120g) brown sugar

1 scant cup (120g) all-purpose (plain) flour

Heaped ⅓ cup (50g) oats

1 teaspoon baking powder

1 teaspoon vanilla extract

1 teaspoon ground cinnamon

Pinch of allspice

Pinch of salt

Preheat the oven to 350°F/180°C/Gas 4. Line a baking sheet with baking parchment. Then combine the beer and raisins in a cup or bowl and leave to soak for a few minutes.

In a large bowl, cream together the butter and brown sugar with a wooden spoon. Then add all the other ingredients, including the beer and raisins, and stir to fully combine.

Scoop 10–12 balls of cookie dough onto the baking parchment and bake for 12–15 minutes. Allow to cool a little before you eat them. They'll keep in an airtight container for a few days.

TRIPEL APRICOT AND PISTACHIO CRUMBLE WITH TRIPEL AND APRICOT ICE CREAM

One evening, I was drinking a glass of Tripel and snacking on some salted pistachios and dried apricots. It was so good that I created several recipes using that combination, and this one was the best. I make it with Tripel Karmeliet as that's one of the sweeter, more honeyed versions of the style, and I picked out flavors in the dish to specifically match the beer.

Vegan option

Serves 4

Takes 45–60 minutes (plus the time to make the ice cream)

Eat it with: sweet Belgian Tripel, Hazy DIPA, or Irish Whiskey

For the ice cream

1 cup (120g) cashew nuts

10-12 dried apricots (ideally unsulfured)

6 tablespoons (90ml) oat milk (or milk of your choice)

4 tablespoons (60ml) Tripel

1 cup (250ml) oat cream or heavy (double) cream

6 tablespoons honey or agave syrup

¼ teaspoon orange zest

¼ teaspoon lemon zest

Pinch of salt

For the Tripel apricots

3 tablespoons (40g) butter

6 tablespoons honey, agave syrup, or packed (soft) light brown sugar

6 tablespoons (90ml) Tripel Karmeliet

4 dried apricots (ideally unsulfured), chopped

¼ teaspoon orange zest

¼ teaspoon lemon zest

2 cardamom pods, crushed open

4-6 fennel seeds

4-6 whole coriander seeds (don't replace with ground coriander, just omit if you don't have seeds)

1 crack of black pepper

8-10 fresh apricots, halved and pitted

For the pistachio crumble

¾ cup (100g) all-purpose (plain) flour

¼ cup (25g) ground almonds

4 tablespoons (60g) cold and cubed butter

5 tablespoons (60g) demerara sugar

½ cup (50g) salted pistachios (or add ½ teaspoon salt), shells removed, nuts crushed

1oz (25g) toasted hazelnuts, crushed

Make the ice cream in advance. Soak the cashew nuts and apricots in the oat milk and beer for 4–12 hours, then put them and all the other ingredients in a powerful blender and blitz until perfectly smooth. Transfer the mixture to an ice cream machine, or put into the freezer in a container and stir every hour to break up the ice chunks.

To make the Tripel apricots, preheat the oven to 350°F/180°C/Gas 4. In a small pan, gently melt the butter and honey, agave syrup, or sugar over a low heat for a minute or two (but don't let it get too warm), then add all the other ingredients, apart from the fresh apricots, and take it off the heat. Leave in

the pan to infuse all the flavors while you prepare the apricots and make the crumble.

Place the apricots in a 9in (24cm) baking dish, some flesh up, some skin up.

To make the crumble, put the flour, ground almonds, and butter in a bowl and rub together with your fingertips until it's a sand-like texture. Then add the sugar and the nuts and mix through.

Using a sieve, strain the spiced apricot mix over the fresh apricots. Sprinkle the crumble topping over the fruit and bake for 35–45 minutes, until bubbling from below and brown on top. Serve with the ice cream.

DOPPELBOCK KAISERSCHMARRN

Not vegan

Serves 4

Takes 30 minutes

Eat it with: Doppelbock, Quadrupel, or Weizenbock

Kaiserschmarrn are Bavarian shredded pancakes and make a light dessert thanks to the whipped eggs in the recipe. They are served with a fruit compote typically made from apples, plums, or cherries. I use a Doppelbock, Quadrupel, or Weizenbock in the recipe.

⅓ cup (50g) raisins

⅓ cup (100ml) Doppelbock, plus 2-3 tablespoons (30-45ml)

4 eggs, separated

2 tablespoons superfine (caster) sugar

1 heaped cup (150g) all-purpose (plain) flour

⅓ cup (100ml) milk (I use unsweetened almond milk)

1 teaspoon vanilla extract

Pinch of salt

2 tablespoons (30g) butter

Confectioners' (icing) sugar, to serve

Whipped cream, vanilla ice cream, or Beer Ice Cream (see opposite), to serve

For the compote

1 tablespoon (15g) butter

7oz (200g) fruit (such as apples, plums, cherries, or mixed berries), peeled if appropriate, pitted (stoned), and diced

2-3 tablespoons brown sugar (depending on fruit sweetness)

1 teaspoon vanilla extract

1 teaspoon ground cinnamon

5 tablespoons (75ml) Doppelbock or Quadrupel

Start by soaking the raisins in 2–3 tablespoons of beer, and set aside.

Make the compote by heating the butter, fruit, and sugar in a small pan, stirring until the sugar dissolves. Add the rest of the ingredients and stew until thick and soft—10–20 minutes, depending on the fruit—then set aside.

To make the Kaiserschmarrn, beat the egg whites into stiff peaks. In a separate large bowl, hand-whisk the egg yolks and the sugar until thick and creamy, then add the flour and the milk, whisking to combine. Add the rest of the beer, vanilla extract, and salt and whisk into a thick batter. Then, very carefully, fold in the egg whites.

In a large skillet (frying pan) with a lid, melt the butter over a low heat, then add the pancake batter so it's a thick layer about ⅜in (1cm) deep (it'll rise when you cook it, so you might want to use two pans or cook in two batches). Drain any excess beer from the raisins and sprinkle them over the pancake. Place the lid on the pan and cook over a low heat for 4–6 minutes, or until it's cooked enough to flip over, making sure it doesn't burn. Flip the pancake, put the lid on, and cook for another 4–6 minutes. Using a palette knife, spatula, or scissors, tear the pancake into small pieces, taking care not to damage the pan, and then cook for a further minute.

Dust over some confectioners' (icing) sugar and serve with the fruit compote and some whipped cream, vanilla ice cream, or your preferred flavor of Beer Ice Cream.

Here is a template for a simple vegan ice cream recipe that's really easy to adapt to different flavors and different beers. Below I've given some variations that really work, plus some of the recipes in this book also have a beer ice cream on the side—Bock and Hazelnut (see page 214), or Tripel and Apricot (see page 209). You can use an ice cream machine, if you have one, and it tastes best when it's still a little soft. If you don't have an ice cream machine, you can just make it in the freezer; it'll taste best after 4–5 hours of freezing, so plan ahead for that.

BEER ICE CREAM

Vegan option

Serves 4

Takes 5 minutes active cooking time (but needs preparing and freezing—8 hours)

1 cup (120g) cashew nuts

5 tablespoons (75ml) oat milk (or milk of choice)

5 tablespoons (75ml) beer

1 cup (250ml) cream—oat cream, vegan heavy (double) cream, or full-fat coconut milk

6 tablespoons maple syrup, honey, agave syrup, or malt extract

1 teaspoon vanilla extract

Pinch of salt

Any other flavorings

Soak the cashew nuts in the milk and beer for 4 hours, or overnight if making the next day.

Combine all the ingredients in a powerful blender and blitz until perfectly smooth.

Freeze in an ice cream machine, or put into the freezer in a container and stir every hour to break up the ice chunks.

IMPERIAL STOUT, CHOCOLATE AND COCONUT ICE CREAM

Use Imperial Stout for the beer and full-fat coconut milk for the cream, and add ¾ cup (75g) cacao powder.

BRUNE AND CINNAMON ICE CREAM

Use Belgian Brune or Quadrupel for the beer and oat cream for the cream, and add 1 teaspoon ground cinnamon and a pinch of allspice. Stir in a handful of raisins or sultanas after blending.

DOUBLE CHERRY ICE CREAM

Use Sweet Kriek or another cherry beer for the beer and oat cream or full-fat coconut milk for the cream. Use 4 tablespoons of maple syrup and 2 tablespoons Luxardo cherry syrup (or 6 tablespoons maple syrup, if you don't have Luxardo). Add 1 teaspoon ground cinnamon and ½ teaspoon almond extract. Stir in a handful of pitted (stoned) fresh cherries or dried cherries after blending.

Tart à la bière is a traditional regional recipe from the north of France and across into northern Belgium. It's an improbable recipe which pretty much just uses beer, sugar, and eggs, but it's a brilliant one—I made it out of curiosity, but I loved it. It's somewhere between an English egg custard tart and a brown-sugar pie, but with beer. I used Leffe Brune and it was a great choice—it has a brown-sugar sweetness and a depth of dried fruit. Most sweeter Belgian dark beers will work fine in this. Serve with thick heavy (double) cream, clotted cream, or the Brune and Cinnamon Ice Cream on page 211. And you can make your own pastry if you want—it's just a standard pie dough (shortcrust). There's no vegan option with this dessert, as the eggs are essential.

BEER TART

Not vegan

Serves 6–8

Takes 1 hour

Eat it with: Imperial Stout or Belgian Quadrupel

18oz (500g) pie dough (shortcrust pastry) or one 9in (23cm) ready-made pie crust

1 cup (200g) packed (soft) light brown sugar

3 eggs

1 cup (250ml) beer (French or Belgian Brune)

½ teaspoon ground cinnamon

½ teaspoon salt

Pinch of nutmeg

2 tablespoons (30g) butter, cubed

Preheat the oven to 350°F/180°C/Gas 4. If not using a ready-made pie crust, line a 9in (23cm) tart tin with pastry. Trim away any excess pastry, and prick the base several times with a fork. Line the tart with baking parchment and fill with baking beans. Bake for 15 minutes, then remove the beans and paper and bake for another 5 minutes.

In a large bowl, whisk together the sugar and eggs, then add the beer, ground cinnamon, salt, and nutmeg.

When the pastry is ready, remove from the oven and let stand for a minute or two, then pour in the sugar-egg-beer mix and dot the cubes of butter over the top. Bake for 30–35 minutes, then allow to cool for 30 minutes before serving. It's best eaten the day that it's made.

SALVATOR BANANA TART
WITH BOCK & HAZELNUT ICE CREAM

Vegan option

Serves 4

Takes 15 minutes
(plus time to make and freeze
the ice cream)

Eat it with: Doppelbock and
hazelnut schnapps

For the ice cream

1 cup (120g) cashew nuts

2oz (50g) toasted hazelnuts, lightly
crushed

5 tablespoons (75ml) oat milk
(or milk of your choice)

5 tablespoons (75ml) Doppelbock

1 cup (250ml) oat cream or heavy
(double) cream

1 tablespoon hazelnut schnapps

1 tablespoon smooth hazelnut butter
(or almond butter)

6 tablespoons maple syrup

1 frozen banana (optional—if you really
love the flavor of banana)

Pinch of salt

For the Salvator bananas

¾ cup (80g) packed (soft) light
brown sugar

5½ tablespoons (80g) butter

2 tablespoons hazelnut schnapps

1 tablespoon white miso (or
½ teaspoon salt)

½ cup (120ml) Doppelbock

4 or 5 ripe bananas, sliced into 1in
(2.5cm) pieces

1 pack vegan puff pastry (10-12oz/300-
350g), rolled out and cut to just larger
than the shape of your pan (optional)

This is sort of inspired by the traditional
American dessert Bananas Foster, but given a
Bavarian flavor by using Salvator, a strong and
malty Doppelbock lager, and some hazelnut
schnapps because I love hazelnut schnapps.
If you don't have hazelnut schnapps then a
hazelnut liqueur should work fine, but I haven't
tested that. You could also just omit it and use
a little more beer. This recipe includes a spoon
of white miso, which is a brilliant flavor with
sweet desserts and adds a delicious richness.
If you want to skip the tart part of the recipe
(as shown opposite), then there are some
instructions below—it is a quicker recipe, and
it still works well with the ice cream.

Start by making the ice cream. Soak the cashew nuts and hazelnuts
in the oat milk and beer for at least 4 and up to 12 hours. Combine
this with the rest of the ingredients in a powerful blender and blitz
until perfectly smooth. Churn in an ice cream machine or put into
a container in the freezer and stir every hour to break up the ice
chunks. Aim to have this in the freezer 4–5 hours before you
want dessert.

If making a tart, preheat the oven to 400°F/200°C/Gas 6. Put the
sugar and butter in a large ovenproof skillet (frying pan) over a
medium heat. Dissolve the sugar and leave it for 1–2 minutes to
caramelize. Once it's all bubbling and rich, carefully add the
hazelnut schnapps (watch out in case it flames up in the pan),
then stir in the miso. Add the beer and cook for a couple of
minutes, then place the bananas in the pan. If making a tart,
place the pastry on top, make two small slits in the middle, then
bake for 15 minutes. Alternatively, cook without pastry (as shown
opposite) on the stovetop for 2–4 minutes until the bananas soften,
but don't let them turn mushy.

Serve either version with the ice cream.

When beers are aged in oak barrels which previously held bourbon, they often have a depth of coconut and vanilla to them. This cheesecake is designed to go perfectly with that flavor. When you make it, open the beer you want to serve with it, pour out what you need, then place the cap back on the bottle or cover it in plastic wrap (clingfilm)—it'll keep for a few hours in the refrigerator (alternatively, save some from the bottom of a bottle to use in the recipe). The toasted coconut makes this cheesecake even better. Either buy it pre-toasted or use coconut flakes (not dried shredded/desiccated) and gently heat them in a dry skillet (frying pan) until golden.

IMPERIAL STOUT COCONUT CHEESECAKE

Vegan option

Serves 6–8

Takes 4–6 hours (active cooking time 15 minutes)

Eat it with: barrel-aged Imperial Stout

For the base

4½oz (130g) Graham crackers (digestive biscuits)

¼ cup (50g) melted coconut oil

⅓ cup (15g) toasted coconut flakes

Pinch of salt

For the filling

1½ cups (350g) cream cheese

14oz (400ml) can coconut cream

2 tablespoons coconut oil, melted

3 tablespoons maple syrup

3 tablespoons (45ml) Imperial Stout

Seeds of 1 vanilla pod (or 1 tablespoon vanilla extract)

⅓ cup (15g) toasted coconut flakes, to serve/decorate

Line a 9in (23cm) cake pan with baking parchment. In a food processor, pulse the base ingredients until they are a fine rubble and then press into the pan. Place in the refrigerator.

Beat together the ingredients for the filling. Spoon the mixture onto the cheesecake base. Cover and refrigerate for at least 4 hours.

Sprinkle the toasted coconut flakes over the top before serving.

DUBBEL CHOCOLATE MALT PUDDING AND CHOCOLATE SAUCE

Vegan option

Serves 6–8

Takes 45–60 minutes

Eat it with: Imperial Stout or barrel-aged Quadrupel

1½ cups (200g) dates, pitted (stoned) and chopped

½ cup (120ml) milk

4 tablespoons malt extract

1 tablespoon barley miso (or 1 teaspoon salt)

7 tablespoons (100g) butter

¼ cup (50g) packed (soft) dark brown sugar

1 heaped cup (150g) self-rising (self-raising) flour

½ cup (50g) cacao powder

1 teaspoon baking soda (bicarbonate of soda)

1 teaspoon baking powder

1 tablespoon malted drink powder, such as Ovaltine®, Horlicks®, or Milo® (optional, not vegan)

1 teaspoon ground cinnamon

1 tablespoon apple cider vinegar

1 teaspoon vanilla extract

Scant ¾ cup (180ml) Dubbel

For the chocolate sauce

1 cup (250ml) cream

2 tablespoons (30g) butter

2 tablespoons cacao powder

3 tablespoons malt extract

4 tablespoons (60ml) Dubbel

1 tablespoon barley miso

⅔ cup (100g) dark chocolate, broken into small pieces

Imagine a sticky toffee pudding combined with a chocolate pudding, made sweet with malt extract, and all smothered in chocolate sauce, and that's what this recipe is. The beer comes through with a rich and fermented depth which is enhanced by adding the barley miso, which I think is a really important ingredient in this recipe. If there's leftover pudding, it'll be good for the next few days, like a brownie. Serve with the strongest Imperial Stout or barrel-aged Quadrupel that you can find.

Preheat the oven to 350°F/180°C/Gas 4 and line a 9in (23cm) square baking pan with baking parchment.

In a small pan, heat the dates and milk, simmering gently for 5–10 minutes as the milk evaporates and the dates soften. Stir well so that the dates break apart and become paste-like. Add the malt extract and miso, then remove from the heat.

In a large bowl, cream together the butter and sugar. Add the rest of the ingredients and then the date mixture, stirring to combine into a thick batter. Pour into the baking pan and cook for 35–45 minutes. When you remove it from the oven, make the sauce.

To make the sauce, heat the cream, butter, and cacao powder in a small pan, whisking to get rid of any lumps in the cacao. When it comes to a simmer, cook for a couple of minutes, allowing it to reduce a little, then add the malt extract and remove from the heat. Pour in the beer and the barley miso and then add the chocolate, stirring until all the chocolate melts.

Pour the sauce over the pudding and serve immediately.

Carrot cake and pineapple upside down cake are both great with Double IPAs, so I've brought them together into one super-cake and made them with the fruitiest Hazy DIPA I could find, aiming for one with high sweetness, low bitterness, and a tropical fruitiness. You can serve this cake hot with vanilla ice cream but it's also good cold, and will keep for a day or two (it's actually better the next day if you want it cold).

CARROT & PINEAPPLE UPSIDE DOWN IPA CAKE

Vegan

Serves 6–8

Takes 1 hour

Eat it with: Hazy DIPA, American DIPA, or Tripel

1½ cups (200g) all-purpose (plain) flour

1 heaped cup (200g) superfine (caster) sugar

1 teaspoon baking powder

1 teaspoon baking soda (bicarbonate of soda)

1 teaspoon salt

1 teaspoon ground cinnamon

½ teaspoon ground ginger

½ teaspoon allspice

⅔ cup (150ml) coconut oil, melted (or olive oil)

½ cup (120ml) Hazy IPA or DIPA

1 tablespoon apple cider vinegar

1½ cups (200g) carrots, grated, plus 1 carrot peeled and sliced into thin rings

15oz (425g) can of pineapple rings

6–8 tablespoons maple, golden, or agave syrup

1 tablespoon stem ginger syrup (optional)

Preheat the oven to 325°F/170°C/Gas 3. Grease a shallow baking pan roughly 14 x 10in (35 x 25cm) with coconut or olive oil.

In a large bowl, combine all the dry ingredients and stir together. Then add the oil, beer, and apple cider vinegar, and stir to properly combine into a thick batter. Add the grated carrot. Finely chop 3½oz (100g) of the pineapple, then add that in too and stir.

Pour the maple syrup (and ginger syrup, if using) into the baking pan until it covers the bottom. Place as many rings of pineapple as you can in a single layer in the tin, then put rings of raw carrot in any gaps. Pour the cake batter over the top and bake for 45–50 minutes, or until a skewer inserted into the middle comes out clean. (If it starts to get too brown on top while baking, cover with aluminum foil.) Let the cake cool slightly and then tip it out onto a wire rack to cool further.

INDEX

Index entries in *italics* are recipes.

ACKNOWLEDGMENTS

This book is for Emma. I wrote it during the first Covid-19 lockdown in early 2020, and developing and cooking recipes and focusing on great beer was the perfect distraction for that strange, sad time. I couldn't have done it without Emma's excitement and happiness at being my recipe tester.

Thanks also to Penny Craig for all her great and thoughtful work on producing this book; to Cindy Richards who commissioned this book and continues to let me write books about beer—it's a pleasure to work with you and the rest of the team at Dog 'n' Bone; to the photographer and stylists who made my recipes look so delicious; and to Joe Todd for recipe testing and great feedback.